COMMON QUESTIONS AND
POWERFUL ANSWERS FOR LDS YOUTH

JOHN HILTON III AND ANTHONY SWEAT

DESERET
BOOK

SALT LAKE CITY, UTAH

Design by Ken Wzorek and Barry Hansen

Visit us at DeseretBook.com

Library of Congress Cataloging-in-Publication Data

Names: Hilton, John, III, author. | Sweat, Anthony, author.
Title: Q & A : common questions and powerful answers for LDS youth / John Hilton III and Anthony Sweat.
Other titles: Q and A
Description: Salt Lake City, Utah : Deseret Book, [2016] | Includes bibliographical references. | Compilation of selections from the authors' previous books "How?," "Why?," and "The big picture."
Identifiers: LCCN 2016017333 | ISBN 9781629722344 (paperbound)
Subjects: LCSH: Mormon youth—Religious life. | Mormon youth—Conduct of life. | LCGFT: FAQs.
Classification: LCC BX8643.Y6 S94 2016 | DDC 248.8/3088289332—dc23
LC record available at https://lccn.loc.gov/2016017333

Printed in China
RR Donnelley, Shenzhen, China

10 9 8 7 6 5 4 3 2 1

To our students throughout the years—
Thank you for your incredible questions.
Keep them coming!

"My dear young friends, we are a question-asking people because we know that inquiry leads to truth."

—President Dieter F. Uchtdorf

Introduction

In 2006, we (John Hilton III and Anthony Sweat) met at a session of Especially for Youth in Gainesville, Georgia, and we quickly became good friends. One day while talking about questions that we had been asked by our seminary students, we realized that although one of us lived in Utah and the other in Florida, we were getting the same types of questions. In fact, they were the same questions we received year after year, no matter where we happened to be teaching.

Out of this conversation grew the idea of writing a book for youth that addressed their key questions. That book was *WHY?* After we wrote *WHY?*, we realized that although many youth need to understand *why* they should keep the commandments, they also look for practical ideas about *how* to do so. Thus the book *HOW?* was born.

We intended to write another sequel in the series called *WHAT?* that would focus on doctrinal questions like "What is agency and what does it mean for me?" or "What can I do to prepare for the Second Coming?" However, it was decided that this book should have a different format to focus on lessons for families, and it was instead called *The Big Picture.*

In 2015, Deseret Book approached us with the idea of doing a "best of" *WHY?* and *HOW?* that would bring together the most relevant chapters from these books under one cover called *Q&A: Common Questions and Powerful Answers for LDS Youth.* We also thought it was a good opportunity to update some content in the book that had become a little outdated (like pictures of old flip-phones) and quotes from the *For the Strength of Youth* pamphlet that was updated by the Church in 2012. We also decided to add some new chapters about issues faced by contemporary teens (that's you!) to address issues that are becoming increasingly important.

In this book, we've updated fifteen chapters from *WHY?* and fourteen chapters from *HOW?* We then added two chapters from *The Big Picture,* formatted in the style of *WHY?* and *HOW?* and added two brand-new chapters on timely topics for teens today—mobile devices and same-sex marriage. You'll notice that the *WHY?* chapter titles are blue, the *HOW?* chapter titles are orange, and the other chapter titles are green.

We testify to you that God cares about you and wants to answer your sincere questions about living the teachings of the Church. Ultimately the answers you need will come from the scriptures, modern prophets, and the Holy Ghost. We hope that this book can also help you find some of the answers you seek.

John Hilton III
Anthony Sweat
Provo, Utah, May 1, 2016

How Can I Increase My Faith in Jesus Christ?

"Remember that faith and doubt cannot exist in the same mind at the same time, for one will dispel the other. Cast out doubt. Cultivate faith." —President Thomas S. Monson[1]

A young man named Junior recently shared in a testimony meeting his experience attending a soccer camp in North Carolina. He impressed the coaches there and was offered a full-ride scholarship. When he asked about the timing of the scholarship in regards to serving a mission, he was told that if he accepted the scholarship he would have to play four years in a row—and then go on his mission. "But you won't want to go," the coach told him, "because after four years I guarantee that you'll get picked up by a professional team." This was very tempting for Junior because playing professional soccer was his dream. After fasting and praying, he called the coach back and said, "I'm sorry, I won't be joining your team. I'm putting my mission as my top priority."

Although Junior might not have realized it at the time, when he made the decision to decline the scholarship, he was exercising faith in Jesus Christ—the first principle of the gospel.

In the book *True to the Faith,* we read, "Having faith in Jesus Christ means relying completely on Him—trusting in His infinite power, intelligence, and love. It includes believing His teachings."[2] But how do we develop faith in our Savior that allows us to trust him completely? This chapter will focus on three primary elements of developing and increasing our faith: creating *hope* in, taking *action* on, and seeing the *evidence* of the promises of Jesus Christ's atonement and teachings. Using the life of Joseph Smith as an example, we can see how, even as a teenager, he implemented all three of these elements to increase his faith in Jesus Christ.

Create Hope through Hearing the Word of God

Paul taught that "faith cometh by hearing, and hearing by the word of God" (Romans 10:17). Hearing, reading, and learning about the promises of God are critical steps in increasing our faith because it naturally creates hope. One reason for this is because the scriptures and words of the prophets are full of promises for the faithful. Jacob wrote, "We search the prophets, . . . and having all these witnesses we obtain a hope, and our faith becometh unshaken" (Jacob 4:6). As we search the scriptures we will find promises that God has made to us—promises that create hope.

WHAT SCRIPTURES CREATE HOPE FOR YOU?

Do you have a favorite scripture that gives you hope? One that promises you blessings if you act in obedience and faith? Post your favorite scripture on social media and share it with the world!

Joseph Smith understood how the scriptures can create hope. During his time of confusion regarding which church was true, he came across the Epistle of James and read this now-famous verse: "If any of you lack wisdom, let him ask of God, that giveth to all men liberally, and upbraideth not; and it shall be given him" (James 1:5). Reading the promise in that verse created hope for Joseph—hope that his question would be answered. This was a critical first step for him, and for us, toward increasing faith.

EVER HAD EXPIRED MILK? HOW ABOUT EXPIRED FAITH?

"Great faith has a short shelf life." —President Henry B. Eyring[3]

Just as milk goes bad after a short amount of time, our faith must continually be renewed or it can sour as well.

Faith
Must be replenished each day

Take Action and Experiment upon the Word

All promised gospel blessings are conditional upon our obedience (see D&C 130:20–21). In other words, if we hope to obtain any blessing, we need to take action and obey what the gospel requires of us to obtain that blessing. This truth is one reason why Joseph Smith said that faith is "the principle of action in all intelligent beings."[4] Elder David A. Bednar said, "True faith . . . always leads to action."[5] It is kind of like the scientific method used in experiments: After a hypothesis is formed, then a righteous experiment must be performed to test it. Our hope in Jesus Christ naturally leads us to act and conduct our own spiritual experiments. The prophet Alma tells us that if we want to increase our faith, we must "awake and arouse [our] faculties, even to an *experiment* upon my words, and *exercise* a particle of faith" (Alma 32:27; emphasis added).

The Spiritual-ific Method

Take a look at the scientific method below. Instead of using it to test *scientific* truths, we can do what Alma says and use the steps to test *spiritual* truths. Notice how Joseph Smith's experience could follow this spiritual-ific method

Ask a question
Which church is true? (Joseph Smith-History 1:10)

Do background research
Study the scriptures (Joseph Smith-History 1:8, 11)

Construct hypothesis
If I ask God in faith, he'll answer my question
(Joseph Smith-History 1:12-13)

Test with a righteous experiment
Go to the woods and pray (Joseph Smith-History 1:14)

Analyze results/draw conclusions
Received a vision of the Father and the Son
(Joseph Smith-History 1:17-19)

Hypothesis is *true*
"I had found the testimony of James to be true"
(Joseph Smith-History 1:26)

Report results
"I then said to my mother, 'I have learned for myself that Presby-terianism is not true'" (Joseph Smith-History 1:20)

HOW *is faith related to testimony?*

When Lehi and his family left Jerusalem, his wife, Sariah, did not know for sure that it was the right thing to do. However, she followed in faith anyway. She experimented upon the word and waited for the evidence. Notice what she says when her sons return with the brass plates: "And she spake, saying: *Now I know of a surety* that the Lord hath commanded my husband to flee into the wilderness" (1 Nephi 5:8; emphasis added). If we obey in faith like Sariah did, *then* our testimonies will be confirmed so we too can say, "Now I know of a surety."

As a teenager, Joseph Smith took his hope from a scriptural promise that God would answer his questions, and he decided to act on it. He *did something* with what he had learned. He said, "I at length came to the determination to 'ask of God.' . . . I retired to the woods to make the attempt. . . . I kneeled down and began to offer up the desires of my heart to God" (Joseph Smith–History 1:13–15). It is our "attempts" in righteous experiments that will produce the results that lead to increased faith, for "faith without works is dead" (James 2:20).

> "Although your beginning fire of faith may be small, righteous choices bring greater confidence in God, and your faith grows. The difficulties of mortality blow against you, and evil forces lurk in the darkness, hoping to extinguish your faith. But as you continue to make good choices, trust in God, and follow His Son, the Lord sends increased light and knowledge, and your faith becomes settled and unwavering. President Thomas S. Monson said: 'Fear not. . . . The future is as bright as your faith.'"—Elder Neil L. Andersen[6]

DO TRY THIS AT HOME!

You know how in movies, people can move things with their mind? Have you ever wished you could do that? Did you know that if you have enough faith, Jesus says you can move things—even entire mountains (see Matthew 17:20)? Take a look around you and locate an object (like a lamp or a book or something on the table). Now, move it with your faith!

What happened? Did the object move?

We're guessing not. We're guessing all that happened is that you got a headache from focusing your eyes like laser beams really hard.

Moving an object with your faith doesn't have to do with mental focusing or laser-beam eyes. Elder James E. Talmage said, "Faith implies such confidence and conviction as will impel to action. . . . Faith is active and positive, embracing such reliance and confidence *as will lead to works.*"[7]

In other words, faith is doing something. That is why the apostle James says, "Faith without works is dead" (James 2:20).

So, what's the easiest way to move the object with your faith?

Get up and move it!

GET IN THE WHEELBARROW!

There is an apocryphal story of a famous tightrope walker who walked on a tightrope across the Niagara Falls. The story goes that crowds gathered around to watch the man, who not only made it across the rope, he also did it blindfolded! Then he walked back along the tightrope, across the Falls, but this time, wheeling a wheelbarrow. He said that for his next stunt, he would cross the rope with the wheelbarrow again, but this time he would safely carry a person in the wheelbarrow.

"Do you think I can do it?" he asked the crowd.

The crowd cheered and shouted, "We believe you can do it!"

"Okay," the man said. "Who is willing to get in the wheelbarrow?"[8]

The moral of the story is obvious—we may say that we believe, but true faith requires action. Do we believe enough to "get in the wheelbarrow" and experiment on God's word?

Look for Evidence of Its Truthfulness

Just like in a science experiment, we must look at the results of our obedience. We must analyze the evidence of our faithful action and determine if our hope is confirmed. The scriptures tell us that "faith is . . . the *evidence* of things not seen" (Hebrews 11:1; emphasis added). As you look back over your life, you can probably see a lot of evidence that will strengthen your faith. Can you remember a time when a prayer was answered? When a priesthood blessing provided comfort or healing? When you felt peace while reading the scriptures? That is evidence!

Alma taught us what type of evidence to look for after we have performed our "experiment" upon the word (see Alma 32:27):

"Now, if ye give place, that a seed may be planted in your heart, behold, if it be a true seed, . . . behold, it will begin to *swell* within your breasts; and when you feel these swelling motions, ye will begin to say within yourselves—It must needs be that this is a good seed, or that the word is good, for it beginneth to *enlarge* my soul; yea, it beginneth to *enlighten* my understanding, yea, it beginneth to be *delicious* to me" (Alma 32:28; emphasis added).

The spiritual evidences to look for can easily be remembered and understood by the acronym **SEED:**

S—Swell within us. Look at the evidence of our *feelings.* Does the action produce the fruits of the Spirit, such as love, joy, and peace (see Galatians 5:22)? If it does, it is a good seed.

E—Enlarge our soul. Look at the evidence of what the action does to us as a person. Are we more kind, more energetic, less selfish? Has the action helped us put off the natural man and become more of a spiritual man (see Mosiah 3:19)? If it does, it is a good seed.

E—Enlighten our understanding. Look at the evidence in our mind. Does the action help us see things more clearly? Does it help us understand more deeply? Does it help us have "Aha!" moments of pure knowledge and enlightenment (see D&C 6:15)? If it does, it is a good seed.

D—Delicious to our souls. Look at what kind of appetite the action creates in us, and what kind of hunger it fills. Does the experiment feed us spiritually (see John 6:35)? Does it help us "hunger and thirst after righteousness" (Matthew 5:6)? If it does, it is a good seed.

When we have these feelings it is evidence that what we are experimenting on is true.

HOW *does knowing about God affect our ability to have faith in him?*

The degree to which we have a correct understanding of God significantly affects our ability to have faith in him. For example, if we mistakenly believe that anything bad that happens in our life is a sign that God is angry with us, then when things go wrong, we might become angry toward God and lose faith. *Lectures on Faith* states that in order to exercise faith in God we must have a correct idea of the kind of being he is.[9] As we come to better know God's true nature and character, we will be able to exercise more faith in him.

"Every time you *try your faith,* that is, act in worthiness on an impression, you will receive the confirming evidence of the Spirit. Those feelings will fortify your faith. As you repeat that pattern, your faith will become stronger."
—Elder Richard G. Scott[11]

Look at the evidence of the SEED in Joseph Smith's words of his First Vision. He said, "My Soul was filled with love and for many days I could rejoice with great joy and the Lord was with me."[10] We know that Joseph's mind was enlightened from the answer he received (see Joseph Smith–History 1:16–18), but his soul was also filled with joy. If we act in righteousness and spiritually discern the evidence of our action, our faith will be confirmed and increase as well.

Elder David A. Bednar called this three-step process a "helix" of faith. He said, "These three elements of faith—assurance [hope], action, and evidence—are not separate and discrete; rather, they are interrelated and continuous and cycle upward. . . . As we again turn and face forward toward an uncertain future, assurance [or hope] leads to action and produces evidence, which further increases assurance. Our confidence waxes stronger, line upon line, precept upon precept, here a little and there a little."[12]

THE HELIX OF FAITH
How to increase your faith

Hope (assurance) in something unseen
Action (experiment) and put it to the test
Evidence (results) of your action

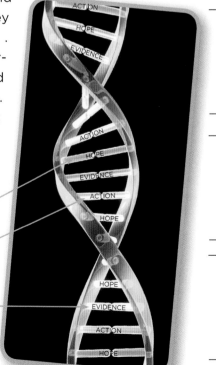

increase in faith

increase in faith

increase in faith

Invitation to Act

Search the scriptures

or the words of the living prophets (such as in *For the Strength of Youth* or a recent general conference address) and find a promise that is connected to living the gospel. Put the three steps in this chapter—hope, action, evidence—to work and record your experience of how your faith increased.

Ultimately faith is a gift that comes from God. As we continue to create *hope* in, take *action* on, and see the *evidence* of the promises of Jesus Christ's atonement and teachings, our faith will grow bit by bit, brighter and brighter until we have a sure knowledge for ourselves. As Alma observed, "Now behold, would not this increase your faith? I say unto you, Yea" (Alma 32:29).

TELL ME ONE MORE TiME!

How Can I Increase My Faith in Jesus Christ?

- **Create hope through hearing the word of God**
- **Take action and experiment upon the word of God**
- **Look for evidence of its truthfulness**

Why Should I Keep the Commandments?

Pretend for a moment that you had to walk through a minefield with hidden explosives buried all around you. Luckily, you have a map that can show you all the potential bombs. There are explicit instructions on the map, telling you exactly which paths lead to destruction and which paths lead to safety. Would you follow the map or ignore it and say, "I don't need anyone telling me what to do. I hate all these restrictions and rules. Just let me walk where I want to walk! I can figure it out for myself!"?

WOULD YOU RATHER CROSS A MINEFIELD LIKE THIS?

The red sign designates a minefield.

OR LIKE THIS?

Each stick marks an unexploded land mine.

The commandments of God are similar to that minefield map. God knows which steps in life will hurt and even kill us spiritually, and which steps will lead us along a path of safety and happiness. When he tells us, "Don't lie" or "Serve your neighbor," he is saying, "Don't step there—it will lead to tragedy" and "Do step here, it's a better path." Ignoring God and his divine commandments is like ignoring the map and walking blindly through a minefield. Let's take a look at why that is true.

Commandments and Happiness

Although people who break commandments may seem to be momentarily happy, eventually their disobedience causes them to become miserable. One reason why we should keep the commandments is that "wickedness never was happiness" (Alma 41:10). Since this is a book

about why we should keep the commandments, we could almost end the discussion right here. Most everyone wants to be happy. Not many people wake up and say, "I hope I can be miserable today." The problem is that sometimes people seek happiness from the wrong sources. Some people think that money, fame, popularity, or physical beauty will make them happy. Sadly, some even believe sin will bring happiness.

YOU CAN'T REALLY BUY HAPPINESS

A study on happiness printed in the *Washington Post* said:

"A wealth of data in recent decades has shown that once personal [savings] exceeds about $12,000 a year, more money produces virtually no increase in life satisfaction. From 1958 to 1987, for example, income in Japan grew fivefold, but researchers could find no corresponding increase in happiness."[1]

In reality, none of those things will ever make anyone truly happy. Possessions get lost, beauty fades, money is spent, and after high school nobody really cares who the head cheerleader or captain of the football team was. Similarly, sin only produces sorrow, guilt, and regret.

FALLING STARS

Although they have talent, money, fame, and beauty, many celebrities live lives that are out of control and seem to be the opposite of happiness. We should keep our focus on the true source of light—the Son of God—and not on celebrity stars that can fade or fall.

So what *does* make people truly happy? Elder Dale G. Renlund taught, "Obedience to God's laws preserves our freedom, flexibility, and ability to achieve our potential. The commandments are not intended to restrict us. Rather, obedience leads to increased spiritual stability and long-term happiness."[2]

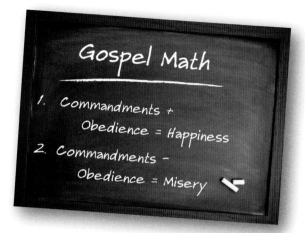

It really is that simple—obedience brings happiness. No calculus required to figure this one out.

IF YOU'RE HAPPY AND YOU KNOW IT . . . DON'T DO METH

The following pictures show a drug addict and the toll that meth took on her in just a ten-year period. It is obvious that doing drugs does *not* produce happiness.

Start

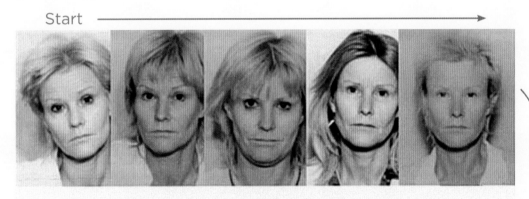

10 Years of Meth Use

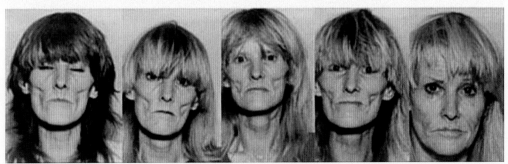

Provided by the Drug Enforcement Administration

End

Please note that Elder Renlund used words like "happiness," "freedom," and "spiritual stability" when he spoke about obedience, and not words like "fun," "entertaining," and "exciting." Sometimes people think that just because something is fun or exciting that it will produce happiness. Some sins appear fun or enjoyable, but that doesn't mean they bring long-lasting joy.

It is impossible to find true happiness in sin, as deceivingly appealing and fun as it may appear, because being in the "bonds of iniquity" is "contrary to the nature of happiness" (Alma 41:11). As you read the different commandments outlined in this book, you can put them to the test by living them and discovering this truth for yourself: The more we obey God's laws, the more happiness, peace, and joy we will have in our lives.

Guidance, Direction, and Protection

A second reason to keep the commandments is that they give us needed guidance. The Lord taught, "I give unto you a new commandment. . . . Or, in other words, I give unto you *directions*" (D&C 82:8–9; emphasis added). The commandments show us the right way and are for our benefit and protection. Returning to the minefield analogy, we can either ignore our all-knowing and wise Heavenly Father and get hurt in the process, or we can be obedient and free from unnecessary pain.

WARNING: DON'T HEAD-BUTT THE ANIMALS

John Says:

Once when I went to the zoo with my children, we came to a station where we could feed the giraffes.

Although a sign was posted warning us that the giraffes could be dangerous, I thought it would be fun to take a picture with a giraffe.

As I stood posing next to one, the giraffe pulled his head away from me, and then with surprising speed, he moved his neck in a circular motion, whacking me on the head. It hurt! If you think giraffes are wimps, you're wrong. In the final picture, I kept my distance from the giraffe.

The sign mentioned above warning zoo guests to be cautious of the giraffes was meant to give helpful guidance and keep visitors safe. It's the same with the commandments—they are there to direct us to stay safe from those things which will inevitably bring pain and sorrow.

EVERY WARNING HAS A REASON . . .

TOUCHING WIRES CAUSES INSTANT DEATH
☠ $200 FINE ☠

IF DOOR DOES NOT OPEN
DO NOT ENTER

CAUTION
THIS SIGN HAS SHARP EDGES

Please Be Safe.

Do not stand, sit, climb, or lean on zoo fences.
If you fall, animals could eat you and that might make them sick.
Thank you.

Obedience and Freedom

A third reason why keeping the commandments is so important is because of the following truth: Obedience leads to freedom, and disobedience leads to slavery. When we obey God's commandments, we can avoid many of those limiting, addictive, and controlling practices and behaviors that can take away our freedom. Elder Bruce C. Hafen taught:

"Curiously, the invitation to submit to God's will initially looks like a restriction on our freedom, yet ends by bringing us the full-blown liberty of eternal life. Laws and rules may seem to limit rather than free us; but it is only because of the law of gravity that we can walk. Only by adhering to the laws of physics can we compose beautiful music and send up spaceships. Obedience is liberating, not confining.

"By contrast, Satan's invitation to disobey God's laws initially looks like an expansion of our freedom; yet, if we follow Satan, we will end up in bondage to him."[3]

According to the U.S. Department of Justice, as of December 31, 2013, there were more than 1,574,700 prisoners in state and federal prisons in the United States. The leading causes of imprisonment were violent offenses (54%)—such as murder, rape, sexual assault, and robbery. Property offenses—such as burglary, fraud, and vandalism—accounted for 19%. And drug offenses were another 16%. Can you think of any crime that does not break some sort of commandment? Talk about sin taking away our freedom . . . literally![4]

Keeping commandments helps us remain in control of ourselves, our desires, our passions, and the direction of our lives. As the Savior taught, "The truth shall make you free" (John 8:32).

COMMANDMENTS AND KITE STRING

Here is an interesting thought: Does the string on a kite hold it down, or keep it up, so it can fly? How is that similar to having commandments? What happens to a kite when someone cuts the string? What happens when someone breaks the commandments? Think about it . . . there are a lot of similarities.

That Which We Persist in Doing . . .

DO TRY THIS AT HOME!

Pull out an old board game that you don't know how to play, and try to play it *without reading the rules or instructions.* Or, if you do know the rules, play the game with someone who doesn't know them. See how long it takes before they start to ask questions about how the game should be played. Compare this to the commandments of God. How hard would life be if we were left on our own without God giving us guidance, rules, and commandments so that we can know how to play the "game" of life successfully?

A fourth reason why keeping the commandments is so important is that the more we obey, the easier it is to continue obeying. This is because each time we obey, we are blessed with an increased amount of the Spirit of the Lord, which strengthens us to withstand temptation. As you read these next verses keep in mind that the word "light" in the scriptures can be a synonym for the Spirit of Jesus Christ (see D&C 84:45).

"He that keepeth his commandments receiveth truth and light, until he is glorified in truth and knoweth all things" (D&C 93:28).

We can invite the Light of Christ into our life by living the commandments. Notice what happens when we receive light:

"He that receiveth light, and continueth in God, receiveth more light; and that light groweth brighter and brighter until the perfect day" (D&C 50:24).

In other words, when we gain light and continue to do what is right, we will receive more light—and that light continues to grow brighter. One of the great things about receiving light is that it makes us less likely to want to do bad because "light and truth forsake that evil one" (D&C 93:37). Truly, the more we obey, the easier it is to be obedient, and to be more like our Savior.

SPIRITUAL ACCLIMATIZATION

Have you ever noticed yourself breathing hard at higher altitudes? It's because your body isn't acclimatized, or used to the thin amount of oxygen in the air. But, if we stay at the new altitude, we will get used to it. For example, if a person hikes to 10,000 feet and spends several days at that altitude, their body acclimatizes. If the person then climbs to 12,000 feet, their body will acclimatize again in another 1 to 3 days.[5] Keeping the commandments is similar. Living a "higher" way of life, although it may be hard at first, becomes easier the more time we spend doing it.

When we obey now, we increase our capacity to obey in the future by receiving an increased amount of the Spirit—like an upward spiral of light.

HOW DO YOU VIEW THE COMMANDMENTS?

One indicator of our spirituality is how we view the commandments. President Ezra Taft Benson taught, "When obedience ceases to be an *irritant* and becomes our *quest,* in that moment God will endow us with power."[6] The way we view obedience affects our power to be obedient.

Commandments can be seen as an *irritant*, like blurred vision, or . . .

Commandments can be seen as a focused *quest* . . . either way, our view affects our ability to follow them clearly.

Ye Shall Prosper in the Land

Another reason why we should be obedient is explained repeatedly in the scriptures. Put simply, each time we obey the commandments we will be blessed. Lehi taught his sons the Lord's words: "Inasmuch as ye shall keep my commandments ye shall prosper in the land" (2 Nephi 1:20). This promise is repeated numerous times throughout the scriptures. We are blessed with happiness, peace, freedom, and the Spirit of God. Even in the inevitable times of trial, God will "expand [our] vision, and strengthen [us]. He will give [us] the help [we] need to meet [our] trials and challenges"[7] if we are faithful.

These blessings will not only be rewarded in the next life, but in our life *now*. King Benjamin taught that when we obey, God will "immediately" bless us (Mosiah 2:24).

Why Should I Keep the Commandments?

1. **When we obey, we experience true happiness. On the negative side, "wickedness never was happiness" (Alma 41:10).**
2. **The commandments give us needed guidance and direction that help us avoid unnecessary pain and sorrow.**
3. **Obedience leads to freedom, and disobedience leads to slavery.**
4. **The more we obey, the more of the Spirit of the Lord (light) we receive in our lives making it easier for us to obey in the future.**
5. **Each time we keep the commandments, we are blessed.**

NOW that we have reviewed some of the *principles*, let's answer some of the questions regarding the *practices* connected to why we should keep the commandments:

Why are there so many commandments and rules?

As the first three principles in the chapter emphasize, God's commandments primarily exist to produce happiness for his children and to help them avoid unnecessary pain. There are many ways we can produce sorrow through our actions. Therefore, our loving Heavenly

Father commands us to avoid those practices that produce unhappiness (adultery, dishonesty, anger, etc.), and he also commands us to do those things that produce happiness and will help us become like him (forgive, love, serve, be humble, etc.). There are a lot of commandments, but that also means there are a lot of blessings.

Why do some people who break the commandments appear happy?

The key word in that question is *appear.* While those who break commandments may have momentary pleasure through disobedience, eventually disobedience leads to sorrow, suffering, or slavery. Remember the analogy of the kite string from earlier in the chapter—when the kite breaks away from the string, it might appear "free," perhaps even suddenly darting up higher in the sky, but it won't take long before it spins out of control and crashes to the ground. Remember, there is an eventual consequence to all disobedience, some consequences just take longer than others to become apparent.

Why are some commandments more important than others—or are they?

The Savior said that the most important commandments were to love God and to love our neighbor (see Matthew 22:36–40). There are obviously some commandments that hurt God or hurt our fellow man more than others. According to Alma 39:5, the three worst sins that can be committed are denying the Holy Ghost, murder where innocent blood is shed, and sexual immorality.

Why Should I Listen to and Follow the Prophet?

Imagine a beautiful river scene like this one.

Wouldn't you love to be canoeing along this river, enjoying the view? But what if we expand our view of this scene?

Suddenly the river trip takes on a whole new meaning. This object lesson, adapted from a talk by Elder Neil L. Andersen, shows one reason why it is so important for us to follow the prophets—because they see things we cannot.

Do You See What I See?

Just like an expanded view of the river changes our perspective, prophets can give us an expanded view of the world, which helps us avoid equally dangerous pitfalls. One of the gifts given to prophets is this gift of vision; thus, prophets are called seers, or *see*-ers. The Book of Mormon says that "A seer can know of things which are past, and also of things which are to come, and by them shall all things be revealed, or, rather, shall secret things be made manifest, and hidden things shall come to light, and things which are not known shall be made known by them, and also things shall be made known by them which otherwise could not be known" (Mosiah 8:17).

Consider all the ways people try to "see" the future.

Only one comes with a guarantee. (See D&C 1:37-38 for the promise.)

Through revelation, prophets are able to see things before they happen. The scriptures repeatedly demonstrate how those who listened to seers were blessed. Whether it was Joseph in Egypt seeing the seven-year famine, or Noah building his ark before the flood, or Lehi and his family leaving Jerusalem before the city was destroyed, blessings came to those who obeyed what they could not see themselves.

Prophecies Fulfilled

We have many modern examples of how seers have seen and told of events before they unfolded. For example, Joseph Smith prophesied of the Civil War thirty years before it happened—he even named where the rebellion would begin (see D&C 87). Years before his martyrdom and the Saints moved west to Utah, Joseph saw in a vision that some members of the Church would "live to go and assist in making settlements and build cities and see the Saints become a mighty people in the midst of the Rocky Mountains."[1]

Joseph also saw the worldwide growth of the Church. Speaking at a time when all the priesthood holders in the world could fit in a log cabin, he prophesied, "This Church will fill North and South America—it will fill the world."[2] Today, we are literally seeing this prophecy fulfilled.

LDS CHURCH GROWTH WORLDWIDE

"This Church will fill North and South America—it will fill the world." —Joseph Smith

The gift of seership is alive and well today. In general conference, we sustain each member of the First Presidency and Quorum of the Twelve as a prophet, *seer,* and revelator. "The Family: A Proclamation to the World," given in 1995, provides a recent example of their prophetic power to see.

The first sentence of the Proclamation reads: "We, the First Presidency and the Council of the Twelve Apostles of The Church of Jesus Christ of Latter-day Saints, solemnly proclaim that marriage between a man and a woman is ordained of God."[3] At the time this Proclamation was made there was little public debate that marriage should be defined as being "between a man and a woman," and at that time no government on earth had redefined marriage to include same-gender relationships.

However, within six years of the Proclamation, the Netherlands became the first country to legalize same-sex marriage, followed by Belgium, Spain, Canada, and South Africa.[4]

In 2015, the United States Supreme Court ruled to legalize same-sex marriage in the whole country. Modern-day seers saw this increased global pressure to redefine marriage and called "upon responsible citizens and officers of government everywhere to promote those measures designed to maintain and strengthen the family as the fundamental unit of society."[5]

DO TRY THIS AT HOME!

We're not prophets, but we've made a prediction. We need your help to see if it's correct. Pick a number between one and ten in your head. Multiply that number by nine. Then add the two digits of your answer together (for example, if you got 42, 4+2=6). Now subtract five from that number (for example, 6-5=1). Have your new number? Now, think of the alphabetical equivalent to the number (1=A, 2=B, 3=C, etc.). Now, think of a country that starts with your

letter (Albania, Bosnia, Croatia, etc.). Take the last letter in the country's name and think of an animal whose name starts with that letter. (It must be a one-word animal—"black widow," for example, would not count.) Finally, take the last letter of the animal's name and think of a color that starts with that letter. (If you had "bear," the color could be "red.") So you should have a color, an animal, and a country. We think we've predicted what you picked. Turn to page 24 and see if we were correct!

Dodging Destruction and Being Protected from Plagues

Another reason why we should follow the prophet is because those who heed the prophet's counsel have been promised safety and protection from many of the foretold calamities and problems of the last days. Some people are afraid of the Second Coming because of the widespread destruction and misery that has been foretold will accompany it. In the words of Elder Bruce R. McConkie, "There will be earthquakes and floods and famines. The waves of the sea shall heave themselves beyond their bounds, the clouds shall withhold their rain, and the crops of the earth shall wither and die.

"There will be plagues and pestilence and disease and death. An overflowing scourge shall cover the earth and a desolating sickness shall sweep the land. Flies shall take hold of the inhabitants of the earth, and maggots shall come in upon them. (See D&C 29:14–20.) 'Their flesh shall fall from off their bones, and their eyes from their sockets' (D&C 29:19).

"Bands of Gadianton robbers will infest every nation, immorality and murder and crime will increase, and it will seem as though every man's hand is against his brother."[6]

That sounds scary! But one theme repeated in the scriptures and in the words of the prophets is that the people who follow God's prophet will be safe from many of the problems that await the wicked and rebellious (see 1 Nephi 22:16–17). There was terrible devastation and death in the Americas following Christ's crucifixion, but as Mormon teaches us, "It was the *more righteous* part of the people who were saved, and it was *they who received the prophets* and stoned them not; and it was they who had not shed the blood of the saints, who were spared" (3 Nephi 10:12; emphasis added). Although *all* the righteous will not be spared *all* of the destructions that will come, it is certain that following the prophet will maximize our protection.

Elder McConkie also promised, "We do not say that all of the Saints will be spared and saved from the coming day of desolation. But we do say there is no promise of safety and no promise of security except for those who love the Lord and who are seeking to do all that he commands."[7]

Much of the protection that will come to the Saints in the last days will be "Noah-like," meaning that as we follow prophetic counsel, we will be prepared in order to make it through potential trials and problems (such as the counsel to store food and stay out of debt). Some of the protection will also be "Moses and Pharaoh-like," in that obedience will help us avoid many modern-day plagues (such as sexually transmitted diseases).

Given the prophesied calamities that will happen before the Second Coming, the divine safety, preparation, and peace promised to the righteous is another powerful reason why we should follow the counsel of God's living prophets in the latter days.

Never Led Astray

On May 11, 1996, eight people died trying to summit Mount Everest, making it one of the deadliest days in the mountain's history. One factor that led to this disaster was that the guides permitted their climbers to try to summit the mountain after the 2:00 PM turn-around time that had been designated. Being that close to the success of summiting the world's tallest peak caused some of the guides to put pleasing their clients ahead of their expedition's safety.[8]

Who's guiding you?

A KEY THAT WILL NEVER RUST

Joseph Smith said, "'I will give you a key that will never rust—if you will stay with the majority of the Twelve Apostles . . . you will never be led astray.' The history of the Church has proven this to be true."[9]

DO TRY THIS AT HOME!

Go to http://lds.org and re-read the prophet's most recent counsel from general conference. You may also want to download some conference talks and listen to them. What insights do you gain from the living prophet?

Fortunately, we have been promised that the latter-day prophets will never bend to the pressures of society and lead the people of God astray. Prophets and apostles will *always* lead the Church and its members in a straight course. President Wilford Woodruff promised, "The Lord will never permit me or any other man who stands as President of this Church to lead you astray. It is not in the program. It is not in the mind of God. If I were to attempt that the Lord would remove me out of my place, and so He will any other man who attempts to lead the children of men astray from the oracles of God and from their duty."[10]

If we follow the prophet, we will never be led astray as we strive to find our way back into the presence of our Heavenly Father.

TELL ME ONE MORE TiME!

Why Should I Listen to and Follow the Prophet?

1. **Prophets can see coming events more clearly and direct us accordingly—they are see-ers!**
2. **Those who follow the prophet have been promised safety from and preparation for many of the calamities of the last days.**
3. **When we follow the prophet, we will never be led astray.**

NOW that we have reviewed some of the *principles*, let's answer some of the questions regarding the *practices* connected to following the prophet:

Why is it so important to listen to general conference?

General conference is the time when the Lord's prophets publicly declare God's will for the worldwide Church. President Harold B. Lee said, "If you want to know what the Lord would have the Saints know and to have his guidance and direction for the next six months, get a copy of the proceedings of this conference, and you will have the latest word of the Lord as far as the Saints are concerned."[11] It is also a time when we can publicly raise our hands to sustain the living prophets and leaders of the Church and express our faith that they are truly prophets, seers, and revelators.

Why do modern prophets sometimes teach things that are different from what past prophets taught?

In times past, as new circumstances have arisen, the Lord, through his prophets, has directed inspired changes to meet the new challenges and opportunities of the day. Since this is a "true and living church" (D&C 1:30), change is a sign of continuing revelation, and we should expect more changes in the future. Although programs, practices, and policies of the Church might change because of new revelation, the eternal truths that those practices are based on—the doctrines of the gospel—don't change.

Why should I listen to prophets who are so much older than I am? They don't know what it's like to be a teenager today.

You might be surprised how much Church leaders *do* know about what it's like to be a youth in today's world. Consider this: God the Father, the Savior, and the Holy Ghost—the Godhead—know more about being a teenager today than you do because they have the knowledge and experience of ALL the world's teenagers combined, and you just have yourself! If we believe that prophets truly do receive revelation and that they are truly seers, then there is no doubt that they know exactly what spiritual issues are facing teenagers today.

THERE ARE NO ORANGE KANGAROOS IN DENMARK!

Let's see, you picked the number 4, the letter D, Denmark as the country, kangaroo as the animal, and orange as the color. We were right, weren't we?

Again, we are *not* prophets. This is a simple math trick, and real prophets don't use tricks. How blessed we are to live in a time when seers walk the land.

How Can I Know When the Holy Ghost Is Speaking to Me?

Please sincerely answer the following question in your mind: When was the last time you remember really feeling the Spirit or having been influenced by the Holy Ghost?

Got your answer?

So when was it? How long ago was the event that you immediately thought of? What was the event? We have asked this question to many youth over the years, and we hear common answers such as: "It was at our testimony meeting at camp" or "When I received my patriarchal blessing" or "I really felt the Spirit at EFY." However, it's less common for a youth to answer this question by saying, "I really felt the Spirit this morning when I prayed," or "About ten minutes ago when we sang the opening hymn and I felt peace," or "Just this morning when I received a subtle impression to say 'hi' to a person without many friends." Why is that so?

Each week when we partake of the sacrament we are promised to "always have [God's] Spirit to be with [us]" (Moroni 4:3). Notice the word *always.* The promise is not that we will have the Holy Ghost with us *sometimes,* or just in Church buildings, or during major life events. No, we are promised that the Spirit will be with us *always*—at school, at practice, in our home, with our friends, at work, and at play. Always. So why then do we at times have to search back months or years into the deep recesses of our memories to recall the last time we think the Spirit influenced us?

Elder David A. Bednar said, "Sometimes as Latter-day Saints we talk and act as though recognizing the influence of the Holy Ghost in our lives is the rare or exceptional event" when the reality is that "the Holy Ghost can tarry with us much, if not most, of the time—and certainly the Spirit can be with us more than it is not with us."[1]

Perhaps the problem is not that we aren't being influenced by the Holy Ghost in our daily lives, but simply that we don't recognize it and are overlooking it.

Looking for a SPECTACULAR SPIRITUAL EXPERIENCE?

You might be missing something . . .

President Kimball taught, "Expecting the spectacular, one may not be fully alerted to the constant flow of revealed communication from the Holy Ghost."[2]

HOW long will it take for an answer to come or for me to receive the revelation I need?

The answer to this question depends on the situation, and on the Lord's divine timing (see D&C 88:68). Elder Richard G. Scott gave a great insight to receiving answers from the Spirit through prayer when he taught: "Often when we pray for help with a significant matter, Heavenly Father will give us gentle promptings that require us to think, exercise faith, work, at times struggle, then act. It is a step-by-step process that enables us to discern inspired answers. . . . Seldom will you receive a complete response all at once. It will come a piece at a time, in packets, so that you will grow in capacity. As each piece is followed in faith, you will be led to other portions until you have the whole answer."[3] Revelation often comes in pieces—a little at a time (see 2 Nephi 28:30).

Perhaps we are even like the Lamanites who "were baptized with fire and with the Holy Ghost, *and they knew it not*" (3 Nephi 9:20; emphasis added). If we are missing the subtle daily guidance of the Spirit because we are looking for something more incredible, we might even mistakenly think that we aren't feeling the Holy Ghost at all! So how can we know and recognize when the Holy Ghost is speaking to us? We will use D&C 8:2 as our foundational scripture to answer this question. It says, "Yea, behold, I will tell you in your *mind* and in your *heart,* by the Holy Ghost" (emphasis added). The Holy Ghost will speak to our minds through our *thoughts,* and to our *hearts* through our feelings.

Let's look at how that can happen.

The Holy Ghost Will Give Us Instructions in Our Mind

Have you ever had a thought pop into your mind to *do* something? Maybe you saw your mom clear off the dinner table and thought, "I should help her," or perhaps you came home from school and were ready to sit down and watch some TV but thought, "I should get my homework done first so I don't get behind." Maybe you've had a clear warning voice of instruction in your mind, such as, "This show isn't good . . . turn it off" or "Don't do that" or "I should get out of this situation now." The Lord taught us, "As often as thou hast inquired thou *hast received instruction of my Spirit*" (D&C 6:14; emphasis added). These instructions in our mind often come in the form of "Do this . . ." "Don't do that . . ." "Go here . . ." "Don't go there . . ." "Look into this . . ."

Elder Richard G. Scott testified that "sometimes the direction [from the Holy Ghost] comes so clearly and so unmistakably that it can be written down like spiritual dictation."[4] The spiritual instructions that come to our minds will lead us to follow Christ, obey his gospel, and draw closer to him. If we receive an instruction in our mind to do something we know is wrong, we can know it is not of God (see chapter 9).

The Holy Ghost Will Enlighten Our Mind

To enlighten means "to give spiritual or intellectual insight to."[5] When Oliver Cowdery wanted to have a clearer knowledge and understanding of Joseph Smith's work on the Book of Mormon, the Lord said, *"I did enlighten thy mind;* and now I tell thee these things that thou mayest know that thou hast been *enlightened by the Spirit of truth"* (D&C 6:15, emphasis added). An easy way to notice when this is happening is when we have those "Aha!" moments. Those moments when we understand something more clearly, or more deeply. It is often noticed in statements such as "That makes sense" or "I get it now" or "I understand that better." For example, if you are reading a book about how the Holy Ghost enlightens our mind, and you think "That makes sense," then you were just enlightened by the Spirit! The Holy Ghost enlightened you about how he can enlighten you. Pretty cool.

The Holy Ghost can not only enlighten your mind regarding gospel principles, but also regarding any truth. Our Savior taught, "Howbeit when he, the Spirit of truth, is come, he will guide you into all truth" (John 16:13). That includes truths in math, truths in science, truths in sociology. *All truth.* If you understand a truth more clearly, you are being influenced by the Holy Ghost.

The Holy Ghost Will Help Reassure Our Mind

Have you ever been going through a difficult time or having a bad day and then as you studied the scriptures, or prayed, or heard a gospel talk or lesson the thought came to you, "I'm going to be okay," or "Everything will work out," or "Stay positive," or "God is aware of you and your situation. He loves you and will help you." Reassuring thoughts similar to those are another way the Lord speaks to our mind through the Holy Ghost.

> ### PAY ATTENTION TO WHEN YOU DON'T HAVE THE SPIRIT WITH YOU
>
> Elder David A. Bednar shared an important key that can be helpful for us as we try to always have the Spirit with us. He said, "Precisely because the promised blessing is *that we may always have His Spirit to be with us,* we should attend to and learn from the choices and influences that separate us from the Holy Spirit. The standard is clear. If something we think, see, hear, or do distances us from the Holy Ghost, then we should stop thinking, seeing, hearing, or doing that thing."[6]

Once again, to Oliver Cowdery, the Lord said, "Verily, verily, I say unto you, if you desire a further witness, *cast your mind upon the night* that you cried unto me. . . . Did I not *speak peace to your mind* concerning the matter? What greater witness can you have than from God?" (D&C 6:22–23; emphasis added). If we will pay attention to these different ways the Holy Ghost speaks to our mind (enlighten, instruction, reassurance) we can say with the prophet Enos, "The voice of the Lord came into my mind again, saying . . ." (Enos 1:10).

❓ **HOW** do desire and worthiness affect my ability to receive revelation on a daily basis?

Our desire to receive instruction and personal worthiness will affect the revelation we receive. President Spencer W. Kimball said: "The Lord will not force himself upon people; and if they do not believe, they will receive no visitation. If they are content to depend upon their own limited calculations and interpretations, then, of course, the Lord will leave them to their chosen fate. . . . If there be eyes to see, there will be visions to inspire. If there be ears to hear, there will be revelations to experience. . . . Revelation can come to every good, faithful [person]. . . . The Lord will give you answer to your questions and to your prayers if you are listening. . . . All people, if they are worthy enough and close enough to the Lord, can have revelations."[8]

♥ The Holy Ghost Gives Us Divine Feelings

When some people are asked what it is like to *feel* the Holy Ghost they say, "I get a burning in my bosom!" This comes from D&C 9:8: "If it is right I will cause that your bosom shall burn within you; therefore, you shall feel that it is right." Does this mean your chest is on fire? Like heartburn? Maybe. But probably not. Remember, the Spirit often works through the quiet, the subtle, the delicate, and not usually through the intense or dramatic. Elder Dallin H. Oaks explained the burning in the bosom this way: "Surely, the word 'burning' in this scripture signifies a feeling of comfort and serenity."[7]

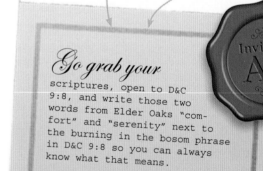

Go grab your scriptures, open to D&C 9:8, and write those two words from Elder Oaks "comfort" and "serenity" next to the burning in the bosom phrase in D&C 9:8 so you can always know what that means.

Invitation to Act

IS *HOMEWARD BOUND* TRUE?

Just because we feel *emotion* doesn't mean we are feeling the Holy Ghost. Just because we might cry when Shadow comes over the hill in *Homeward Bound* doesn't mean that *Homeward Bound* is true. President Howard W. Hunter explained: "I get concerned when it appears that strong emotion or free-flowing tears are equated with the presence of the Spirit. Certainly the Spirit of the Lord can bring strong emotional feelings, including tears, but that outward manifestation ought not to be confused with the presence of the Spirit itself."[9]

If we don't understand this principle we might mistakenly bear our testimony that we know something is true, just because we shed a tear.

One of the great gifts of God is divine feelings. Feelings such as love, peace, joy, hope, faith, humility, gentleness, gratitude, comfort, and serenity. These feelings can only come from God, and cannot come through wickedness, rebellion, or from the adversary. If we are experiencing those divine feelings, they come through the Holy Ghost and we are being influenced by him. This is a burning in the bosom! If we are looking for fire, we might miss the divine.

DO TRY THIS AT HOME!

To do this activity you must purchase an "Air Zooka" (you can find them online or at major retail stores in their toy section), or you can simply use a powerful fan. The Air Zooka is a large bucket-looking gun that compacts and shoots balls of air across the room. The ball of air is powerful enough to turn pages of scripture, shake the leaves of a tree, or send someone's hair flying. Shoot a few things with it. Shoot it past some family members and friends and let them feel it and hear it. After playing with it, answer this question: How is the air or wind like the Spirit? Read John 3:7-8 where the Savior compares the Spirit to the wind. Just because we can't see or touch something, doesn't mean it isn't real!

Here are some answers we thought of: You can't see it but you can feel it. You can hear it. It can be soothing or powerful. You can't touch it but you can see its effect on things.

♥ The Holy Ghost Gives Us Feelings of Warning

It is important to know that God is not the author of fear, doubt, and discouragement (see 2 Timothy 1:7). But sometimes we are about to head in the wrong direction, and God knows it. So in his love, he warns us through our feelings by the power of the Holy Ghost. The scriptures simply put it this way, "If it be not right you shall have no such feelings [of comfort and serenity], but you shall have a stupor of thought" (D&C 9:9). Elder Franklin D. Richards said the stupor of thought is "a questionable feeling."[10] President Boyd K. Packer taught: "If ever you receive a prompting to do something that makes *you feel* uneasy . . . do not respond to it!"[11] Remember, these feelings of uneasiness usually come when we are about to head in a direction that leads us into spiritual or physical danger. They are usually accompanied by thoughts of instruction to stop or to leave. If we are feeling uncomfortable with a situation, it may be a stupor of thought, with the Holy Ghost telling us not to proceed.

DON'T LET A JALAPEÑO OVERPOWER YOUR GRAPE

"The inspiring influence of the Holy Spirit can be overcome or masked by strong emotions, such as anger, hate, passion, fear, or pride. When such influences are present, it is like trying to savor the delicate flavor of a grape while eating a jalapeño pepper. Both flavors are present, but one completely overpowers the other. In like manner, strong emotions overcome the delicate promptings of the Holy Spirit."—Elder Richard G. Scott[12]

We have been promised that the Holy Ghost can be with us *always*—each day of our lives, not just each major event in our lives. We testify that this is true, and that we all can be spiritually influenced and led each day—multiple times each day. The next time somebody asks, "When was the last time you felt the Spirit?" you want to be able to respond by saying, "Well, what time is it?"

TELL ME ONE MORE TIME!

How Can I Know When the Holy Ghost Is Speaking to Me?

- **The Holy Ghost will give us instructions in our mind.**
- **The Holy Ghost will enlighten our mind.**
- **The Holy Ghost will help reassure our mind.**
- **The Holy Ghost gives us divine feelings.**
- **The Holy Ghost gives us feelings of warning.**

How Can I Strengthen My Testimony?

What is it that causes a young man or woman to get up hours before school starts each day to go to seminary and learn the scriptures? What is it that leads missionaries to voluntarily give up eighteen to twenty-four months of their lives to go to foreign lands and preach the gospel, and pay their own way? What is it that motivates Latter-day Saints to freely give 10 percent of their income to the Church?

President Hinckley gives the answer: "This thing which we call testimony is the great strength of the Church. It is the wellspring of faith and activity. . . . [It] is the element which motivates the membership to forsake all in the service of the Lord. . . . This testimony . . . is of the very essence of this work. It is what is moving the work of the Lord forward across the world."[2]

Since testimony is the critical element to activity and faithfulness in the Church, the question becomes: *How* can we gain or strengthen our testimony?

> ## PROPHETIC TESTIMONY
>
> "I declare that God lives and that He hears and answers our prayers. His Son, Jesus Christ, is our Savior and our Redeemer."
>
> **PRESIDENT THOMAS S. MONSON**[1]

"HOW DO WE KNOW WHAT REALLY IS TRUE?"

Elder Robert D. Hales taught the following points:

"Cultivate a diligent desire to know that God lives.

"This desire leads us to ponder on the things of heaven—to let the evidence of God all around us touch our hearts.

"With softened hearts we are prepared to heed the Savior's call to 'search the scriptures' and to humbly learn from them.

"We are then ready to ask our Heavenly Father sincerely, in the name of our Savior, Jesus Christ, if the things we have learned are true."[3]

Study the Book of Mormon

President Ezra Taft Benson called the Book of Mormon the "keystone of testimony."[4] That means that if we can gain a testimony of the truthfulness of the Book of Mormon it will be the key to obtaining the rest of our testimony. If we know the Book of Mormon is true, then we will know that Jesus is the Christ, for it testifies of his divinity. If we gain a testimony of the Book of Mormon, then we'll have a testimony of Joseph Smith—because he translated it—and a testimony of the Church he founded, The Church of Jesus Christ of Latter-day Saints. Having a testimony of the Book of Mormon helps everything else fall into place.

IF THE BOOK OF MORMON IS TRUE . . .

Having a testimony of the Book of Mormon helps everything else fall into place.

1. If the Book of Mormon is true,

then Joseph Smith was a prophet.

2. If Joseph Smith was a prophet,

then The Church of Jesus Christ of Latter-day Saints is the true church.

3. If The Church of Jesus Christ of Latter-day Saints is the true church,

then it is led by a true prophet today.

PROVE IT TO ME!

Have you ever had people say to you something like: "Well, I want proof that there is a God" or "Show me some real evidence that Joseph Smith was a prophet, then I'll believe." Have you ever wished that there was some sort of proof, some sort of real, touchable thing that could prove that Jesus is the Christ, that Joseph did see God, and that Joseph was a prophet? Oh, wait, God already gave us something!

President Benson said: "I testify that through the Book of Mormon God has provided for our day *tangible evidence* that Jesus is the Christ and that Joseph Smith is His prophet."[5]

If someone doubts your testimony or asks for proof, hand them a copy of the Book of Mormon and say, "There's your proof! It's either true, or it's not. I testify it is."

Since the Book of Mormon is the keystone of our testimony we need to know how to gain a testimony of the Book of Mormon. At the end of the book, Moroni gives us a promise: "And when ye shall receive these things, I would exhort you that ye would ask God, the Eternal Father, in the name of Christ, if these things are not true; and if ye shall ask with a sincere heart, with real intent, having faith in Christ, he will manifest the truth of it unto you, by the power of the Holy Ghost" (Moroni 10:4).

If we read the Book of Mormon and pray about it with a sincere heart, with real intent to obey its teachings, having faith in Christ, the Spirit will tell us through our mind and heart that the Book of Mormon is true (see chapter 8). Each of us can have this divine and sacred experience! President Hinckley said, "Without reservation I promise you that if you will prayerfully read the Book of Mormon, regardless of how many times you previously have read it, there will come . . . a stronger testimony of the living reality of the Son of God."[6] Obtaining a testimony comes through prayer and scripture study, but particularly through a study of the Book of Mormon.

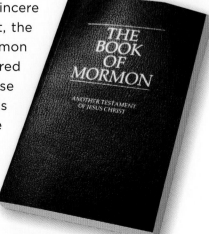

WHAT WOULD IT TAKE TO MAKE UP THE BOOK OF MORMON? . . . HOW 'BOUT YOU START WRITING ABOUT OUTER MONGOLIA?

Those who claim that the Book of Mormon is not true are by default claiming that the book was made up—fabricated by Joseph Smith, his friends, or someone else and pulled off as one of the great hoaxes of this world. Here is roughly what it would take to make up the Book of Mormon:

- You must write the religious, social, and political history of some ancient people, like the Mongols or people from Greenland.

- You must write the book off the top of your head, using no reference material—no Google in Joseph's day!

- You must complete the whole book in 65 to 75 working days.

- You must invent over 280 new names the world has never heard, and they must be properly derived from your ancient people's language, a language which you don't know. Have fun with that one.

- Your book must include the fullness of the gospel of Jesus Christ, including sermons that are so inspiring that people willingly read them again and again and again.

- Your book must be over 500 pages long and 300,000 words.

- Your first draft must stand forever (other than minor grammatical changes).

- You must be willing to give your life, and the life of a family member, for the book you write.[7]

Our testimony to the world is that the Book of Mormon was not made up by Joseph Smith. As Elder Jeffrey R. Holland's grandfather President George Q. Cannon said, "No wicked man could write such a book as this; and no good man would write it, unless it were true and he were commanded of God to do so."[8] Logic tells most rational people the book is true, but the Spirit provides an even more powerful witness: The book is of God.

Live What We Learn; Live the Gospel

The Savior taught, "If any man will *do* his will, he shall *know* of the doctrine" (John 7:17; emphasis added). In other words if we want to *know* if a gospel principle is true, we need to *live* that principle (*do* the things we are supposed to do).

PROPHETIC TESTIMONY

"I know that my redeemer liveth, and that he shall stand at the latter day upon the earth."

JOB (Job 19:25)

For example, a young woman we know said that she never read her scriptures. She didn't think they would help in her life. Then she starting having some problems and began to read the scriptures on a daily basis. As she read the scriptures every day, she felt different. She felt better and though she still had problems she was able to work through them. She bore her testimony of the value of scripture study. She gained her testimony of scripture reading by reading the scriptures.

HOW can I know if something I learn in school is true or false?

Most of the things you will learn in your formal education will be true, but—unfortunately—sometimes the theories, philosophies, and values of the world are mixed in and presented as facts or absolute truths, when they are not. There are two primary ways to be able to discern what is and is not true.

Study the Book of Mormon: President Ezra Taft Benson said: "God, with his infinite foreknowledge, so molded the Book of Mormon that we might see the error and know how to combat false educational, political, religious, and philosophical concepts of our time."⁹ Match what you hear and learn against the standards and truths taught in the Book of Mormon, the holy scriptures, and with what the current prophets are teaching. If the ideas and values you learn in school contradict what the scriptures and prophets plainly teach, then stick with the scriptures and prophets.

Listen to the Holy Ghost: The Savior taught: "Howbeit when he, the Spirit of truth, is come, he will guide you into all truth" (John 16:13). Pay attention to how you *feel* when learning something. If it doesn't feel right, it probably isn't.

Example of step #4.

DO TRY THIS AT HOME!

There are many levels of testimony:

I hope it's true . . .
I think it's true . . .
I believe it's true . . .
I know it's true . . .

What if we told you that your ring finger is less flexible than your other fingers? Do you hope, think, believe, or know that is true? What is the only way to move from "hope" to "know"? Experiment and test it out! Do the following:

1. Put your hands together, palm to palm.

2. Keeping your palms together, see if you can separate your pointer fingers. Can you do it? Good, now keeping your palms together, fold your pointer fingers over.

3. With your palms together and pointer fingers folded over, try to separate your pinky fingers. Can you do it? Good. Now fold those over.

4. What about your thumbs, and your middle finger? Good. Fold those over.

5. Now with your palms firmly pressed together and all your fingers folded over *except your ring fingers*, try to separate your ring fingers from each other. Interesting, isn't it?

So how many of you now "know" your ring finger is less flexible than your others? Gaining a witness of spiritual things is much the same: When we first experiment and act in obedience, then the testimony comes.

President Howard W. Hunter taught, "Action is one of the chief foundations of personal testimony. The surest witness is that which comes firsthand out of personal experience.

". . . This, then, is the finest source of personal testimony. One knows because he has experienced."¹⁰

Notice that we must act in faith first, then the witness comes (see chapter 1). It is not the other way around. There are some who say, "When God gives me a testimony of tithing, then I'll pay it." However, that simply is not the way the Lord works. We first act, then our testimonies will grow.

HOW come I can't try the bad stuff (sin) to learn if it's bad and gain my testimony that way?

Some think they can gain a testimony of the Word of Wisdom by drinking alcohol or doing drugs to see how bad it is, or gain a testimony of the need to be chaste and morally clean by being immoral. Remember, the Savior taught, "If any man will *do* [God's] will, he shall know" (John 7:17; emphasis added). The Holy Ghost will only testify to us that something is true if we are obedient and live what God teaches. The Spirit can't testify that something is true when we are rebelling against God and being disobedient.

Share What You Know and Believe with Others

John Says: I can still remember the first time I bore my testimony. I was about ten years old and was in our Primary room. I was wearing a dirty coat and didn't want to bear my testimony. But everyone else was doing it, so I got up and said (and this is about how I said it), "I'dl iketobearmytestimonythatIknowthischurchistrue, I'mthankfulformyfamilyinthenameofJesusChristAmen."

Have you ever shared or heard a testimony like that?

I remember the second time I bore my testimony. I was twelve years old and it was at the end of a ward youth conference. I was a deacon at the time, and every other deacon in my quorum had already borne his testimony. All the older deacons were saying, "John, go bear your testimony!" I didn't want to, but I did because of the peer pressure. That testimony was about as meaningful as my first.

I can also clearly remember the third time I shared my testimony. I was fifteen at the time and was at EFY. Going into the testimony meeting, I really didn't plan on bearing my testimony, but as the meeting went on, I really started to feel the Spirit. Finally, I got up and began to explain the feelings I had in my heart for the gospel. A feeling of warmth came over me as I shared my testimony, and I felt the Spirit like I never had before. My testimony got stronger because I bore it. When I sat down, I felt so good. I learned for myself that a testimony was found in the bearing of it.

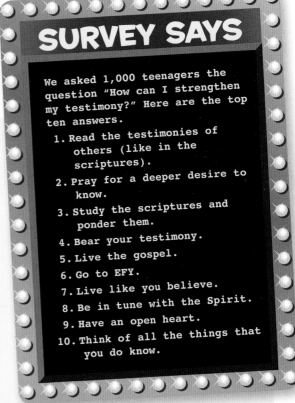

SURVEY SAYS

We asked 1,000 teenagers the question "How can I strengthen my testimony?" Here are the top ten answers.

1. Read the testimonies of others (like in the scriptures).
2. Pray for a deeper desire to know.
3. Study the scriptures and ponder them.
4. Bear your testimony.
5. Live the gospel.
6. Go to EFY.
7. Live like you believe.
8. Be in tune with the Spirit.
9. Have an open heart.
10. Think of all the things that you do know.

When Brigham Young called a new leader over the young men of the Church, he told him, "At your meetings you should begin at the top of the roll and call upon as many members as there is time for to bear their testimonies and at the next meeting begin where you left off and call upon others, so that all shall take part and get into the practice of standing up and saying something. Many may think they haven't any testimony to bear, but get them to stand up and they will find the Lord will give them utterance to many truths they had not thought of before. More people have obtained a testimony while standing up trying to bear it than down on their knees praying for it."[11]

We can bear our testimonies at any time, not just in testimony meetings. We can share our knowledge of truth in conversations with friends, at home with our families, and using technology. We don't have to wait for fast and testimony meeting to bear a testimony.

Invitation to Act

How is your testimony? Answer these questions posed by Elder Richard G. Scott. He said, "Honestly evaluate your personal life. How strong is your own testimony? Is it truly a sustaining power in your life, or is it more a hope that what you have learned is true? . . . Does your testimony guide you to correct decisions?"[12]

Take a moment and answer his questions. How is *your* testimony?

"I'd like to bear my testimony. My dad knows this church is true. My mom has read the Book of Mormon . . ."

You've got to find out for yourself. Share what you know and you'll know it as you share.

A Testimony Is Like Spinning a Basketball

How do people spin a basketball on their finger for a long time? The key is in not letting the ball slow down, but to keeping it spinning on your finger by tapping it. If we don't tap the ball, it will eventually slow down, lose its momentum, and fall. Our testimonies are similar: once we get them up and going, we keep them going by "tapping" them on a consistent basis through daily scripture study, prayer, living the gospel, and sharing our testimony with others. If we don't do those things, our testimonies can eventually get spiritually weak, lose momentum, and perhaps fall apart altogether.

For most, receiving a testimony takes time—it doesn't come overnight. We might be doing all the right things and still feel like we don't have a testimony or that our testimony is not strong enough. Don't get discouraged. Someone who is six-foot four didn't become that height overnight, nor do talented piano players play Bach's *Minuet in G* their first day. Remember that sometimes when we are seeking our testimonies, it's not that we're not doing the right things—we just haven't done the right things long enough.

Alma the Younger said, "I have fasted and prayed *many days* that I might know these things of myself" (Alma 5:46; emphasis added). This teaches us that not only can fasting help us gain a testimony, but perhaps more importantly that it may take *many days,* or weeks, or months, or years.

We know that as we gain a testimony of the Book of Mormon, live the gospel, and share what we know with others our testimonies will slowly grow and strengthen into a powerful witness of the truths of the gospel.

TELL ME ONE MORE TIME!

How Can I Strengthen My Testimony?

- **Study the Book of Mormon.**
- **Live what we learn; live the gospel.**
- **Share what you know and believe with others.**

What Is Agency and What Does It Mean to Me?

If I have my agency, then why do my parents tell me what to do?

My mom makes me so mad!

It's my life—I can do whatever I want!

I can't go to mutual; I have to finish my homework.

Have you ever heard or said any of those statements? Each of them reflects a misunderstanding of what agency is and why it's been given to us. What *is* agency? President David O. McKay frequently referred to agency as "God's greatest gift to man."[1] Simply stated, agency is "the ability and privilege God gives people to choose and to act for themselves."[2]

In *Gospel Principles*, we read, "When we follow the temptations of Satan, we limit our choices. The following example suggests how this works. Imagine seeing a sign on the seashore that reads: 'Danger—whirlpool. No swimming allowed here.' We might think that is a restriction. But is it? We still have many choices. We are free to swim somewhere else. We are free to walk along the beach and pick up seashells. We are free to watch the sunset. We are free to go home. We are also free to ignore the sign and swim in the dangerous place. But once the whirlpool has us in its grasp and we are pulled under, we have very few choices. We can try to escape, or we can call for help, but we may drown."[3]

DANGER— WHIRLPOOL. NO SWIMMING ALLOWED HERE.

In order for agency to take effect, certain conditions have to be present. We'll call these the four aspects of agency: Law, Knowledge of Good and Evil, Opposition, and the Power to Choose. Let's check them out with the help of the prophet Lehi's great discourse that he gave to his sons in 2 Nephi 2.

The Four Aspects of Agency

Let's use an analogy to see how these four aspects are necessary for agency to exist.

Law

Suppose we offered you a can of beer and a can of lemonade.

Now imagine that the Word of Wisdom had never been given, and there was no prophetic or legal guidance on drinking alcohol. You wouldn't be able to choose which of the two drinks was the "right" drink because there would be no eternal law. The prophet Lehi taught that if "there is no law . . . there is no sin" (2 Nephi 2:13). But, as Lehi's son Jacob taught, God "has given a law" (2 Nephi 9:25). Having designated laws of God is a key part of our ability to exercise our agency. The law designates which choice is right.

Knowledge of Good and Evil

Have you ever done something wrong and didn't know it was wrong? This happens all the time in our youth, and especially with little children. (Bless their little souls, they have no idea it's wrong to color the walls with crayons.) It isn't until we know something is right or wrong that we can purposefully choose to obey or disobey the law and therefore be accountable for our righteousness or wickedness.

Using these same two drinks, we can illustrate the importance of knowledge of good and evil in terms of exercising agency. Even if God has designated the law (don't drink alcohol), if we don't know what God's law is, we will be less able to make the right choice. The scriptures teach us that because of the light of Christ, "men are instructed sufficiently that they know good from evil" (2 Nephi 2:5).

Opposition

Now suppose we offered you two drinks to choose between, but both were cans of beer. Well, another key part of agency is having choices that are in opposition to each other. If our only choice is between two cans of the same beer, then it's pretty hard to exercise our agency. The prophet Lehi taught us: "For it must needs be, that there is an opposition in all things. If not so . . . righteousness could not be brought to pass, neither wickedness" (2 Nephi 2:11). Having choices that are in opposition to each other gives us the opportunity to exercise our agency and make the right choice.

Power to Choose

Let's consider one last aspect of agency: the power to choose. Even if we have a law, a knowledge of the law, and opposites to choose between, if we are not able to choose we cannot exercise our agency. Even if we know the lemonade is the correct choice, if the lemonade is put impossibly out of our reach and we are forced to drink the beer, we cannot exercise our agency because we have no power to do so. Without the power to choose what we will do, there can be no agency and therefore no accountability. Thankfully, God has given us the power to choose, teaching us that we "are free to choose" (2 Nephi 2:27).[4]

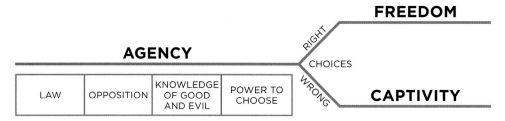

What Does Agency Have to Do with Me?

There are lots of ways that the doctrine of agency affects us in our lives. Elder Robert D. Hales taught, "Some may remember the old adage: 'The devil made me do it.' Today I want to convey, in absolutely certain terms, that the adversary cannot make us do anything."[5]

Perhaps the greatest blessing of agency is that we are free to make our own choices and control our own destiny. The prophets teach us, "Heavenly Father has given you agency, the ability to choose right from wrong and to act for yourself. Next to the bestowal of life itself, the right to direct your life is one of God's greatest gifts to you."[6] However, with that freedom comes responsibility. The prophets call this "accountability" and teach that "you are responsible for the choices you make."[7]

Let's look at how we can be better and more responsible agents.

Agency and Excuses

When we truly understand agency, we realize that when we make excuses we are denying our agency. We are saying that something or someone else controls us and our actions and that we aren't in control, which is contrary to the doctrine of agency. When we make an excuse, we are saying that we don't have a choice in the thing we are making an excuse for, and thus we deny our power to choose.

For example, at a youth dance a young man asks a young woman to dance and she says,

"I'd love to dance with you, but I can't. I have to go talk to my friend about something." She is essentially saying, "I don't have a choice; I *have* to talk to my friend. I'd love to dance with you if I could, but I *can't*." By making an excuse, she denies her power to choose and her control over her behavior, which she is responsible for independent of any other person.

Here's another example: A young man is asked by his seminary teacher if he read his scriptures. He says, "I couldn't because I had so much homework and was too tired at the end of the night." We hope his seminary teacher would correct the incorrect agency statement with something like, "You mean, you *chose* not to study your scriptures because you *chose* to do your homework, eat dinner, and play basketball before studying your scriptures?"

When you get right down to it, most excuses are an attack on one of the four pillars of agency. Consider this quote from Elder Paul V. Johnson: "Think of some of the excuses people give for their wrong actions: 'I didn't know it was wrong'—a claim they had no knowledge of good from evil. 'I couldn't help it'—claiming they had no personal power to choose. 'There wasn't anything else I could do'—purporting no choices from which to pick. 'Don't push your morals on me'—assuming there is no eternal law."[8]

Here is a key principle: when we make excuses, we weaken ourselves. Making excuses hurts us because by attacking those pillars of agency, we trick ourselves into thinking that we really *aren't* free to choose, or that there is no real eternal law. We should avoid making excuses. Alma taught his son, "Do not endeavor to excuse yourself *in the least point*" (Alma 42:30; emphasis added). The moment we take responsibility for our actions is the moment we gain power over the course of our lives.

No Excuses

Look at the following statements and figure out which ones deny agency:

- My little sister is such a pest. She really makes me mad.
- I'd love to go on a date with you, but I have to stay home with my sick cat.
- I won't sub for you, because I will not work on Sundays.
- Sorry, that's just the way I am.
- I was going to read my scriptures, but I couldn't. My dog ate them.
- That offends me.
- I choose not to watch R-rated movies.
- I want to do missionary work but I can't. I'm too shy.
- I'm sorry this is late. It's my fault; I'll do better next time.

What Does Agency Have to Do with My Emotions?

One area of agency that is sometimes overlooked is that to a large extent we choose our emotions. Here are a few of the emotions we can choose:

We have the power to choose the emotion of happiness. President Harold B. Lee taught, "Happiness does not depend on what happens outside of you but on what happens inside of you; it is measured by the spirit with which you meet the problems of life."[9]

Take the "No Excuses Challenge" for twenty-four hours. Refrain from phrases like "I have to" or "He made me" or "I couldn't help it." What changes do you notice in your life because you took this challenge?

VIDEO BONUS

Visit "Watch Tour Step" at http://www.youtube.com/watch?v=gWQ5dPeixdw to see the powerful effects of what our agency can lead to.

Now consider the emotion of anger. Can anybody *make* us mad? President Thomas S. Monson answered this question, saying, "No one can *make* us angry. It is our choice. If we desire to have a proper spirit with us at all times, we must choose to refrain from becoming angry. I testify that such is possible."[10]

Sometimes people say that something "offends" them. Can something offend us, or are we choosing to take offense? Elder David A. Bednar taught, "It ultimately is impossible for another person to offend you or to offend me. Indeed, believing that another person offended us is fundamentally false. To be offended is a *choice* we make; it is not a *condition* inflicted or imposed upon us by someone or something else."[11]

Another example of an emotion we can choose is "love." Sometimes we hear a married person say they "fell out of love" with their spouse.

Is that true? Can we "fall out of love," or do we choose to stop loving somebody?

Elder Lynn G. Robbins answered this question by saying, "Any commandment by God involves agency. We can obey or disobey, but there is always a choice. When the Lord uses the command form of the verb *love* in 'Thou shalt love thy wife will all thy heart, and shalt cleave unto her and none else' (D&C 42:22), He is not leaving this love in Cupid's hands. . . . You can't fall out of love if it's a commandment to stay in love."[12]

DO TRY THIS AT HOME!

Try the following experiment to see what we mean by choosing our emotions.

All right, get ready to loosen up your facial muscles, and give the biggest, cheesiest smile ever. (This activity works best if you have other people do it with you.) Now, give your best smile for a full minute. Ready, set, go!

If you smiled for a full minute, odds are you feel better. You may have even laughed with each other. Notice how something as simple as choosing to smile affected you? We can choose our attitudes, and we can choose to smile!

How Would You Feel in a Nazi Concentration Camp?

Are you in control of how you feel? Could you control your feelings even if you were in a Nazi concentration camp? A man named Viktor Frankl was in a concentration camp, and he wrote, "We who lived in concentration camps can remember the men who walked through the huts comforting others, giving away their last piece of bread. They may have been few in number, but they offer sufficient proof that everything can be taken from a man but one thing: the last of the human freedoms—to choose one's attitude in any given set of circumstances, to choose one's own way."[13]

Acting as Agents

A key part of understanding agency is that we are "agents." To be an agent means we are authorized to act. God has "given unto the children of men to be agents unto themselves" (Doctrine and Covenants 104:17), which means we should be responsible for the things God has given us.

We are agents over our choices, our bodies, our attitudes, our time, our talents, our resources, and much, much more. Being an agent means that we don't just avoid bad things, we proactively choose to do good (meaning nobody has to tell us to do it). The Lord has said: "For behold, it is not meet that I should command in all things; for he that is compelled in all things, the same is a slothful and not a wise servant; wherefore he receiveth no reward. Verily I say, men should be anxiously engaged in a good cause, and do many things of their own free will, and

bring to pass much righteousness; for the power is in them, wherein they are agents unto themselves. And inasmuch as men do good they shall in nowise lose their reward" (Doctrine and Covenants 58:26–28).

Let us never forget that God has given us our agency. We have the ability to act and not merely to be acted upon (see 2 Nephi 2:14). Let us choose to be good agents by choosing to "use [our] agency to show [our] love for God by keeping His commandments."[14]

WHAT'S THE BIG DEAL WITH AGENCY IF GOD ALREADY KNOWS EVERYTHING I WILL DO?

God does know what is going to happen to us ahead of time (see Abraham 2:8), but that doesn't mean we "have" to do it. For example, are you going to close this book right now, or are you going to keep reading? We're not sure what you're going to do, but God knows. Still, it's your choice whether you close the book or not.

Just because God knows does not mean He is choosing for you. Understanding that God knows what we will do without forcing us to do it is difficult to grasp. In fact, even Elder Richard G. Scott said that he didn't fully comprehend it. He said, "The Lord has placed currents of divine influence in your life that will lead you along the individual plan He would have you fulfill here on earth. . . . I do not fully understand how it is done, but this divine current does not take away your moral agency. You can make the decisions you choose to make."[15]

TELL ME ONE MORE TiME!

What Is Agency and What Does It Mean to Me?

- **There are four "pillars" necessary for agency: Law, opposition, knowledge of good and evil, and the power to choose.**
- **Excuses we make are often an attack on one of these four pillars of agency.**
- **Others don't offend us or make us mad. We choose our emotions.**
- **To be an agent means we are authorized to act. Let's proactively do good!**

How Can I Set Standards That Will Keep Me Spiritually Safe?

WHAT WOULD YOU DO FOR 10 MILLION DOLLARS?

President Monson reported on a survey that asked people what they would do for 10 million dollars. Let's see what YOU would do for that amount of cash.

"For ten million dollars in cash, would you leave your family permanently?"

"Would you marry someone you didn't love?"

"Would you give up all your friends permanently?"

"Would you serve a year's jail term on a framed charge?"

"Would you take off your clothes in public?"

"Would you take a dangerous job in which you had a 1-in-10 chance of losing your life?"

"Would you become a beggar for a year?"

"Of the people polled, 1 percent would leave their families, 10 percent would marry lovelessly, 11 percent would give up friends, 12 percent would undress in public, 13 percent would go to jail for a year, 14 percent would take the risky job, and 21 percent would beg for a year."[1]

From the example above, obviously money cannot be the driving force in the standards that we keep. In order to set firm standards we need to base them on the truths found in the doctrines of the gospel. Elder Richard G. Scott said, "Firmly establish personal standards. Choose a time of deep spiritual reflection, when there is no pressure on you, and you can confirm your decisions by sacred impressions. Decide then what you will do and what you will not do. . . . The Spirit will guide you. Then do not vary from those decisions no matter how right it may seem when the temptation comes. . . . The realization of your dreams depends upon your determination to never betray your standards."[2]

Let's look at three keys from this statement that give counsel on how we can set standards that will keep us spiritually safe.

"Choose a Time of Deep Spiritual Reflection, When There Is No Pressure on You"

An important part of setting standards is to make them in a spiritual setting. For example, we might be more able to set a powerful spiritual goal in a quiet room, in the temple, or in nature, rather than somewhere noisy or distracting. We could find a private place where we could have the scriptures, *For the Strength of Youth*, and a paper and pen to write down impressions we feel as we pray about our standards. It is also important to have enough time set aside that we can wait for impressions to come. Perhaps approaching such a setting with a fast would be appropriate.

Invitation to Act

It is also wise to make sure there is no pressure on us at the time we set our standards. The time to decide whether or not we will view pornography is before our friend says, "Look at this picture." The time to decide whether or not you are going to kiss is before somebody gives you "the kiss look." President Spencer W. Kimball said, "Right decisions are easiest to make when we make them well in advance. . . . The time to decide on a mission is long before it becomes a matter of choosing between a mission and an athletic scholarship. The time to decide on temple marriage is before one has become attached to a boyfriend or girlfriend who does not share that objective."[3]

"Confirm Decisions by Sacred Impressions . . . the Spirit Will Guide You"

There is power that comes when the Holy Ghost gives us direction. Suppose a young man goes to Sunday School and hears the teacher say, "You shouldn't watch R-rated movies." Compare this with a young man who prays about his standards and feels the Holy Ghost tell him that he shouldn't watch R-rated movies. Which will leave a more powerful impression upon the young man's mind and heart?

Speaking of the youth of the Church, President Henry B. Eyring said, "They must choose obedience to the Lord's commandments in the face of greater temptations and trials. They must do it out of faith in Jesus Christ. *And that faith can only come through the witness of the Spirit.*"[4] Elder Richard G. Scott has repeatedly told of a sacred experience he had receiving inspiration during a Church meeting. Of the process he said, "I received further impressions, and the process of writing down the impressions, pondering, and *praying for confirmation* was repeated."[5] The Spirit confirmed revelation to Elder Scott, and it can impress the standards we should commit to live in our minds more powerfully than anything else.

HOW can I set a standard I will keep for the rest of my life?

Maybe right now you don't need to set a standard that you will keep for the rest of your life. For example, think about the law of chastity. You don't need to say "I will never kiss anybody in my life" (because someday you'll kiss your future spouse, we hope!), but you may be inspired to set a personal standard like, "I will not engage in passionate kissing before marriage. And I am not going to kiss anybody until I am in a meaningful relationship that could lead to marriage."

As another example, you could say, "Between now and the time I am sixteen, I will never watch a PG-13 movie." When you turn sixteen, you could seek inspiration about whether or not you should continue with that standard.

DO TRY THIS AT HOME!

Take a look at the picture below. How tall would you say this person is?

Now, guess how tall the person is, but this time guess in "spans."

Don't know what a span is? It's the distance between the end of the thumb to the end of the little finger when your fingers are extended.

Why was it easier to guess "feet and inches" compared to spans? Because we all know and accept the standard of feet and inches. When a standard is defined and accepted, it becomes easy to judge whether you are on or off. Spans differ depending on the size of a person's hand (my span might be bigger than your span), so there is inconsistency and error. Additionally, some people don't know what a span means, so they don't know the standard to judge from.

The standards of the Church are more like measuring in feet and inches than measuring in spans. The measurements are clear. The more we are familiar with those standards and accept them, the easier it is to know if our lives are on the mark. However, if we use the world's ever-shifting standards, it is much like a span . . . you never really know if you are truly correct!

"Do Not Vary from Those Decisions No Matter How Right It May Seem When the Temptation Comes"

There is always a temptation to vary from our standards. Let's look at two stories from the scriptures and compare what Lehonti and Nehemiah did as they were faced with continual temptation.

Lehonti led a group of Lamanites who didn't want to fight Nephites. The Lamanite king wanted to fight the Nephites and sent an evil man named Amalickiah to make Lehonti and his group go to war. Lehonti and his men were safe on a mountain. Now notice what happens.

"And it came to pass that when it was night [Amalickiah] sent a secret embassy into the mount Antipas, desiring that the leader of those who were upon the mount, whose name was Lehonti, that *he should come down to the foot of the mount,* for he desired to speak with him. And it came to pass that when Lehonti received the message he durst not go down to the foot of the mount. And it came to pass that *Amalickiah sent again the second time,* desiring him to come down. And it came to pass that Lehonti would not; and *he sent again the third time.* And it came to pass that when Amalickiah found that he could not get Lehonti to come down off from the mount, *he went up into the mount, nearly to Lehonti's camp;* and *he sent again the fourth time his message unto Lehonti,* desiring that he would come down, and that he would bring his guards with him. And it came to pass that . . . Lehonti [came] down with his guards to Amalickiah" (Alma 47:10–13; emphasis added).

So the first three times Lehonti refused to come down from his place of safety. But on the fourth time, Amalickiah went up, almost to where Lehonti was, and said, "Just come down a little bit—and bring your guards." That might be like Satan tempting us today saying, "It's not that big of a deal. As long as you're with your friends, it won't hurt you to do this."

On the fourth time, Lehonti gave in. Within a short period of time, he had been murdered, and Amalickiah was in command of the army.

Compare that account with that of Nehemiah. Nehemiah was in charge of rebuilding a wall around Jerusalem. His enemies, Sanballat, Tobiah, and Geshem, wanted to stop the wall from being built and devised a plan to harm Nehemiah. They asked him to come to the plains of Ono and "thought to do [him] mischief" (Nehemiah 6:2).

OH NO!

Nehemiah's enemies wanted to meet him in the plain of "Ono." If you're asked to go somewhere or do something that would make your parents say, "Oh no!"—don't do it!

Nehemiah refused to go to Ono. He said, "I sent messengers unto them, saying, I am doing a great work, so that I cannot come down: why should the work cease, whilst I leave it, and come down to you?" (Nehemiah 6:3).

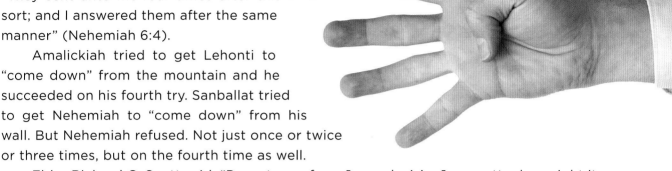

Notice what happens next. He said, "They sent unto me *four times* after this sort; and I answered them after the same manner" (Nehemiah 6:4).

Amalickiah tried to get Lehonti to "come down" from the mountain and he succeeded on his fourth try. Sanballat tried to get Nehemiah to "come down" from his wall. But Nehemiah refused. Not just once or twice or three times, but on the fourth time as well.

Elder Richard G. Scott said, "Do not vary from [your decision] no matter how right it may seem when the temptation comes."[6] The difference between Lehonti and Nehemiah is what they did "the fourth time." In life, our standards will be challenged repeatedly. We must decide now that on the fourth, fifth, and every time we will hold fast to our standards.

DON'T LET DOWN!

In the 2006 Winter Olympics, Lindsey Jacobellis competed in the Women's Snowboard Cross event. She was in the lead and clearly going to win the gold medal. But on the last jump she was showing off and attempted a method grab. She didn't land it, and as a result, she lost the gold medal, settling for silver. She had been in the lead the whole time, but a small mistake at the end cost her. When it comes to your standards, don't ever let your guard down. Keep strong to the end![7]

Set a Standard That Will Help Keep You from Ever Getting Close to the Line

Another important part of setting firm standards is that we set a standard that will help us keep from ever getting close to the line of sin. For example, when it comes to the law of chastity, *For the Strength of Youth* says, "Do not participate in passionate kissing."[8] The question isn't,

"How long can I kiss before it's passionate?" but "What standard can I set to keep far away from passionate kissing?" What matters isn't how close can we get to the line, but rather, how we can avoid even getting close.

The question "How far can I go and not sin?" is *not* the important question. President Henry B. Eyring, when he was a member of the Quorum of the Twelve, taught, "The question that really matters is this: 'How can I learn to sense even the beginning of sin and so repent early?'"[9]

As we set standards for ourselves we must make sure that they are standards that will help keep us *far away* from the line of sin, not right next to it.

HOW strict should I be when I set a standard for myself?

Perhaps it's less important that you be super-strict with yourself, and more important that you try hard to receive personal revelation for what your standards should be. You could get really strict and say, "I'm setting a standard to never watch a movie" (and maybe some people would feel inspired to set that standard). But instead of focusing on being strict (or on trying to get away with as much as you can), try to focus on what you think your Father in Heaven would have you do to stay far away from the line of sin.

So don't set a standard to go right up to the line of sin. For example, when it comes to the law of chastity, the line might look like this:

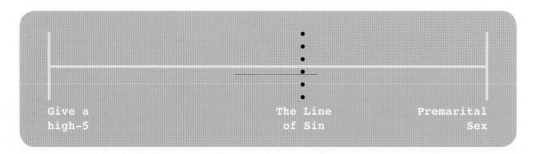

Give a high-5 — The Line of Sin — Premarital Sex

Instead, set a standard that will keep you from even getting close to the line of sin.

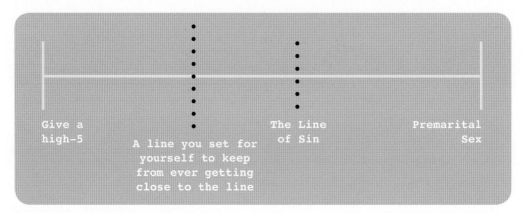

Give a high-5 — A line you set for yourself to keep from ever getting close to the line — The Line of Sin — Premarital Sex

The same principle applies to other standards.

TELL ME ONE MORE TIME!

How Can I Set Standards That Will Keep Me Spiritually Safe?

- "Choose a time of deep spiritual reflection, when there is no pressure on you."
- "Confirm decisions by sacred impressions . . . the Spirit will guide you."
- "Do not vary from those decisions no matter how right it may seem when the temptation comes."
- Set a standard that will help keep you from ever getting close to the line.

8 ch How Can I Break Bad Habits?

Swearing. Complaining. Being critical of others. Losing your temper. Being late. Overeating. Procrastinating your homework. Squeezing the toothpaste tube from the top.

Bad habit #64: There is a lot of toothpaste in the bottom of the tube . . . maybe I should rethink this . . .

DO TRY THIS AT HOME!

Fold your arms. Take a look at how they are folded. Did you fold your left arm over your right arm, or your right arm over your left? Now, try folding your arms, but put the opposite arm on top of the one you naturally did. How did that feel? How long do you think it would take before that didn't feel weird anymore and just became natural? Remember, when breaking a bad habit, you are going to feel a little different at first. Stick with it, and soon enough the positive habit will feel normal and natural.

There are all kinds of bad behaviors that people try to overcome. Most of us have some sort of habit or sin that we have tried to break in our lives—over and over and over again. Yet sometimes we struggle to actually get over it. While squeezing the toothpaste from the top of the tube might not be a big deal, there are bad habits that are sinful in nature. We want to stop repeating our bad behavior—but how can we do it in such a way that we don't start it up again? Elder Richard G. Scott tells us how:

"Suppose a small child were to run in front of your car. What would you do? Careful analysis of each step taken will teach you how to overcome your serious habit:

"First your mind decides to stop. Nothing else can happen until that decision is made.

"Then you take your foot off the accererator. Can you imagine stopping a car with one foot on the accelerator and the other on the brake?

"Finally you firmly apply the brake.

"The same pattern is followed to overcome your entrenched habit. Decide to stop what you are doing that is wrong. Then search out everything in your life that feeds the habit, such as negative thoughts, unwholesome environment, and your companions in mischief. Systematically eliminate or overcome everything that contributes to that negative part of your life. Then stop the negative things permanently."[1]

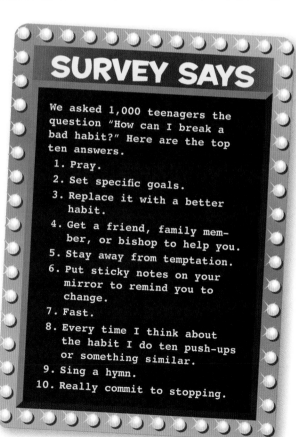

Decide to Stop

As Elder Scott said, the first thing we can do to change a negative behavior is to decide to stop the bad behavior. And then we must desire to change. Not merely say, "I'd like to change," but seriously decide that change is necessary. One message that is often repeated in the scriptures is what the Lord said to Enos: "I will grant unto thee according to thy desires" (Enos 1:12, see also Alma 29:4–5; D&C 7:8). Notice that it doesn't say, "I will grant unto thee according to thy *wishes*" or "according to thy *dreams*." Do we *really* desire to change our behavior? Until we see that the benefits of breaking the habit outweigh the gratification that comes from the behavior, we will have little desire to change.

SURVEY SAYS

We asked 1,000 teenagers the question "How can I break a bad habit?" Here are the top ten answers.

1. Pray.
2. Set specific goals.
3. Replace it with a better habit.
4. Get a friend, family member, or bishop to help you.
5. Stay away from temptation.
6. Put sticky notes on your mirror to remind you to change.
7. Fast.
8. Every time I think about the habit I do ten push-ups or something similar.
9. Sing a hymn.
10. Really commit to stopping.

HOW can I learn to control my temper?

Many of the things we'll talk about in this chapter can help you in controlling your temper. But more important than any technique is the understanding that you *can* control whether or not you get angry. President Thomas S. Monson taught, "To be angry is to yield to the influence of Satan. No one can *make* us angry. It is our choice. If we desire to have a proper spirit with us at all times, we must choose to refrain from becoming angry."[2] Perhaps the best way to learn to control our temper is to first understand that nothing can make us angry—it is our choice.

Change the Environment

After we decide to stop a bad habit, Elder Scott tells us to "search out everything in your life that feeds the habit, such as negative thoughts, unwholesome environment, and your companions in mischief."[3] In other words, we need to change the stimulus that prompts the habit. Studying Ivan Pavlov's famous psychology experiment on conditioned responses can help us learn how to break bad habits. Pavlov noticed that dogs began to salivate when those who were to feed them appeared. He predicted that if a stimulus (like ringing a bell) was present when the dogs were given food, then soon the dogs would associate the sound of a bell ringing with getting food. Sure enough, after a few repetitions, the dogs began to salivate when hearing the bell, even if no food was present.[4]

Many of our bad habits are Pavlovian in nature: a conditioned stimulus leads to a conditioned response. When the bell rings, dogs salivate. When we come home, we turn on the television (thus procrastinating our homework). When we hang out with certain friends, we swear or drink. If we can change the environment—change the stimulus (going to the library to study for an hour after school, or changing the group of friends we hang out with)—we will find it easier to change the response and thus, change the habit.

PAVLOV'S DOG AND HABITS

Change the stimulus—change the response!

Make It Difficult to Continue the Bad Habit

Elder Scott mentions another key to help us stop doing bad things: make those bad things difficult to do, or, as he says, "systematically eliminate or overcome everything that contributes to that negative part of your life."[5] For example, if we are trying to eat less candy or sweets, we could put them in a hard-to-reach place.

CHOCOLATE!

One study showed that when chocolates were placed on a worker's desk, that worker would eat more than twice as much chocolate each day compared to when the chocolates were six feet away from the worker's desk.[6]

On desk   Six feet away

The Anti-Nephi-Lehis provide a powerful example of this principle in action. They made a choice to never take another person's life. Notice what they did to make it more difficult for them to change their minds later: "We will hide away our swords, yea, even we will bury them *deep in the earth,* that they may be kept bright, as a testimony that we have never used them, at the last day; and if our brethren destroy us, behold, we shall go to our God and shall be saved" (Alma 24:16; emphasis added).

The weapons were buried *deep in the earth,* or in other words, they were very difficult to access. What would have happened if the Anti-Nephi-Lehis had buried their weapons shallowly in the earth? It might have been much more tempting for them to reach for their weapons when they were faced with opposition. Take a look at how this might be applied to us today:

Bad habit	Bury it shallowly	Bury it deep
Watching bad movies	Hide them under your bed	Dump, delete, discard them
Eating junk food	Put it in the cupboard	Give it away or don't buy it
Visiting bad Internet sites	Decide not to visit them	Install a filter with a password only your parents know

Think for a moment about a bad habit you have. What would it take to bury it deep? Now, go do it!

Get Help from Friends, Leaders, and God

Finally, Elder Scott tells us to "stop the negative [habit] permanently."[7] Seeking help from those around us, and from God, greatly contributes to our ability to stop our habit permanently. There are many different ways we can get others to help us overcome our negative behavior. One approach is to find a friend who is also trying to stop the same habit and work together. Friends can report to each other and set goals together (see chapter 27).

HOW STEEP IS THIS HILL?

The *New York Times* reported on a 2008 study in which students were taken to the base of a steep hill and asked to estimate how steep the hill was. Some students stood by themselves while others had a friend standing by them. Those who had friends standing by them estimated that the hill was less steep than did those students who were standing alone. In other words, having a friend close by made the challenging hill—or for us, the challenging habit to break—appear to be less difficult.[8]

Another powerful key for breaking bad habits completely is to seek heavenly help. Heavenly Father wants to help us overcome the bad habits we have, and the atonement of Jesus Christ can give us the strength to change our habits. Some of us might say, "I can't change!" and we might agree with you! Maybe we *aren't* strong enough to change—by ourselves. However, with the help and power of Jesus Christ, we can change. Elder David A. Bednar taught, "The enabling and strengthening aspect of the Atonement helps us . . . to become good in ways that we could never recognize or accomplish with our limited mortal capacity."[9]

HOW should I act if I feel that I was "born with" the source of my temptations—if it's just the way I am?

Just because we feel we are born with certain sources of temptation doesn't mean we have to act on those temptations. Elder Dallin H. Oaks taught:

"Perhaps there is an inclination or susceptibility to such feelings that is a reality for some and not a reality for others. But out of such susceptibilities come feelings, and feelings are controllable. If we cater to the feelings, they increase the power of the temptation. If we yield to the temptation, we have committed sinful behavior. That pattern is the same for a person that covets someone else's property and has a strong temptation to steal. . . .

"Feelings can be controlled and behavior can be controlled. The line of sin is between the feelings and the behavior."[10]

OH, NO! TOOTH DECAY!

Tooth decay isn't pretty. How does one prevent it? By brushing and flossing regularly. But what happens if one slips out of the habit of brushing and flossing? The tooth decay grows and, over time, becomes progressively worse. Simple good habits like brushing and flossing can help prevent tooth decay.

Similarly, simple good habits like sincere prayer and scripture study can help prevent the *spiritual* decay of forming bad habits.

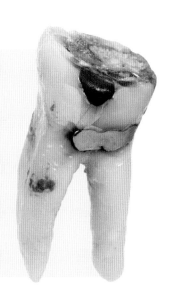

Replace Bad Habits with Good Ones

Fill the empty space with something good before it gets filled back up with junk.

President Boyd K. Packer said, "Do not try merely to *discard* a bad habit or a bad thought. *Replace* it. When you try to eliminate a bad habit, if the spot where it used to be is left open it will sneak back and crawl again into that empty space. . . . When you discard it, fill up the spot where it was. Replace it with something good. Replace it with unselfish thoughts, with unselfish acts. Then, if an evil habit or addiction tries to return, it will have to fight for attention. . . . You are in charge of you. I repeat, it is very, very difficult to eliminate a bad habit just by trying to discard it. Replace it."[11]

IT'LL COST YA!

Another way to break bad habits is to create consequences for yourself. For example, you might have heard of a "Swear Jar" where you put a set amount of money into the jar every time you swear. You can have a similar jar for any kind of habit you're trying to break. If you're trying to stop complaining, you could make a commitment to yourself that every time you complain you'll put a quarter into the jar—and at the end of the month you'll use the money to buy something for someone else.

The consequences don't always have to be negative though. You can also give yourself positive consequences when you make good choices that move you toward breaking your bad habits. For example, if you're trying stop being sarcastic, reward yourself with a treat when you go for two days without making a sarcastic comment.

HOW can I better control my language?

When it comes to changing the words we say, Elder L. Tom Perry offers this suggestion, "If you slip and say a swear word or a substitute word, mentally reconstruct the sentence without the vulgarity or substitute word and repeat the new sentence aloud."[12] So, for example, suppose you're walking and you stub your toe and say a swear word on accident. What should you do? Stop, think about what you could say differently, and then repeat the new sentence out loud. Perhaps, "Ouch. That hurt." ☺ If we consistently do this, Elder Perry tells us, "Eventually you will develop a non-vulgar speech habit."[13]

Study Matthew 4:1-11

(and pay attention to the Joseph Smith Translation in the footnotes). Analyze and highlight how the Savior implemented the following principles in overcoming his temptations:

1. Following the whisperings of the Holy Ghost
2. Fasting
3. Leaving the place of temptation
4. Memorizing scriptures
5. Standing in holy places

How can you apply these same principles to the bad habits you have? Take action!

Invitation to Act

TELL ME ONE MORE TiME!

How Can I Break Bad Habits?

- **Decide to stop**
- **Change the environment**
- **Make it difficult to continue the bad habit**
- **Get help from friends, leaders, and God**
- **Replace bad habits with good ones**

How Can I Know When I've Been Forgiven?

What do a pile of stones and tearing a roof apart have to do with each other?

Both of them are connected to one of the greatest miracles Jesus performed in his lifetime—and still performs today: *the miracle of forgiveness.*

To a woman about to be stoned for her sins, the Lord rebuked her accusers and told the woman, "Hath no man condemned thee? . . . Neither do I condemn thee: go, and sin no more" (John 8:10–11). On another occasion, Jesus was in a house and the friends of a sick man broke up the roof in order to get their friend to him, and "when Jesus saw their faith, he said unto the sick of the palsy, Son, thy sins be forgiven thee" (Mark 2:5).

One of the greatest blessings in the entire gospel is that through the Atonement of Jesus Christ we too can be forgiven of the sins and mistakes in our lives. Doctrine and Covenants 58:42 states, "Behold, he who has repented of his sins, the same is forgiven, and I, the Lord, remember them no more."

However, even after we have truly repented (see chapter 3), sometimes we are left wondering: "Have I actually been forgiven?" Here are a few principles that teach us how we can know when the miracle of forgiveness has taken place in our lives, just as it did for those in Jesus' time.

We Have Peace of Mind

Elder F. Burton Howard of the First Quorum of the Seventy counseled with a young man through the repentance process. The young man asked, "'How can I ever know the Lord has really forgiven me?'

"'That is the easy part,' [Elder Howard] replied. 'When you have fully repented, *you feel an inner peace.* You know somehow you are forgiven because the burden you have carried for so long, all of a sudden isn't there anymore. It is *gone* and *you know* it is gone. . . .

"'I wouldn't be surprised,' [Elder Howard] said, 'if when you leave this room, you discover that you have left much of your concern in here. If you have fully repented, the relief and the peace you feel will be so noticeable that it will be a witness to you that the Lord has forgiven you.'"[1]

Another form of this peace of mind is peace of conscience. *For the Strength of Youth* puts it this way: "When you do what is necessary to repent and receive forgiveness, . . . you will feel the peace of the Lord Jesus Christ."[2]

HOW can I enjoy the blessings of forgiveness if I still remember my sins?

Some mistakenly think that just because they can still remember their sins, they haven't been forgiven. This isn't true. Elder Jeffrey R. Holland had this to say about remembering our sins: "You can remember just enough to avoid repeating the mistake."[3] The scriptures say that the Lord will remember our sins no more (D&C 58:42), not that we won't!

WORLD PEACE? FIND INNER PEACE FIRST

It is a cliché that pageant contestants say they want world peace for our society. However, as the Dalai Lama said, "We can never obtain peace in the world if we neglect the inner world and don't make peace with ourselves. World peace must develop out of inner peace."[4]

Finding inner peace through repentance and forgiveness can be the first step we all can take toward establishing world peace.

World peace!

The Sin Has Lost Its Appeal

One key to knowing if we have been forgiven is that we have lost the desire to commit the sin we have repented of. We may still be *tempted* to commit that sin, but now we don't *want* to commit that sin—we don't desire it anymore. When King Benjamin's people were moved to repentance they said, "we have no more disposition to do evil, but to do good continually" (Mosiah 5:2). They had lost their *desire* to sin. Alma taught, "Now they, after being sanctified by the Holy Ghost, having their garments made white, being pure and spotless before God, *could not look upon sin save it were with* abhorrence" (Alma 13:12; emphasis added). When the sin begins to lose its appeal, we begin to find forgiveness.

abhorrence (ab-hor-rence): to loathe or hate.

DOES THIS LOOK APPEALING TO YOU?

When we begin to lose the desire for our sins on the same level that we don't desire a fly in our soup, then we can know we are on the path to being forgiven.

We Enjoy the Gift of the Holy Ghost and Fruits of the Spirit

One of the roles of the Holy Ghost is to sanctify, or purify, us of sin. Christ taught the Nephites that we are "sanctified by the reception of the Holy Ghost" (3 Nephi 27:20). If we are enjoying the gifts of the Holy Ghost, then we generally are enjoying the gift of forgiveness as well because the Holy Ghost cleanses, sanctifies, and purifies us. Similarly, President Henry B.

WATER ON YOUR BACK

Imagine that you are on your hands and knees with several cups of water on your back and legs. How could you stand up without getting wet? The answer is, you probably can't—on your own. When it comes to being forgiven we must understand that it is a gift from Jesus Christ. Symbolically speaking, he will take away those cups of water and give us the strength to stand on our feet.

Eyring taught, "Reception of the Holy Ghost is the cleansing agent as the Atonement purifies you. . . . That is a fact you can act on with confidence. . . . And when he is your companion, you can have confidence that the Atonement is working in your life."[5]

DO TRY THIS AT HOME!

Do you think we have been commanded to forgive others for *their* benefit? Think again. This activity might help you see why: Pick up a large, heavy object like a book (or a chair if you are feeling really tough!). Carry it around with you for a while. Try to do some simple tasks while holding on to it, like tying your shoe. You can't set down the object at any time, or rest it on anything. You need to hold on to it and carry it all the time!

Do you want to set it down yet? We thought so.

Now read Doctrine and Covenants 64:9–11 and ask yourself: Why does the Lord command us to forgive others? It is usually not until we "let go," forgive, and "put down" our grudges that we can move on with our lives. The commandment to forgive is just as much for our benefit as it is for others. When we forgive, we let go of a burden and feel greater peace.

"Your Sins Are Forgiven You"

Over and over in the scriptures, the Lord tells people, "Your sins are forgiven you" (see D&C 36:1). As a matter of fact, the phrase "sins are forgiven" appears in the scriptures *fifteen different times*. Truly, the Lord is willing and able "to make you holy, and your sins are forgiven you" (D&C 60:7).

We Are Willing to Forgive Others

Another key to knowing if we have truly enjoyed the gift of forgiveness is that we are willing to extend forgiveness to others. The Savior stated on multiple occasions "for if ye forgive men their trespasses, your heavenly Father will also forgive you" (Matthew 6:14; see also D&C 64:9–10; Ephesians 4:32). To be forgiven, we must forgive.

HOW can I forgive others if they aren't sorry for what they've done?

Our willingness to forgive others should not depend on whether or not they forgive us. President Gordon B. Hinckley shared the story of a woman who was driving her car when a young man threw a frozen turkey that smashed into her windshield. As a result, the woman had to undergo hours of surgery and learned that it would take years of physical therapy to return to normal. But she frankly forgave the young man who had injured her and worked to reduce the penalties he would face.[6] One lesson we can gain from this story is that we can forgive others—even if they have done terrible things to us. Whether or not they are sorry does not really matter.

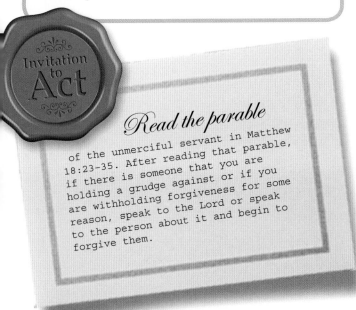

Invitation to Act

Read the parable of the unmerciful servant in Matthew 18:23–35. After reading that parable, if there is someone that you are holding a grudge against or if you are withholding forgiveness for some reason, speak to the Lord or speak to the person about it and begin to forgive them.

HOW FORGIVING AM I?

Forgiving others means more than just accepting an apology or saying, "It's okay." Here are a few questions to ask ourselves to see how forgiving we might be:

1. Do I ever say, "I will forgive, but never forget?"

2. Am I ever secretly happy when something unfortunate happens to someone I don't like?

3. Do I try to "get even" with people for something they have done to me?

4. Is there anyone with whom I refuse to speak?

5. In arguments, do I bring up things that others have done in the past?

6. When I disagree or get angry with someone, do I sulk and pout and take a few days to get over it?

7. Do I talk unkindly to others about someone who has hurt or offended me?

8. Do I ever justify my grudges by rationalizing, "If they would say they are sorry, then I would forgive them"?

9. When someone does apologize to me, do I ever think or say, "It'll take more than just words to make it right"?

10. When I hear a certain person's name, do I still feel bitterness or anger inside?

Our Priesthood Leader Says We Are Worthy to Participate in Gospel Ordinances

For the Strength of Youth points to the critical role bishops play in repentance and forgiveness: "Serious sins, such as sexual transgression or use of pornography, need to be confessed to your bishop. Be completely honest with him. He will help you repent."[7] To be clear, bishops do not forgive us. Only the Lord can forgive sins. However, the bishop acts as the Lord's agent and as a judge in Israel. Specifically, he has the authority to judge when we are worthy to participate in gospel ordinances. When a bishop judges us worthy to participate in gospel ordinances after we have repented, we can know that the Lord has freed us from the guilt of our sin. Elder Richard G. Scott said, "I testify that when a bishop or stake president has confirmed that your repentance is sufficient, know that your obedience has allowed the Atonement of Jesus Christ to satisfy the demands of justice for the laws you have broken. Therefore you are now free. Please believe it."[8]

We Are Willing to Keep All the Commandments

The scriptures teach us that another indicator that we have been forgiven of a particular sin is that we are willing to keep *all* the commandments, not just the one we have broken: "Nevertheless, he that repents and *does the commandments* [note the plural] of the Lord shall be forgiven" (D&C 1:32; emphasis added; see also Mosiah 5:5). When President Henry B. Eyring was a bishop, a young man asked him how he could know if he had been fully forgiven. Bishop Eyring later saw Elder Spencer W. Kimball (who was then a member of the Quorum of the Twelve), and asked him how the young man could receive revelation to let him know if he had been forgiven. The following transcript is President Henry B. Eyring's account of what transpired:

"I thought Elder Kimball would talk to me about fasting or prayer or listening for the still small voice. But he surprised me. Instead he said, 'Tell me something about the young man.'

"I said, 'What would you like to know?'

"And then he began a series of the most simple questions. Some of the ones I remember were:

"'Does he come to his priesthood meetings?'

"I said, after a moment's thought, 'Yes.'

"'Does he come early?'

"'Yes.'

"'Does he sit down front?'

"I thought for a moment and then realized, to my amazement, that he did.

"'Does he home teach?'

"'Yes.'

"'Does he go early in the month?'

"'Yes, he does.'

"'Does he go more than once?'

"'Yes.'

"I can't remember the other questions. But they were all like that—little things, simple acts of obedience, of submission. And for each question I was surprised that my answer was always yes. Yes, he wasn't just at all his meetings: he was early; he was smiling; he was there not only with his whole heart, but the broken heart of a little child, as he was every time the Lord asked anything of him. And after I had said yes to each of his questions, Elder Kimball looked at me, paused, and then very quietly said, 'There is your revelation.'"[9]

If we are alive with an all-around righteous life, then the guilt of a specific sin may be dying.

As we see these principles of forgiveness working in our lives, they will become indicators that we have been forgiven. We can experience what Enos felt when he said, "And there came a voice unto me, saying: Enos, thy sins are forgiven thee, and thou shalt be blessed. And I, Enos, knew that God could not lie; wherefore, my guilt was swept away" (Enos 1:5–6).

TELL ME ONE MORE TiME!

How Can I Know When I've Been Forgiven?

- **We have peace of mind.**
- **The sin has lost its appeal.**
- **We enjoy the gift of the Holy Ghost and fruits of the Spirit.**
- **We are willing to forgive others.**
- **Our priesthood leader says we are worthy to participate in gospel ordinances.**
- **We are willing to keep *all* the commandments.**

How Can I Have More Meaningful Prayers?

ROAST, ROAST, ROAST!

To see a short video that teaches what roast has to do with having effective prayers, visit http://johnhiltoniii.com/qa.

President Henry B. Eyring, then a member of the Quorum of the Twelve, said, "Most of us have had some experience with self-improvement efforts. My experience has taught me this about how people and organizations improve: the best place to look is for small changes we could make in things we do often. There is power in steadiness and repetition. And if we can be led by inspiration to choose the right small things to change, consistent obedience will bring great improvement."[1]

Improving our prayers is one of the "small changes" we can make in something that we do often. Many people pray at least a couple of times each day, offering hundreds and hundreds of prayers a year. However, as we've all experienced, some of those prayers are more powerful than others. Why is that the case? How can we have more effective prayer on a daily basis?

Follow the Prophets: Go Somewhere Private, Kneel, and Pray Out Loud

We can gain powerful insight into how to make our prayers more meaningful by studying the prayers of prophets. Notice some patterns of prayer in these three scriptures. (We've highlighted some of them for you.)

Enos: "Behold, **I went** to hunt beasts in the forests; and the words which I had often heard my father speak concerning eternal life, and the joy of the saints, sunk deep into my heart. And my soul hungered; and **I kneeled down** before my Maker, and **I cried unto him** in mighty prayer and supplication for mine own soul" (Enos 1:3–4).

Joseph Smith: "In accordance with this, my determination to ask of God, **I retired to the woods** to make the attempt. It was on the morning of a beautiful, clear day, early in the spring of eighteen hundred and twenty. It was the first time in my life that I had made such an attempt, for amidst all my anxieties I had never as yet made the attempt to **pray vocally**. **After I had retired to the place where I had previously designed to go**, having looked around me, and finding myself alone, **I kneeled down** and began to offer up the desires of my heart to God" (Joseph Smith–History 1:14–15).

HOW do I know if I should kneel, stand, or sit when I pray?

Have you ever been in bed and wondered if you can just pray while lying down? Or have you ever been in a meeting and somebody was asked to give the closing prayer, and the person asked, "Should I stand up?" Sometimes it can be awkward.

There's a common rhyme, "A prayer in bed is a prayer unsaid." While that's probably technically not true, the point is that when we are privately praying to God at night or in the morning we should usually kneel or show respect in some form, rather than just lying down in bed and closing our eyes.

But what if you're in a public meeting? Elder David A. Bednar shared an experience in which Elder David B. Haight (at the age of 97) refused to sit down while praying. Elder Bednar said, "There was simply no way that mighty Apostle was going to sit and pray in the presence of the First Presidency and his colleagues of the Twelve. And of greater importance, he was not going to sit as he communicated with his Heavenly Father."[2]

When we are called on to pray in public it is best to stand. Although there may be some situations where it is appropriate to sit while praying (for example, if you are driving a vehicle ☺), as a general rule kneeling (in private prayer) or standing (in public prayer) may be more appropriate.

Nephi: "[Nephi] went out and bowed himself down upon the earth, and cried mightily to his God in behalf of his people, yea, those who were about to be destroyed because of their faith in the tradition of their fathers. And it came to pass that he cried mightily unto the Lord all that day" (3 Nephi 1:11–12).

Did you catch the patterns? First, these prophets went somewhere private when they prayed. Second, they knelt down to pray. Kneeling is a sign of submissiveness to God, a willingness to do what God tells us, and a show of respect and reverence. Finally, the prophets cried out, or prayed vocally. There is great power in vocal prayer: it helps us to concentrate and verbally express our true feelings and desires. Perhaps it isn't coincidental that Joseph Smith's First Vision burst upon him after his first vocal prayer on the subject (see Joseph Smith–History 1:14). The Lord has also instructed us to pray vocally: "And again, I command thee that thou shalt pray vocally as well as in thy heart; yea, before the world as well as in secret, in public as well as in private" (D&C 19:28).

CAN YOU STAY FOCUSED?

Try to think of nothing but vanilla ice cream for one minute straight. Ready? Go!

How did you do? Odds are, your thoughts started to wander, didn't they? Maybe your thoughts ran something akin to this:

Vanilla ice cream, vanilla ice cream, vanilla ice . . . hey, wasn't there a rapper named Vanilla Ice? Whatever happened to him? He's probably hanging out with MC Hammer. Hammer time! Hammers. Where is our hammer in our house? I need to hang up a picture. Oh, yeah, vanilla ice cream!

Sometimes it can be hard to keep our concentration, especially when we are praying silently. Praying vocally can help us focus on our prayer.

ON YOUR KNEES!

Our friend Laurel Christensen shared the following insight with us. A couple thousand years ago a Chinese emperor had his people create an army of more than 8,000 terra-cotta soldiers. These warriors were hand-made statues; each one was unique. There were five different types of statues. Over time many of the warriors were damaged and in need of repair. Only one type of warrior has been discovered that did not need any repair work. Any guesses to which one it was? The archer. *And he was on his knees.*

Choose one of the principles discussed in this chapter and implement it in your personal prayers over the next week. For example, you could try saying your personal morning and evening prayers on your knees.

Invitation to Act

SAY WHAT?

Look at these letters. In your mind, try to figure out what they mean:

1. SA
2. XS
3. NV
4. NTT
5. DK
6. XTC

If you're struggling to figure it out, simply say each letter *out loud* and listen to the words they make. Notice how you got more meaning when you spoke out loud? Vocal prayers are much the same.

Answers: 1. Essay 2. Excess 3. Envy 4. Entity 5. Decay 6. Ecstasy

Speak to God Openly as Your Loving Father

Elder Richard G. Scott said, "Don't worry about your clumsily expressed feelings. *Just talk to your Father.*"[3] In the same talk he also said, "What seems most helpful [in prayer] is seeing in my mind a child approaching trustingly a loving, kind, wise, understanding Father, who wants us to succeed."[4] When "the Lord spake unto Moses face to face," he spoke "as a man speaketh unto his friend" (Exodus 33:11). God is both our friend (see D&C 84:63), and our Father; our prayers are more effective when we speak to him openly and freely as we would our closest friends. Speaking to God in this way will also help us avoid using "vain repetitions" (Matthew 6:7), or prayers without meaning.

Although we should speak to God freely and openly, we should still do it with respect and reverence in our language. Elder Dallin H. Oaks said, "When we go to worship in a temple or a church, we put aside our working clothes and dress ourselves in something better. This change of clothing is a mark of respect. Similarly, when we address our Heavenly Father, we should put aside our working words and clothe our prayers in special language of reverence and respect."[5]

Pray for Others

DO TRY THIS AT HOME!

One of the glasses in the picture above has sugar mixed in it. One has salt mixed in it. Since you can't taste them, how can you tell the difference?

Answer: If you are coming up with complicated science experiments, you are missing the easiest way. Just ask us! We created the picture. The glass on the right has the sugar in it. Remember, Heavenly Father is in charge of everything. Turning to him in prayer and asking him for answers makes solving life's problems a little easier.

Another pattern we can find in the prayers of prophets is that they prayed for others. Notice this pattern in the following verses:

- "Lehi . . . prayed unto the Lord, yea, even with all his heart, *in behalf of his people*" (1 Nephi 1:5; emphasis added).
- "[Enos] prayed unto him with many long strugglings *for [his] brethren, the Lamanites*" (Enos 1:11; emphasis added).
- "[Captain Moroni] prayed mightily unto his God for the blessings of liberty to rest upon *his brethren*" (Alma 46:13; emphasis added).

Sometimes, in the midst of our problems and needs, the greatest solution is to focus on the needs of others. In doing so, we not only serve others, but we find solutions to our own needs. Remember, the Lord promised that "he that loseth his life for my sake shall find it" (Matthew 10:39).

Thank More

For many years Elder F. Michael Watson served as the secretary to the First Presidency. Elder Watson said, "Each morning in the meeting of the First Presidency, the Brethren take turns praying. I always liked to listen to President Ezra Taft Benson pray. His prayers were almost entirely in thankfulness instead of asking for blessings."[6]

Once Elder David A. Bednar and his wife were instructed by a member of the Quorum of the Twelve to offer a prayer in which they only gave thanks. Although they had some pressing matters they wished to pray for, they followed his counsel. Elder Bednar said that as they prayed, only expressing thanks, not asking for any blessings, that they received both insight and inspiration.[7]

"The most meaningful and spiritual prayers I have experienced contained many expressions of thanks and few, if any, requests. . . . Let me recommend that periodically you and I offer a prayer in which we only give thanks and express gratitude. Ask for nothing; simply let our souls rejoice and strive to communicate appreciation with all the energy of our hearts."—Elder David A. Bednar[8]

Texting or Morse Code—Which Is Faster?

A television show had a competition between two people doing Morse code and two people texting each other to see which pair could communicate more quickly. Which method do you think was the fastest? (Hint: it wasn't texting.) The host of the show joked to the texters that they had been beaten by a 170-year-old technology.[9] But there's something even better than texting or Morse code for communicating important messages—prayer!

Listen More

Imagine if your friend called you and said, "Hi, (insert your name)! Thanks for being my friend. Could you please help my acne go away and also get me some money? And while you're at it, could you help me do better in school? Bye." And then your friend hangs up before you can respond. How would you feel?

In a similar way, we sometimes do this with our prayers. President Gordon B. Hinckley said, "The trouble with most of our prayers is that we give them as if we were picking up the telephone and ordering groceries—we place our order and hang up."[10]

Don't hang up too soon! Elder M. Russell Ballard wrote, "The most important part of prayer is not what we say but how well we listen."[11] We need to take time after we pray to really listen for communication from the Lord. Prayer, after all, should be a *two-way* conversation. If we ask the Lord a question in our prayers, we also need to be still and listen for an answer throughout our prayer and throughout the day.

"My father [President Henry B. Eyring] has told us that there are two things that he prays for every night. The first is, 'What blessings do I have that I am not aware of?' and the second is, 'Whom can I help?' . . . Dad says there has never been a day that his prayers haven't been answered."—Matthew Eyring[12]

Listen to What the Spirit Tells Us to Pray For

Not only do we need to listen for God's *answers* to our prayers, but the best prayers are the ones in which *we listen to what God is telling us to pray for through the Holy Ghost.* Elder Bruce R. McConkie wrote: "Perfect prayers are those which are inspired, in which the Spirit reveals the words which should be used."[13] The Lord's prophets have repeatedly taught this principle of the Holy Ghost telling us what we should pray for. President J. Reuben Clark said, "I should like to testify to the power of prayer, and to say that it is a wise man who knows what to pray for. One of the things that we should seek in going before the Lord and in going upon our knees, *is his inspiration and his wisdom to tell us what to ask for.*"[14]

This may be what Paul meant when he said, "I will pray with the spirit" (1 Corinthians 14:15), and "Likewise the Spirit also helpeth our infirmities: *for we know not what we should pray for as we ought: but the Spirit itself maketh intercession for us*" (Romans 8:26; emphasis added). If we are humble, have faith, and desire to know and follow God's will, as we listen to the promptings of the Holy Ghost we can know what we should and should not pray for, and therefore pray according to what God desires for us.

HOW can I start praying in the morning, and not just at night?

Although all prayers are important, it is possible that our morning prayers are more important than the prayers we say before we go to bed. Why? Because in the morning we are getting ready to start our day, to face the tests and trials of life, and to perform our work. At night, we are usually concluding the day and then getting into bed. We probably don't need a lot of spiritual direction while we snore! However, most youth (and probably adults) admit that they skip their morning prayer more often than their nighttime prayer. This is because they either forget in the morning or are in too big of a hurry.

Something you might consider trying is getting up a few minutes earlier each day and to pray first thing when you get out of bed. Sometimes the hardest part of developing a habit of morning prayer is simply remembering to pray. You could put a sign on your bathroom mirror or in another place where you will see it to remind yourself to pray each morning. We have one good friend whose reminder is the doorknob. If he touches the doorknob to leave in the morning and hasn't prayed, he gets down on his knees there in front of the door and does so before he leaves. Don't skip out on the vital morning prayer!

Does this resemble our prayers? Remember, one of the purposes of prayer is to get ourselves in tune with what God wants for us, and not just to ask what we want for ourselves.

Follow the Pattern Set in the Savior's Prayers

Ultimately, we gain powerful insights into how to make our prayers more meaningful by studying the recorded prayers of our Exemplar, Jesus Christ. His longest prayer in the Book of Mormon is in 3 Nephi 19:

19. And it came to pass that Jesus departed out of the midst of them, and went a little way off from them and bowed himself to the earth, and he said:

Notice that the Savior went to a private place to pray.

Notice that even the Savior showed reverence in his posture.

20. Father, I thank thee that thou hast given the Holy Ghost unto these whom I have chosen; and it is because of their belief in me that I have chosen them out of the world.

The first thing the Savior did after addressing the Father was to express gratitude.

21. Father, I pray thee that thou wilt give the Holy Ghost unto all them that shall believe in their words.

Notice that the Savior is praying for *others*, not himself. The Savior's prayer consisted of expressing gratitude and asking for others to be blessed.

It is also important to note that after this prayer was finished, the Savior offered two more prayers (see verses 27–31). In fact, it appears from the scriptural account that his third prayer was the most powerful prayer of the three. Isn't that interesting? Some of us have had the experience of praying, climbing into bed, and having something else pop into our mind to pray for. We shouldn't say, "Well, I've already prayed tonight." Instead, pray again! The Savior teaches us that we should continually offer prayers and that sometimes it is the second or third prayer that is the most powerful.

Another important lesson from the prayers of the Savior is that he taught we should pray saying, "Thy will be done" (Matthew 6:10). President Boyd K. Packer said, "I have learned to conclude all my prayers with 'Thy will be done.'"[15]

Elder H. Burke Peterson summarizes much of what we have discussed about how to have more effective prayer: "As you feel the need to confide in the Lord or to improve the quality of your visits with him—to pray, if you please—may I suggest a process to follow: go where you can be alone, go where you can think, go where you can kneel, go where you can speak out loud to him. The bedroom, the bathroom, or the closet will do. Now, picture him in your mind's eye. Think to whom you are speaking, control your thoughts—don't let them wander, address him as your Father and your friend. Now tell him things you really feel to tell him—not trite phrases that have little meaning, but have a sincere, heartfelt conversation with him. Confide in him, ask him for forgiveness, plead with him, enjoy him, thank him, express your love to him, and then listen for his answers."[16] We testify that if we will pray in such a manner, we can go from "just saying a prayer" to really praying.

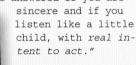

"If you have had trouble getting answers to your prayers, try asking today, 'What is there that you would have me do?' That prayer will be answered if you are sincere and if you listen like a little child, with *real intent to act.*"

—President Henry B. Eyring[17]

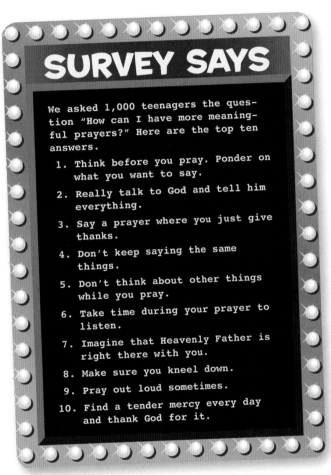

SURVEY SAYS

We asked 1,000 teenagers the question "How can I have more meaningful prayers?" Here are the top ten answers.

1. Think before you pray. Ponder on what you want to say.
2. Really talk to God and tell him everything.
3. Say a prayer where you just give thanks.
4. Don't keep saying the same things.
5. Don't think about other things while you pray.
6. Take time during your prayer to listen.
7. Imagine that Heavenly Father is right there with you.
8. Make sure you kneel down.
9. Pray out loud sometimes.
10. Find a tender mercy every day and thank God for it.

TELL ME ONE MORE TIME!

How Can I Have More Meaningful Prayers?

- **Follow the prophets: Go somewhere private, kneel, and pray out loud.**
- **Speak to God openly as your loving Father.**
- **Pray for others.**
- **Thank more.**
- **Listen more.**
- **Listen to what the Spirit tells us to pray for.**
- **Follow the pattern set in the Savior's prayers.**

11 ch Why Should I Fast?

> "The first and the best victory is to conquer self; to be conquered by self is, of all things, the most shameful and vile."—Plato[1]

PLATO

We all know the feeling. It is Sunday morning, and you have just rolled out of bed. You stagger toward the kitchen like a zombie, anticipating a nice breakfast to fill your stomach and start your engine for the day. You have just poured the cold milk over your cereal and are ready to take your first bite when you hear your mom call from the bedroom and say, "I hope you're not eating . . . it's fast Sunday!" Your heart sinks as you wish you could have just gulped down your food in gluttonous ignorance. You wonder aloud, "Why do I have to fast?"

SCRIPTURE SEARCH

In Doctrine and Covenants 59:14, the Lord gives a synonym for fasting. What word does he use? Why do you think he views these words as synonyms?

You're not alone. Although fasting is one of the oldest-known practices in the Lord's Church—it dates back to Old Testament times—its meaning has been lost to many, including some Latter-day Saints. But when we understand some of the doctrines and principles behind the practice of fasting, we will find that fasting can be a delight, even if we have to momentarily forgo that yummy bowl of cereal.

Fasting Helps Us Overcome Sin

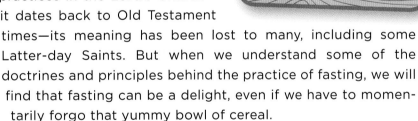

Perhaps the best place to begin a discussion about fasting is with Isaiah's explanation of why we should fast. Many of Isaiah's people were apparently like some of us, because they also voiced their complaints about being asked to fast: "Wherefore have we fasted, say they, and thou seest not? wherefore have we afflicted our soul?" (Isaiah 58:3).

Sound familiar? Are there some of us who see fast Sunday as an "afflicted" day for our soul (and our stomach), instead of a blessed day? Speaking for the Lord, Isaiah responds: "Is not this the fast that I have chosen? to loose the bands of wickedness, to undo the heavy burdens, and to let the oppressed go free, and that ye break every yoke?" (Isaiah 58:6).

What a profound answer! The first and primary purpose that he states regarding why we fast is to "loose the bands of wickedness" or in other words to *help us overcome sin.* That is not the first answer most people give when asked to explain why we fast. Ask the average member of the Church why we fast and they might give you many good reasons, ranging from "it's a commandment" to "because it makes Mom's dinner taste better," but rarely will people say "to conquer sin."

It is significant that Isaiah lists overcoming sin as the first reason why we fast. But how will going without food and drink help us overcome sin?

CHURCH IS AT 9:00 AM . . . SWEET!

Fasting has less to do with what time our church meetings start and more to do with what time we last *ate*.

For the Strength of Youth defines a "fast" as "not eating or drinking for two consecutive meals."[2] *Gospel Principles* helps clarify what that exactly means: "One Sunday each month Latter-day Saints observe a fast day. On this day we neither eat nor drink for two consecutive meals, thus making a fast of twenty-four hours. If we were to eat our evening meal on Saturday, then we would not eat or drink until the evening meal on Sunday."[3]

At the heart of almost all sin is selfishness, coupled with a lack of self-control.[4] President David O. McKay said, "The lack of self-control is one of the most common contributing factors of unhappiness."[5] When we say something we shouldn't have, think something that is not virtuous, or do something that is unholy, we let our "natural man" rule over our "spiritual man."

The spiritual man wants to be morally clean, the natural man doesn't. The spiritual man wants to be honest; the natural man wants to lie a little. The spiritual man wants to serve his fellow man, while the natural man only wants the donuts at the end of the service project.

This is a great service project!

FASTING AND FAITHFULNESS

Not touching this orange juice in the morning . . .

and not touching this alcohol at night . . .

have a lot to do with each other.

Fasting is a tool that the Lord has given us to help us learn how to control our natural man. Elder Joseph B. Wirthlin described how this works: "Each time we fast, we gain a little more control over our worldly appetites and passions."[6]

Did you catch that? Fasting helps us overcome our *worldly* appetites and passions. If we can control our natural desire to sustain ourselves through food, we can better control our natural desire for selfishness. If we can pass on a glass of orange juice in the morning, we will have greater ability to pass on a drink of alcohol at night. If we have the willpower to abstain from pre-mealtime food, we will have increased power to abstain from pre-marital sex. If we have the strength to turn away a steamy meal, we will have the strength to turn off a steamy show. If we have the self-control to not touch the cookies that will ruin our fast, we will have the control to "touch not the unclean thing" (2 Corinthians 6:17) that will ruin our soul.

It isn't a coincidence that our Savior was able to overcome each of the devil's temptations *after* he had "fasted forty days and forty nights" (Matthew 4:2). We truly "loose the bands of wickedness" and "undo every yoke" of sin as we learn to control our appetite. The physical hungering of our stomach will lead to the spiritual hallowing of our soul.[7]

A Way to Help Others

As if overcoming sin were not sufficient enough motivation to fast, there is a second, perhaps more noble reason. Isaiah continues his explanation of fasting by teaching the people: "Is [fasting] not to deal thy bread to the hungry, and that thou bring the poor that are cast out to thy house? when thou seest the naked, that thou cover him; and that thou hide not thyself from thine own flesh?" (Isaiah 58:7).

LESS THAN $1 PER DAY

The following map represents the percentage of those living on less than $1 per day, as of 2007.[8]

2%–5%
6%–20%
21%–40%
41%–60%
61%–80%

Much of fasting has to do with hunger—not just ours, but other people's hunger. For many who live in economically comfortable situations, being without food and feeling the pain of hunger is a rare experience. When the only trial regarding food for many Americans is deciding "*What* will I eat?", it becomes difficult to empathize and relate to the poor, whose daily question is "*Will* I eat?"

HELPING THE HUNGRY

"About 25,000 people die each day from hunger or hunger-related causes, most of them children."[9]

Voluntarily going without food for two meals for one day each month temporarily puts us in the same situation as those who involuntarily go without food for many meals each day. Elder Joseph B. Wirthlin explained, "When we fast, . . . we feel hunger. And for a short time, we literally put ourselves in the position of the hungry and the needy. As we do so, we have greater understanding of the deprivations they might feel."[10]

As we fast, we will feel an increased desire to help those who are hungry, and the Lord has prepared a perfect system for us to do so.

Inherent in fasting is the fact that we do not eat food during the time of our fast, usually for two complete meals.[11] Joseph Smith taught the Saints what to do with the food remaining from the fast when he said: "Let this be an example to all saints, and there will never be any lack for bread: When the poor are starving, let those who have, fast one day and give what they otherwise would have eaten to the bishops for the poor, and every one will abound for a long time. . . . And so long as the saints will all live to this principle with glad hearts and cheerful countenances they will always have an abundance."[12]

What an inspired way to care for the poor and the needy! Each time a fast offering is given to a bishop, he can use that money to help provide for the needs of the poor in his ward. And if there is more money than there is need in the ward, the money is passed on to the stake to help the poor within its boundaries. If more fast offerings are collected in the stake than are needed by its members, then it is passed on to the Church to be distributed across the world. What a beautiful system! It is truly inspired by the Lord, as it costs nothing more than a temporary sacrifice of food and the benefits reach so many. President Gordon B. Hinckley said: "The millions of dollars which are needed for this purpose [of caring for the poor] each year really cost no one anything. It is not a sacrifice for anyone to go without two meals a month and give the equivalent cost, and even more, to his or her bishop for the care of the needy.

"Think, my brethren, of what would happen if the principles of fast day and the fast offering were observed throughout the world. The hungry would be fed, the naked clothed, the homeless sheltered. Our burden of taxes would be lightened. The giver would not suffer, but would be blessed by his small abstinence. A new measure of concern and unselfishness would grow in the hearts of people everywhere. Can anyone doubt the divine wisdom that created this program which has blessed the people of this Church as well as many who are not members of the Church?"[13]

IF THE WEALTHIEST 20% OF PEOPLE IN THE WORLD FASTED . . .

The United Nations estimates that the cost to end world hunger *completely*, along with diseases related to hunger and poverty, is about $195 billion a year.[14]

$195,000,000,000 Cost to end world hunger per year.

$16,250,000,000 Cost to end world hunger per month.

$13.54 Cost per month to end world hunger if 1,200,000,000 (20% of world population) people fasted and gave fast offerings each month.

You cannot control whether 1.2 billion people fast or not, but you can control whether you do your part by giving a generous fast offering each month.

Some teenagers may think that they do not need to pay fast offerings because their parents pay a fast offering, or because they do not buy household groceries. But *For the Strength of Youth* says, "A proper fast day observance includes . . . giving a generous fast offering."[15] Isn't it interesting that this pamphlet for *youth* encourages the payment of fast offerings? The Lord expects even the youth to live their covenants and assist the poor.

The next fast Sunday, fast for a full twenty-four hours. Plan ahead of time to have something specific in mind to pray for. In addition, pay a generous fast offering—even if you still live at home!

DO TRY THIS AT HOME!

Blessings from Fasting

A third reason to obey the law of the fast (which includes paying a generous fast offering) is so the Lord will pour out blessings on those who fast. We should begin and end our fast with a prayer. Often during a fast we pray for something specific, something that we care about very much or for someone in need. Fasting is a way of showing the Lord that we really want something and are willing to sacrifice to obtain his help in receiving it.

A Missionary's Experience

One missionary shared the following experience of how fasting helped him receive an answer to a prayer. He said, "My companion and I had been working hard—and I mean *hard!*—for four weeks without any success. We decided to have a special fast for our area, and that month we gave a more generous fast offering than we had given before. In the following weeks, we felt impressed to fast again that we would be able to see people converted to the gospel. In the weeks after our special fast, we were able to teach and baptize people every week. This experience strengthened my testimony that when I fast and pray for something, the Lord will hear my prayers."

Isaiah promised that when we fast "the Lord shall answer; thou shalt cry, and he shall say, Here I am" (Isaiah 58:9).

Notice that when we fast, the Lord will be more likely to respond to our prayers. He says, "Here I am." We are also promised that through fasting, "the Lord shall guide thee continually" (Isaiah 58:11). He will guide us and we will feel an increased outpouring of the Spirit as we become more connected to him through our fast. What an incredible blessing to have the Lord hear and answer our prayers through a dedicated fast!

The next time fast Sunday rolls around, remember the blessings that come from living the law of the fast. They are even better than that bowl of cereal!

Why Should I Fast?

1. Fasting helps us overcome sin as we learn how to control our appetites and passions.

2. Fasting helps us offer relief to the poor through the payment of fast offerings.

3. Fasting draws us closer to God and helps our prayers be answered.

NOW that we have reviewed some of the *principles*, let's answer some of the questions regarding the *practices* connected to fasting:

Why does what time Church starts have little to do with how long I fast?

Sometimes people think that you should break your fast right after your church meetings, so if church starts at 9:00 AM you don't have to fast as long. That kind of thinking misses part of the purpose of the fast. Fasting means going without food or drink for two meals, and a full fast should last about twenty-four hours. Breaking your fast shouldn't be determined by when church ends, but by when you begin your fast. For example, eating four bowls of cereal at 11:59 PM Saturday night, and then eating "dinner" at 2:30 after church on Sunday would be a less-appropriate fast. It is not when church ends; it is when we last ate that should determine the end of our fast.

Why should I still pay fast offerings if my parents already pay?

One reason is because you can. Even if you don't have a job, there can be no doubt that you eat better than millions of others do. Paying fast offerings allows you—as a disciple of Christ—to help the poor and needy around you. A second reason is that to receive the full blessings of the fast, you need to pay fast offerings. Third, paying fast offerings when you are younger helps you develop a habit that will serve you well throughout your life.

Why should I have something I'm fasting for?

Earlier we quoted Isaiah 58, which says that when we fast the Lord will hear our prayers more easily. Fasting provides an excellent opportunity for us to ponder the needs we have and to turn to the Lord for help. If you don't have anything you need, find somebody who does and fast for them. This will give you a purpose for your fast and make it more meaningful than simply going without food or water. Some of the most beneficial fasts can be when you fast for others.

Why Should I Honor My Parents?

We'll give you 5,475 reasons why we should honor our parents. Not sure what they are? Here's a hint:

That's right—on average your parents changed your diapers 5,475 times. Do you think that was enjoyable for them? Do you think they were excited to change your diapers? Chances are, you have never even thanked them! Those diapers alone ought to be reason enough to say, "Yes, Mom," and do the dishes whenever she asks.

As compelling a reason as diapers may be, there are even better reasons why we should honor our parents.

A Commandment with a Promise

One reason why we should honor our father and mother is that we are promised that we will live longer if we do. The apostle Paul wrote, "Honour thy father and mother; (which is the first commandment with promise)" (Ephesians 6:2). What does that mean, "the first commandment with promise"?

Of the Ten Commandments that God gave to Moses, only one came with a stated promise: the fifth commandment, which says, "Honour thy father and thy mother: *that thy days may be long* upon the land which the Lord thy God giveth thee" (Exodus 20:12; emphasis added). The scriptures don't spell out exactly how it is that your days will be long, but common sense dictates that those who honor their parents will probably live longer than if they didn't.

Parents Say	Honoring Them	Not Honoring Them	Choice that will help you live longer
Don't touch the stove	Don't do it	Give that burner a big kiss!	Honoring parents
Look both ways before crossing the street	Look twice	Run across the street without looking	Honoring parents
Obey traffic laws	Drive the speed limit	Burn rubber, baby!	Honoring parents
Don't do dumb stuff	Use wisdom	Jump off a second-story roof	Honoring parents

Elder Russell M. Nelson shared the following experience that shows one example of how honoring parents could have led to a longer life: "Several years ago, I was invited to give an important lecture at a medical school in New York City. The night before the lecture, Sister Nelson and I were invited to dinner at the home of our host professor. There he proudly introduced us to an honor medical student—his beautiful daughter.

"Some weeks later, that professor telephoned me in an obvious state of grief. I asked, 'What is the matter?'

"'Remember our daughter whom you met at our home?'

"'Of course,' I replied. 'I'll never forget such a stunning young lady.'

"Then her father sobbed and said, 'Last night she was killed in an automobile accident!' Trying to gain composure, he continued: 'She asked permission to go to a dance with a certain young man. I didn't have a good feeling about it. I told her so and asked her not to go. She asked, "Why?" I simply told her that I was uneasy. She had always been an obedient daughter, but she said that if I could not give her a good reason to decline, she wanted to go. And so she did. At the dance, alcoholic beverages were served. Her escort drank a bit—we don't know how much. While returning home, he was driving too fast, missed a turn, and careened through a guardrail into a reservoir below. They were both submerged and taken to their death.' . . .

"This experience will not have been in vain if others can listen and learn from it. Children, honor your parents."[2]

By the Numbers: What Have Your Parents Done for You?

200,000. That's the number of dollars the U.S. Department of Agriculture estimates it costs to raise you.[1] With that kind of money, your parents could have bought a condo on the beach, 200 plasma TVs, 10,000 DVDs, or 400,000 bags of candy—but they got you instead!

Besides a longer life, other important blessings come to those who honor their parents. Speaking of this commandment, President Gordon B. Hinckley said, "I think it is such a great commandment from the Lord. If it were only observed more widely, there would be far less misery in the homes of the people. Instead of backbiting, accusation, argument, there would be appreciation and respect and quiet love."[3]

HONOR

The word "honor" means much more than to just "obey" our parents. Think about the word "honor" in the following contexts and how they apply to honoring our parents:

If you were told to *honor* the flag, what would you do?

What does it mean to *honor* a promise?

If you were told to *honor* someone in a speech, what would you say about them?

"Honor thy father and mother" also implies respect, reverence, honesty, and bringing praise to them.

By the Numbers: What Have Your Parents Done for You?

7,665. The number of meals your parents made for you by the time you were seven. And how did you repay them? By throwing the food all over the floor, no doubt!

The Savior said, "The works which ye have seen me do that shall ye also do" (3 Nephi 27:21). In other words, the Savior has invited us to follow his example.

The Savior gave us the ultimate example of honoring his parents as he hung on the cross. Think of the excruciating pain the Savior must have felt. The previous twenty-four hours had been torture and misery and now he was suffering one of the cruelest deaths possible. Yet even still, he honored his mother. The scriptures record, "Now there stood by the cross of Jesus his mother. . . . When Jesus therefore saw his mother, and [John, the Apostle], he saith unto his mother, Woman, behold thy son! Then saith he to the disciple, Behold thy mother! And from that hour [John] took her unto his own home" (John 19:25–27).

Even in that moment of supreme agony, Jesus was concerned about what would happen to his mother after he died. He showed honor to her by making sure her needs were met.

HONORING YOUR PARENTS

"There come thundering to our ears the words from Mount Sinai: 'Honour thy father and thy mother.' . . .

"How do you honor your parents? I like the words of William Shakespeare: 'They do not love that do not show their love.' There are countless ways in which you can show true love to your mothers and your fathers. You can obey them and follow their teachings. . . .

"Be honest with your mother and your father. One reflection of such honesty with parents is to communicate with them. Avoid the silent treatment. . . . If you are [late], make a telephone call. . . .

"Don't wait . . . before you say, 'I love you, Mother; I love you, Father.' Now is the time to think and the time to thank. I trust you will do both. You have a heritage; honor it."—President Thomas S. Monson[4]

By the Numbers: What Have Your Parents Done for You?

600. That's the number of hours of sleep your parents lost during your first year of life. (That doesn't count the lost sleep while your mother was uncomfortable at night during her pregnancy.)

2,920 hours of sleep per year

2,320 hours of sleep per year

Before you were born

After you were born

Respect and Love

DO TRY THIS AT HOME!

No matter how you look at it, our parents have made untold, uncounted sacrifices for us. Even if they aren't perfect parents, they are probably doing the best they can. The least we can do is honor them for all they have done for us by treating them with the kindness and obedience, respect and love they deserve.

Elder M. Russell Ballard taught, "You do not have the right ever to be disrespectful to your mother or your father. Period. If you haven't had that taught to you before, write it in your journal and in your minds and hearts right now. Write down that I said you do not have the right to be ugly, to raise your voice, to slam doors, to scream or holler within the walls of your own home. Young people, you do have the right to be heard. If you are having difficulty getting your mother and your father to listen to you, in a calm manner just ask: 'Mom and Dad, I've got a different feeling about a matter. Can we set a time to talk about it?'"[5]

The next time your parents ask you to do something, say, "Yes! I will do it right away." (And then do it!)

WHAT ABOUT SIBLINGS?

Some might wonder, do I have to be nice to my siblings too? In a word—yes! Why? President Ezra Taft Benson said, "Your most important friendships should be with your own brothers and sisters and with your father and mother."[6] You might find this hard to believe, but trust us—as time goes on, the friendships that will matter the most to you are the ones you have with your parents and siblings. Thirty years from now they will be the people you most likely talk to on a consistent basis, not your junior high and high school friends. Family relationships are the ones that have been (or can someday be) bound together in the temple for eternity.

TELL ME ONE MORE TIME!

Why Should I Honor My Parents?

1. **Honoring your parents is the first commandment with a stated promise—a longer life.**
2. **The Savior set the example for us of honoring parents.**
3. **Our parents have changed diapers, made meals, lost sleep, and done countless other things for us. The least we can do is honor them by showing kindness and obedience.**

NOW that we have reviewed some of the *principles*, let's answer some of the questions regarding the *practices* connected to honoring our parents:

Why shouldn't I talk back to my parents?

We already gave you 5,475 reasons why. If that's not enough, see the quote by Elder Ballard on page 85.

Why is honoring my parents more than simply obeying them?

The commandment from the Lord is to *honor* our parents—which includes obedience. But as President Ezra Taft Benson said, "To honor and respect our parents means . . . that we love and appreciate them and are concerned about their happiness. . . . We treat them with courtesy. . . . We seek to understand their point of view. Certainly obedience to parents' righteous desires and wishes is a part of honoring."[7]

Why should I listen to my parents even if I think they are wrong?

This is a tough question. After reading this chapter, what do you think the answer is? Write down your thoughts in your journal.

Why Should I Be Grateful?

Do you have a pet peeve? Something that really bugs you? Maybe it's people who have private conversations on their cell phone in public places, or people not changing the toilet paper roll when it is empty, or the dreaded "bed-head."

Do you think the Lord has pet peeves? We think he might. Doctrine and Covenants 59:21 says, "And in nothing doth man offend God, or against none is his wrath kindled, save those who confess not his hand in all things, and obey not his commandments."

Two things that offend God the most, that really kindle his wrath, are ingratitude ("confess[ing] not his hand") and disobedience. That's bad news for some members of the Church because Joseph Smith said that "one of the greatest sins of which the Latter-day Saints would be guilty is the sin of ingratitude."[1] Let's learn why we should be grateful so that we don't offend God and kindle his wrath.

REASON NUMBER 3,243 TO BE GRATEFUL

You are not being chased by a lion. (Somebody, somewhere in the world, probably is!)

Counting Your Blessings—It's More Than Just a Song

You've heard the hymn "Count Your Blessings," but did you know studies show that literally counting your blessings increases your emotional health? In a scientific experiment,

gratitude   happiness

researchers had three different groups of people: one group wrote for twenty minutes each day about things they were grateful for; the second group wrote about things they were angry about; and the third group did nothing.[2] Guess which group was happiest? If you guessed the first group, congratulations, keep reading this chapter. If not, go straight to the telestial kingdom and be grateful you're not going to outer darkness. (Just kidding, you can keep reading too).

DO
TRY THIS
AT
HOME!

Count 100 of Your Blessings

Write a list of 100 things you are thankful for. Too many? Then try writing down:

- 10 living people you are grateful for.
- 10 people who have died you are grateful for.
- 10 physical abilities you are grateful for.
- 10 material possessions you are grateful for.
- 10 things about nature you are grateful for.
- 10 things about today you are grateful for.
- 10 places on earth you are grateful for.
- 10 modern-day inventions you are grateful for.
- 10 foods you are grateful for.
- 10 things about the gospel you are grateful for.

Guess what? A list of 100 blessings doesn't even begin to scratch the surface of all the things God has given you that you could possibly be grateful for.

Elder Joseph B. Wirthlin said gratitude "is a quality I have found in every happy person I know."[3] Think about that. Do you know any happy person who is *not* grateful?

He might be lacking some gratitude!

Being Grateful Leads to More Blessings

There are many blessings that come from being grateful for the good things we enjoy. *For the Strength of Youth* says, "Live with a spirit of thanksgiving and you will have greater happiness and satisfaction in life."[4]

Elder Wirthlin also taught that gratitude will make you "more likable and more at peace."[5]

The Lord himself promised, "He who receiveth all things with thankfulness shall be made glorious; and the things of this earth

REASON NUMBER 6,923 TO BE GRATEFUL

Some time in your life you have tasted chocolate. (Millions of people never have.)

shall be added unto him, even an hundred fold, yea, more" (D&C 78:19).

Elder Marvin J. Ashton shared a specific blessing that can come from gratitude. He taught, "The best way to get your family members active in the Church or to become members is to tell them 'thank you' for all they do to support you and tell them how much you love them."[6] This promise is especially helpful to those who have family members who are not members of the Church.

Another blessing of gratitude is that it increases our ability to see. For example, what do you see in the picture below?

DO YOU SUFFER FROM AFFLUENZA?

It seems obvious that we should be thankful for everything we have. So why do so many people forget to express gratitude? President Henry B. Eyring explained that "whatever we get soon seems our natural right, not a gift. And we forget the giver. Then our gaze shifts from what we have been given to what we don't have yet."[7]

Focusing on what we don't have leads to ingratitude. Sometimes it can be helpful to remember how much we have been blessed. A great video clip that has helped us be more grateful is called "Teenage Affluenza." It talks about a disease many teenagers have. Watch it at http://johnhiltoniii.com/qa and see if you have affluenza.

Chances are you probably noticed the dark flowers first. That's normal because, as Elder Joseph B. Wirthlin said, "Our minds have a marvelous capacity to notice the unusual."[8] But there is a problem! Elder Wirthlin pointed out that unfortunately, "The opposite is true as well, the more often we see the things around us—even the beautiful and wonderful things—the more they become invisible to us.

"That is why we often take for granted the beauty of this world—the flowers, the trees, the birds, the clouds—even those we love.

". . . Because we see things so often, we see them less and less."[9]

Did you notice the blue sky in the picture? The beautiful clouds? The mountains in the background? The dozens of flowers that *weren't* discolored? There are so many beautiful things to be grateful for, and as we practice being grateful, we will notice them more and more.

REASON NUMBER 8,472 TO BE GRATEFUL

You know how to read. (Approximately 1 *billion* people in the world are not so blessed.)[10]

Consequences of Ingratitude

It seems obvious, but when we are grateful, we avoid the consequences of ingratitude. When people are not grateful they tend to complain, and that isn't good for anyone. A story from the Old Testament illustrates this point. The Israelites were wandering in the wilderness and even though the Lord had delivered them from slavery and given them manna to eat, they were not grateful. Notice what happens: "And when the people complained, it displeased the Lord: and the Lord heard it" (Numbers 11:1).

So the Lord hears when we complain, and he does not like it. As a result of Israelites' complaining, a fire swept through the camp and many people died. Throughout the scriptures we see examples of people forgetting to thank the Lord and choosing to complain instead. Often, as in the case of the Israelites, the Lord sends the people trials so that they will humble themselves and remember him. Remember, ingratitude offends God (see D&C 59:21), and while the Lord may not cause a fire to come down on those who complain, ingratitude and complaining have plenty of other consequences.

I'D BE HAPPY IF . . .

Some people have a hard time being grateful for what they have. They say, "I'd be happy *if only I had* (fill in the blank—a new car, an iPod, good hair, etc.). Or like the girl who says, "When I'm 16, I'll be happy." Then she turns 16 and says, "When guys start asking me out, I'll be happy." And then guys start asking her out and she says, "When I get a boyfriend, I'll be happy." Then she gets a boyfriend and says, "When I can *break up* with my boyfriend, I'll be happy," and so it goes. If we say, "I'll be happy when . . . " the happiness may never come. But when we are grateful, we invite happiness to come into our lives immediately.

NIKE OR ADIDAS? NEITHER, THEY'RE GOODYEAR

Some people aren't happy because they don't have the latest style of shoes. Let's be grateful we *have* shoes.

Anthony Says:

When I was in Bolivia, I was amazed to see that the Andean Indians cut up leftover tires and turned them into sandals. These Bolivians were so grateful for "tire sandals"! One man even told me they were guaranteed for 50,000 miles. ☺

Consider the following statements about those who lack gratitude:

"Where there is an absence [of gratitude], there is often sadness, resentment, and futility."—Elder Joseph B. Wirthlin[11]

"Many a family, many a marriage is broken because of a lack of appreciation. . . . Too many times I have heard people say, 'My marriage was terminated primarily because my husband (or wife) didn't appreciate anything I ever did for him. No matter what I did, there was no thanks!'"—Elder Marvin J. Ashton[12]

"Absence of gratitude is the mark of the narrow, uneducated mind. It bespeaks a lack of knowledge and the ignorance of self-sufficiency. It expresses itself in ugly egotism and frequently in wanton mischief. . . .

"Without [gratitude], there is arrogance and evil."—Elder Gordon B. Hinckley[13]

The good news is we can avoid the consequences of ingratitude because gratitude is entirely in our control. We might not be able to make the varsity team, or be elected student body president. We might not get asked out on dates, or have the biggest muscles (we speak from personal experience). But we can control whether we have a grateful attitude or not.

REASON NUMBER 10,003 TO BE GRATEFUL

Indoor plumbing!
(Need we say more?)

PERSPECTIVE

Some get mad when they look at their plate
And only see food which taste they really hate
Others are thankful and ever so nice
Even if their plate contains just a handful of rice.
Some complain their car is too slow
Saying "I've got things to do, I've got to go, go, go!"
Others are grateful for a bicycle that is old
They treasure it like precious gold.

TELL ME ONE MORE TIME!

Why Should I Be Grateful?

1. **When we _aren't_ grateful, we offend God.**
2. **Counting our blessings helps us be more positive and happy.**
3. **Being grateful brings additional blessings.**
4. **When we complain and are ungrateful, the Lord may give us additional problems to help us recognize the blessings we do have. Other negative consequences also come with ingratitude.**

NOW that we have reviewed some of the *principles*, let's answer some of the questions regarding the *practices* connected to gratitude:

Cont.

Why should we thank God for blessings before asking for more blessings?

When you stop to think about it, Heavenly Father has already given us everything. In a way it can seem greedy to ask for more without considering all that we already have. Expressing our gratitude in prayer is an important part of truly acknowledging our thanks to God for the blessings we have received before we ask for more.

Why should I be grateful if there is so much I don't have?

You know the question: "Is the glass half-full or half-empty?" Yes there are probably lots of things that you do not have—but what about all the things that you *do* have? One of the keys to a successful life is to learn to focus less on what you want and more on being grateful for what you have.

Why is saying "thank you" a sign of an educated person?

As part of his classic six "B's" talk, President Gordon B. Hinckley said, "Be grateful. . . . The habit of saying thank you is the mark of an educated man or woman."[14] Why would he say that? Because when we thank others, we recognize and understand our dependence on others. Think of the food you eat . . . someone grew it. Think of the clothes you wear . . . someone made them. Think of the house you live in . . . someone built it and paid for it. Think of everything you know . . . someone taught it to you at some point. All we have and all we are is partly dependent on others. That is why President Hinckley said, "Express appreciation to everyone who does you a favor or assists you in any way"[15] because it shows your true awareness of the world around you.

THANK YOU!

How Can I Get More from My Scripture Study?

John Says:

In junior high school, I was a huge football fan. I grew up in Seattle, and posters of the Seahawks' star wide receiver Steve Largent hung in my room. I played little league football and was a wide receiver. I had big dreams of going pro, but unfortunately I wasn't on Mr. Largent's level. In fact, one day my dad told me that I wasn't going to be a professional football player.

I was really bummed! Why did my dad say that? Aren't your parents supposed to encourage you in your dreams? But my dad taught me an important lesson—he said, "John you won't be a professional football player because you're not willing to put in the required effort."

At first I was offended, but then I realized that he was right. I enjoyed playing football, but I didn't like to do drills or run laps. (I was also afraid of getting tackled!) I wasn't willing to do what it took to go pro.

In a similar way, I have sometimes found myself acting like an "amateur" in my scripture study. I know I'm supposed to read each day, and I do, but do I put in the required effort to *really* be spiritually nourished?

Go Pro

We can use the acronym PRO (as in "professional") to help us know how to get more out of our scripture study.

Pray

Regular Schedule

Obey

The P is for **"Pray."** Praying before we start reading will help us be able to be in tune and learn what the Lord would have us learn. President Howard W. Hunter said, "There is nothing more helpful than prayer to open our understanding of the scriptures."[1]

In addition to praying before studying, we should pray after we read to thank the Lord for the scriptures and to ask for help in remembering what we've learned. The Lord has commanded us to "pray always" to gain an understanding of the scriptures (D&C 32:4).

The R is for **"Regular Schedule."** Instead of saying, "I'll read whenever I have time and can fit it in," we should have a set time of day to study the scriptures. It could be the first thing when we wake up in the morning, or perhaps just before we go to bed, or any time

"Getting good results from your study depends on having a strong desire to learn."

PREACH MY GOSPEL[2]

HOW can I get anything from my scripture study if I don't understand all the big words?

Sometimes the unique vocabulary of the scriptures can make the scriptures hard to understand. One thing you can do is to use the seminary student study guide for the book of scripture you are studying. Ask your local seminary teacher for a copy, or you can download a free copy at http://seminary.lds.org/.

Each chapter has descriptions and definitions of difficult words to help make the language more understandable. It also has good quotes and activities throughout it to help you truly study instead of just read.

Others have found that it helps to listen to somebody read the Book of Mormon out loud while they follow along in their own scriptures. Perhaps the most important thing we can do to understand the words is to pray for the Spirit to enlighten us as we study. Elder Bruce R. McConkie said, "There is only one way to *understand* the scriptures. That way is by the power of the *Holy Ghost*."[3]

in between, but having a set time is very helpful because it establishes a routine or habit.

In addition, we should plan to read for a certain amount of *time* each day. President Howard W. Hunter said, "We should not be haphazard in our reading

"If possible, set a consistent time and place to study when you can be alone and undisturbed."

ELDER M. RUSSELL BALLARD[4]

but rather develop a systematic plan for study. There are some who read to a schedule of a number of pages or a set number of chapters each day or week. This may be perfectly justifiable and may be enjoyable if one is reading for pleasure, but it does not constitute meaningful study. It is better to have a set amount of time to give scriptural study each day than to have a set amount of chapters to read. Sometimes we find that the study of a single verse will occupy the whole time."[5]

Sometimes people ask the question, "What if I'm really busy, so I just read one or two verses a day. Is that okay?" Elder M. Russell Ballard said, "I have heard many well-intentioned Church leaders and teachers instruct congregations to find time for daily scripture study, 'even if it's only one or two verses per day.' Though I understand the point they are trying to teach and applaud the sincerity of that conviction, may I gently

BUT I'M TOO BUSY!

In a study of 103 high school seminary students in Utah who answered the question "When you don't read the scriptures, what is your primary reason for not reading?" the number one response (at 34.95 percent) was "too tired," and the number two reason (at 23.30 percent) was "not enough time" or "too busy."[6]

We need to admit that those aren't the

real reasons why we don't study the scriptures. After all, we almost always find time each day to eat, to dress ourselves, and to shower or bathe (we hope!) no matter how tired or busy we are. When we see that feeding our soul through scripture study is just as necessary as feeding our body through food, we will make it a priority and make the time for scripture study.

suggest that if we are too busy to spend at least a few minutes every day in the scriptures, then we are probably Too Busy and should find a way to eliminate or modify whatever activities are making that simple task impossible."[7]

HOW *can I help my family study the scriptures?*

Modern Church leaders have asked that families give "highest priority" to family scripture study.[8] If your family does not study the scriptures every day, talk to your mom and dad and ask if you can help organize a daily family scripture study. If, for whatever reason, you cannot have scripture study with your parents, consider organizing family scripture study with some of your brothers and sisters.

The O is for **"Obey."** President Henry B. Eyring taught, "The effect of . . . careful scripture study is to *always* feel an urging to *do* things."[9] A major purpose of our study should be to look for insights from the scriptures that help us more fully obey God's commandments. Sometimes the most meaningful parts of scripture study come after we've read the scriptures and ask ourselves, "What can I *do* to apply what I've learned?"

Invitation to Act

Go PRO with your scripture study this week. For the next seven days pray before you study, choose a regular time to study the scriptures each day, and at the end of each study session, decide what you will *do* as a result of your study.

ARE YOU USING YOUR SAFETY EQUIPMENT?

Sister Ann M. Dibb told of a terrible accident where four people were killed while working on a bridge. These individuals had safety equipment, *but chose not to use it.* Sister Dibb taught that Heavenly Father has given us safety equipment—including the scriptures. Are we using it?[10]

"My experience suggests that a specific and scheduled time set aside each day and, as much as possible, a particular place for study greatly increase the effectiveness of our searching through the scriptures."

ELDER DAVID A. BEDNAR[11]

HOW can I get an audio copy of the scriptures to listen to on my digital device?

There are a lot of free audio scripture downloads available on the Internet. The Church has provided a free download for each book at http://scriptures.lds.org/.

Click on the book you want to download and then click on "listen." Instructions are given on how to get a free audio copy to listen to on your digital device.

Write Down What We Learn

Another key to getting more from our scripture study is to write down what we learn. There are more than fifty places in the scriptures where the Lord has commanded his children to write his words. For example, the Lord said, "I command all men . . . that they shall write the words which I speak unto them" (2 Nephi 29:11). The Lord is speaking to us through the scriptures—are we recording the impressions we receive?

We've found that when we study the scriptures with paper and pen in hand we receive direction and revelation more easily. Perhaps having a piece of paper and a pen ready sends a signal to the Lord that we expect to learn things worth being written down. Another form of writing as we learn is simply by marking our scriptures and writing impressions or appropriate thoughts in the margins of the scriptures. We know some people who have even purchased the larger set of the scriptures so they can have more room in the margins to write. Whatever our method of writing, the process of recording impressions and thoughts as we study can lead to greater spiritual guidance in our scripture study.

"Please . . . read more slowly and more carefully and with more questions in mind. . . . Ponder, [and] examine every word, every scriptural gem."

ELDER JEFFREY R. HOLLAND[12]

IS ELDER CHRISTOFFERSON ENVISIONING YOUR SCRIPTURE STUDY?

Sometimes we get confused about the purpose of scripture study and think we're just supposed to "read the scriptures." The purpose of scripture study is not just to read the words on the page, but to get the word of God deep in our hearts. Elder D. Todd Christofferson explained what it could mean to seriously study the scriptures. As you read this description, ask yourself: Does this describe my scripture study? He said, "I see you sometimes reading a few verses, stopping to ponder them, carefully reading the verses again, and as you think about what they mean, praying for understanding, asking questions in your mind, waiting for spiritual impressions and insights that come so you can remember and learn more. Studying in this way, you may not read a lot of chapters or verses in a half hour, but you will be giving place in your heart for the word of God, and He will be speaking to you."[13]

GETTING MORE FROM THE SCRIPTURES

Want to continue learning about how to get more from the scriptures? Check out *Please Pass the Scriptures* by John Hilton III. You can download a chapter of the book for free at http://johnhiltoniii.com/qa.

"Study at a desk or table where you can write (not lying down or sitting on your bed), organize your study materials, and remain alert."

PREACH MY GOSPEL[14]

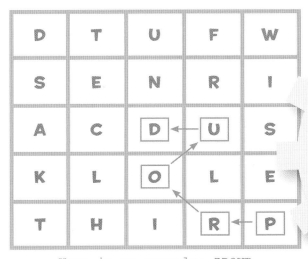

Here is an example: PROUD

DO TRY THIS AT HOME!

Look at the chart to the left. How many words can you find? Here are the rules: 1. You can go in any direction. 2. The letters need to be next to each other (you can't skip over rows or columns to get to the next letter. 3. The words must have at least three letters.

Did you find all the words we found? (See page 98 for answers.)

The Big Picture

Take a look at this picture— what do you see?

Not sure? Let's zoom out a little bit.

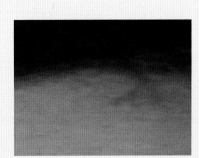

Still don't know? Let's zoom out a little bit more.

At first it was hard to tell what the picture was, but when we zoomed back to see "the big picture" it was much easier. In a similar way, we can sometimes gain more from our scripture study if we stop to see the big picture. One way we can do this after we read from the scriptures is to ask, "What does this mean to me? Why did the Lord put this in the scriptures? What can I learn right now from these scriptures? What do these verses teach me about the Savior? What do these verses teach me about the plan of salvation?"

Answers to "Do Try This at Home" on page 97.

The point of this object lesson is that there are way more words than we think there are. We might have gotten ten words and thought we did pretty well—but there are so many more! (We didn't even list them all here.) In the same way, we may find some insights from the scriptures and think we have found everything—but there is so much more. We need to keep on searching. (Special thanks to Robert Eaton for the idea for this activity.)

hole	house	plod	wiser	dunes	stun	cast
holes	dock	douse	rod	rise	set	core
lode	lock	role	lore	riser	seal	cores
ore	clod	proud	roles	louse	salt	rule
ores	cloud	cent	dole	nurse	ace	rules
teal	clouded	cents	doles	deal	aces	surf
ruler	lace	steal	cod	dolt	dent	cole
hire	laces	tune	send	aloud	colt	dents
our	laced	tunes	hires	end	loud	hilt
ours	scent	ire	tuned	ten	round	dealt
ascent	hour	run	case	rune	tend	rounded
rock	nest	hours	fun	runes	ceased	net
last	sack	old	dour	fund	wise	dune
nets	lasted	lack	hold			

TELL ME ONE MORE TIME!

How Can I Get More from My Scripture Study?

- **Pray before and after you read.**
- **Have a regular schedule.**
- **Find ways to act on or obey the verses you read.**
- **Write down what you learn.**

15 ch How Can I Keep the Sabbath Day Holy?

Perhaps no other commandment is as difficult to interpret as the command to "Remember the sabbath day, to keep it holy" (Exodus 20:8). We know that we should "not do any work" (Exodus 20:10) on that day, but even that can be difficult to figure out. What is *work* after all? If you pick up around the house on Sunday, is that work? The Pharisees in Jesus' time struggled with this question, and started to make strict rules about what is and is not "work" on the Sabbath, and therefore what is and is not keeping the Sabbath day holy.

WALKING AS WORK?

Did you know the Pharisees in Jesus' day used how many steps a person took in a day to define if they "worked" on the Sabbath?[1] What would happen if you hit the walking limit and weren't all the way home yet?

It seems that the Pharisees started to use their *traditions* rather than the *purposes* of the Sabbath to define what is and is not okay to do on the Sabbath (see Mark 7:9).

We may not be so different in the latter days. Instead of using the principles of the Sabbath day to determine what is and is not okay, sometimes we simply use the traditions of our family.

? HOW *should I dress on the Sabbath?*

For the Strength of Youth says, "Show respect for the Lord and yourself by dressing appropriately for Church meetings and activities. This is especially important when attending sacrament services."[2]

Elder David A. Bednar taught, "I know a young man who was taught in his home to dress appropriately for his Sunday meetings—and then to remain in his Sunday attire throughout the entire Sabbath day."[3] Although Elder Bednar made it clear this was not a rule everyone has to follow, it is an idea worth considering.

Should you need further clarification, *For the Strength of Youth* says, "If you are not sure what is appropriate to wear, study the words of the prophets, pray for guidance, and ask your parents or leaders for help."[4]

THERE'S NO SUCH THING AS THE FAMILY CLAUSE

Sometimes we hear teenagers say that something is okay to do on Sunday because they do it with their family. While we should spend quiet time with family on the Sabbath, "family" isn't necessarily the deciding principle of what is or isn't appropriate for the Sabbath. What if the family wanted to skip church and go to a movie instead—is that okay? What if the family wanted to go wakeboarding on Sunday—is that okay? We hate to break it to ya . . . the "Family Clause" may be more a tradition than a truth.

For example, one family might think it's just fine to go on a long Sunday walk, even in the woods, while another family might think that a long walk is like hiking and should be avoided. How do we know which one is Sabbath worthy? Our internal thoughts might go like this: "Going on a walk? That's fine! But what if we go on a walk in the mountains? No, that is not Sabbath approved. That's hiking, and we hike on Saturdays because we get all sweaty. So, not being sweaty is the key to keeping the Sabbath day holy. Yeah, no hiking. That is, unless you live in the mountains and are hiking to church. Then it's fine!"

To alleviate some internal Sabbath difficulty, and to help us make more *principled* decisions regarding keeping the Sabbath day holy, Doctrine and Covenants 59 gives us a few principles by which to judge our Sunday behavior.

"Hey, there's the church over there . . . keep hiking to keep the Sabbath day holy!"

Does the Activity Keep Me "Unspotted from the World"?

Doctrine and Covenants 59:9 says that one of the purposes of the Sabbath is to "more fully keep thyself unspotted from the world." A good question to ask ourselves is: "Does this activity help keep worldly ideas, thoughts, images, and desires out of my mind and heart?"

HOW does doing homework on Sunday affect my ability to keep the Sabbath day holy?

Elder Dallin H. Oaks addressed this question, writing, "I believed that I should labor hard for six days at my work, which was studying law, and should, therefore, refrain from student-like behavior on the Sabbath. . . . Study was my work and the Lord had commanded us to labor for six days and rest on the seventh. . . . I followed my father's example and my mother's gentle teaching, and I was also blessed for it.[5]

President Henry B. Eyring spoke about his experience participating in a very competitive graduate program. He was in a program where one-third of the students would fail— and he did not want to be one of the failing students. The competition was fierce though, and most of his classmates studied on Sunday. But President Eyring said, "For me, there was . . . no studying on Sunday."[6]

Instead, President Eyring devoted his Sunday time to the Lord's service, and he saw the blessings of his obedience: "In the few minutes I could give to preparation on Monday morning before classes, ideas and understanding came to more than match what others gained from a Sunday of study. . . . I cannot promise academic success . . . but I can promise you that if you will go to Him in prayer and ask what He would have you do next, promising that you will put His Kingdom first, He will answer your prayer and He will keep His promise to add upon your head blessings, enough to spare."[7]

Remember, schoolwork is usually the main daily labor for students; the Sabbath is designed to have us rest from our daily labors. When we use Sunday for a homework day, often our thoughts are more on the things of chemistry than the things of eternity.

Does the Activity Allow Me to Attend My Church Meetings and Partake of the Sacrament?

In Doctrine and Covenants 59:9 the Lord says that on the Sabbath we are to "go to the house of prayer and offer up [our] sacraments upon [his] holy day." Of all the meetings and appointments and classes we have during the week, sacrament meeting and partaking of the sacrament is "the greatest and most important meeting in the Church."[8] This is because we are able to renew covenants, recommit ourselves to following the Lord, and "then cometh a remission of your sins by fire and by the Holy Ghost" (2 Nephi 31:17). If an activity prevents us from attending sacrament meeting, it probably isn't an appropriate activity.

The Commandment Is to Keep the Sabbath Day **WHOLLY**

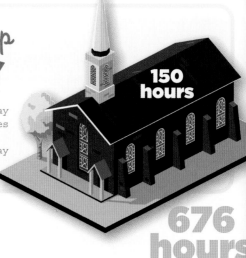

150 hours

676 hours

In one year of going to Church each Sunday, the average Latter-day Saint will spend around 150 hours in Church. But that still leaves us with 676 hours of Sabbath-day activity (if we are awake for sixteen hours a day). There is way more to keeping the Sabbath day *wholly* (for the whole day) than just going to Church.

Does the Activity Help Me Rest from My Regular Work?

Doctrine and Covenants 59:10 teaches that another principle of the Sabbath is "to rest from your labors." We need to ask ourselves: what are my daily labors that this day is designed to allow me to rest from in order to concentrate on more holy things? It seems that resting from our work and drawing closer to the Lord are connected: The more we are able to take a break from our daily work, the more time we have to give ourselves to worship God on the Sabbath. The less we rest from our daily work, the less time we seem to have to worship. That is one of the reasons why the prophets counsel, "Whenever possible, choose a job that does not require you to work on Sundays."[9]

HOW should I respond when my employer wants me to work on Sunday?

For the Strength of Youth simply says, "When seeking a job, share with your potential employer your desire to attend your Sunday meetings and keep the Sabbath day holy. Many employers value employees with these personal convictions. Whenever possible, choose a job that does not require you to work on Sundays."[10] Follow that prophetic counsel and share with your employer your desire to keep the Sabbath day holy by not working on Sunday, and place your faith in the Lord and see what happens.

A young woman named Diane had her dream job—she was a trainer of sea lions and would give performances with them. The only bad thing was that she was required to work on Sundays. After praying about her situation, she felt prompted to tell her boss that she would need to quit if she had to work on Sundays. Her boss told her she had to work Sundays—so Diane quit her job. Later Diane said, "I'm so glad I chose to keep the Sabbath day holy. Although it was hard to leave a job I loved, since then I have been blessed in so many ways." In fact, Diane found a new job, one that allowed her to maintain her standards as well as allowing her to spend time with the man she would eventually marry.

Does the Activity Help Me Draw Closer to God?

One of the primary purposes of the Sabbath day is to "pay thy devotions unto the Most High" (D&C 59:10). A good question to ask ourselves with our Sunday behavior is this: Does the activity help me draw nearer to God? Does it allow me to worship him, make covenants with him (see D&C 59:9), understand him and his purposes more, or help me become more like him?

Invitation to Act

Take a few minutes and plan your entire Sabbath day activities, not just the three hours at Church. Latter-day prophets give some suggestions on how we can fill our Sabbath-day time: "Worship the Lord, attend church, spend quiet time with your family, study the gospel, write letters, write in your journal, do family history work, and visit the sick or homebound."[11] Think of the *best* things that you can do to make the whole day holy.

Does the Activity Allow Me to Serve God's Children?

On the Sabbath we should "offer [our] oblations" of "time, talents, or means, in service of God and fellowman" (see D&C 59:12, footnote *b*). In other words, does a particular Sabbath activity help me give of myself in selfless service to God's kingdom and those around me? Does it help me serve in my calling, visit the needy, and give of myself?

Does the Activity Help Me Repent of My Sins?

Doctrine and Covenants 59:12 says that on Sunday we should be "confessing [our] sins unto [our] brethren, and before the Lord." The Sabbath day is a good day to work on overcoming those sins and temptations that are limiting our progress in becoming more like God. Does the activity we are choosing to do help us repent, or make it more difficult?

DO TRY THIS AT HOME!

To the right are some activities that, depending on the situation, *might* be questionable to some, and *might* be okay to others, if done on a Sunday. Review each activity in light of the six Sabbath-day principles taught in this chapter and discuss with your family if/when each activity might or might not be in harmony with keeping the Sabbath day holy.

1. Surfing the Web
2. Making a purchase online
3. Buying something from a store
4. Playing a board game with your family
5. Going to a friend's house
6. Talking to a friend on the phone
7. Watching sports on television
8. Watching a movie
9. Fixing something that broke
10. Playing sports outside
11. Doing homework
12. Doing yard work
13. Doing the dishes
14. Going on a walk
15. Going on a hike
16. Taking a drive as a family
17. Going boating as a family
18. Helping someone change a flat tire
19. Reading a book
20. Taking a nap

What NOT to Do

It is significant to note that neither the Lord nor his modern prophets gives us lists of hundreds of things we can't do on Sundays. They have simply stated that "Sunday is not a day for shopping, recreation, or athletic events. Do not seek entertainment or make purchases on this day."[12]

If we understand the divine purposes, doctrines, and principles of the Sabbath day, then we will be able to understand how to keep it holy. We testify that as we keep this day pure, blessings flow (see D&C 59:15–19), and it truly becomes a holy day—the highlight and best day of the week.

What's Your Sign?

Elder Russell M. Nelson taught, "How do we *hallow* the Sabbath day? In my much younger years, I studied the work of others who had compiled lists of things to do and things *not* to do on the Sabbath. It wasn't until later that I learned from the scriptures that my conduct and my attitude on the Sabbath constituted a *sign* between me and my Heavenly Father. With that understanding, I no longer needed lists of dos and don'ts. When I had to make a decision whether or not an activity was appropriate for the Sabbath, I simply asked myself, 'What *sign* do I want to give to God?' That question made my choices about the Sabbath day crystal clear."[13]

How Can I Keep the Sabbath Day Holy?

When considering whether you should do a certain activity on Sunday, ask yourself:

- Does the activity keep me "unspotted from the world"?
- Does the activity allow me to attend my Church meetings and partake of the sacrament?
- Does the activity help me rest from my regular work?
- Does the activity help me draw closer to God?
- Does the activity allow me to serve God's children?
- Does the activity help me repent of my sins?

ch

Why Should I Keep the Word of Wisdom?

We could make this a very short chapter just by showing you a few pictures.

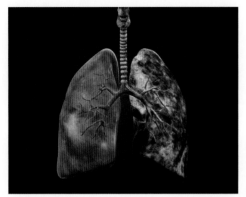

The lung tissue on the left is healthy. The tissue on the right has been damaged by cigarette smoke.[1] Which do you want inside your body?

This picture was taken at the scene of an automobile accident involving a drunk driver.

The three leading causes of death for fifteen- to twenty-four-year-olds are automobile crashes, homicides, and suicides. Alcohol is a leading factor in all three. The question "Why should I keep the Word of Wisdom?" has some pretty obvious answers.

Health Benefits of the Word of Wisdom

First, the health benefits. Although there was little medical evidence in 1833 when the Word of Wisdom was first received, today nobody doubts that it contains good health advice and that living the Word of Wisdom will help us live longer.

The Word of Wisdom says that, "inasmuch as any man drinketh wine or strong drink among you, behold it is not good" (D&C 89:5).

"It is not good" is an understatement! In 2013, alcohol-related impaired driving fatalities accounted for 10,076 deaths (31% of overall driving fatalities).[2]

That definitely doesn't sound good!

As you already know, there is a clear correlation between smoking and cancer: The more you smoke, the likelier you are to get lung cancer.

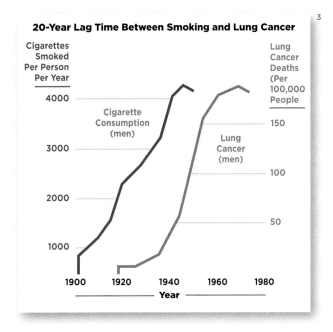

20-Year Lag Time Between Smoking and Lung Cancer [3]

Negative health effects of breaking the Word of Wisdom include nausea, increased stress, loss of muscle control, birth defects, shortness of breath, yellowing of the skin, damaging the liver, and much more.

Numerous studies over the years have shown that those who obey the principles found in the Word of Wisdom enjoy healthier lives and an increased life expectancy. If we live the Word of Wisdom, we are promised that "the destroying angel shall pass by [us]" (D&C 89:21), and we will live longer and healthier lives than if we don't live the Word of Wisdom.

Not only will obeying the Word of Wisdom help us live longer, it will also help us live a life of higher quality and health. A fourteen-year selective study conducted by UCLA epidemiologist James E. Enstrom tracked the health of 10,000 moderately active LDS people in California. Of these non-smoking, monogamous, non-drinkers, Enstrom concluded "that LDS Church members who follow religious mandates barring smoking and drinking have one of the lowest death rates from cancer and cardiovascular diseases—about half that of the general population. . . . Moreover, the healthiest LDS Church members enjoy a life expectancy eight to eleven years longer than that of the general white population in the United States."[4]

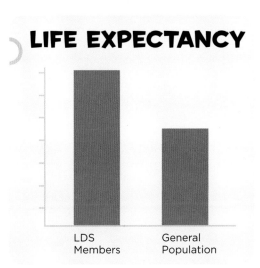

LIFE EXPECTANCY

Intellectual Benefits of the Word of Wisdom

Keeping the Word of Wisdom is not only good for our body, it's good for our brain. Perhaps this is part of what the Lord meant when he promised that those who lived this law would "find wisdom and great treasures of knowledge, even hidden treasures" (D&C 89:19).

President Heber J. Grant taught, "No man who breaks the Word of Wisdom can gain the same amount of knowledge and intelligence in this world as the man who obeys that law. I don't care who he is or where he comes from, his mind will not be as clear, and he cannot advance as far and as rapidly and retain his power as much as he would if he obeyed the Word of Wisdom."[5]

As a second witness, Brigham Young said that if we follow the Word of Wisdom it "will increase [our] intelligence."[6]

In addition to these prophetic words, medical evidence clearly shows that living the Word of Wisdom will make us smarter.

WHICH BRAIN DO YOU WANT?

Drinking alcohol affects our brains. The brain on the left represents one from a healthy, fifteen-year-old non-drinker, the one on the right a fifteen-year-old heavy drinker. The pink and red spots represent brain activity. Whose brain is working better?

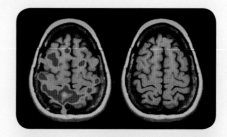

This picture demonstrates what alcohol does to the brain. The image on the left represents the brain of a healthy non-drinker. The one on the right represents a heavy drinker. The holes that appear in the image on the right indicate areas of reduced brain activity.[7] Do you want holes in your brain?

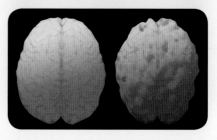

There is even a correlation between drinking alcohol and academic success. A study reported that at both two-year and four-year colleges the heaviest drinkers receive the lowest grades.[8]

ALCOHOL = LOWER GRADES[9]

Percentages of Youth 12-17 Reporting Alcohol Abuse

Grade	%
A	~12%
B	~18%
C	~21%
D or lower	~29%

Average Letter Grade for Reporting Period

Our Heavenly Father desires that we "do many things of [our] own free will" and that we be "agents unto [ourselves]" (D&C 58:27–28). On the other hand, Satan wants to take away our freedom, limit our ability to choose for ourselves, and bind us (see Moses 7:26). One of the ways the adversary does this is through harmful and addictive substances such as drugs, alcohol, nicotine, and caffeine—substances prohibited in the Word of Wisdom. When we keep the Word of Wisdom, we remain in control of our actions and our own free will.

Those who violate the Word of Wisdom run the risk of losing part of their freedom and agency by becoming enslaved to these controlling influences. Also, when we are under the influence of these substances, it becomes increasingly difficult to think clearly and make good decisions. We tend to act more impulsively and emotionally, without realizing the consequences of our behavior. It becomes nearly impossible for us to watch our thoughts, words, and deeds (see Mosiah 4:30) because we are not in complete control of ourselves.

Addiction Isn't Freedom . . .

The following statements were all made by an addict describing how trapped he felt because of his addictions:

"Addiction is missing my mother's birthday because I was high."

"Addiction is the tingling on both sides of my tongue, near the back, when I haven't had a cigarette in 2 hours."

"Addiction is cutting a date short so I can go home and get high."

"Addiction is leaving the party thinking I'm sober enough to drive, backing up the car, and realizing that I'm not."

"Addiction is a box in the back of my closet where I hide my cigarettes."

"Addiction is realizing that I can never introduce my girlfriend to my friends at work, because they know I smoke and she doesn't."

"Addiction is a persistent cough."

"Addiction is never having quiet, much less peace."[10]

Spiritual Benefits of the Word of Wisdom

The spiritual blessings of the Word of Wisdom are perhaps the most important reason why we should obey this divine command. President Boyd K. Packer taught, "The Word of Wisdom was given so that you may keep the delicate, sensitive, spiritual part of your nature on proper alert. . . . And I promise . . . you shall be warned of dangers and shall be guided through the whisperings of the Holy Spirit."[11]

These spiritual blessings are certainly part of the "great treasures of knowledge" promised in Doctrine and Covenants 89.

One of the ways police officers determine whether somebody is under the influence of alcohol is to see how well they follow verbal instructions. Think about it, if somebody who has been drinking struggles to follow verbal instructions, how will they be able to respond to the soft, spiritual promptings of the Holy Ghost?

The Spirit does not shout at us. Coffee, alcohol, tobacco, and other harmful substances create a barrier of insensitivity that prevents us from receiving the revelation we need.

The Lord has promised, "And all saints who remember to keep and do these sayings, walking in obedience to the commandments, shall receive health in their navel and marrow to their bones; And shall find wisdom and great treasures of knowledge, even hidden treasures; And shall run and not be weary, and shall walk and not faint. And I, the Lord, give unto them a promise, that the destroying angel shall pass by them, as the children of Israel, and not slay them" (D&C 89:18–21).

Living the Word of Wisdom will bless you physically, intellectually, and spiritually. There should be no doubt as to why this commandment is so important.

Prophetic Spiritual Promises and the Word of Wisdom

"The Lord . . . gave us the Word of Wisdom . . . that our faith might be strengthened, that our testimony . . . might be increased."
—President George Albert Smith[12]

"I would like it known that if we as a people never used a particle of tea or coffee or of tobacco or of liquor . . . we would grow spiritually; we would have a more direct line of communication with God, our Heavenly Father."
—President Heber J. Grant[13]

"[The] Word of Wisdom . . . was given . . . for the benefit, the help, and the prosperity of the Latter-day Saints, that they might purify and prepare themselves to go nearer into the presence of the Lord."
—President Joseph F. Smith[14]

TELL ME ONE MORE TiME!

Why Should I Keep the Word of Wisdom?

1. **Living the Word of Wisdom will bring better physical health.**
2. **You will be smarter if you keep the Word of Wisdom.**
3. **You will remain in control of your actions and avoid the addictions that are connected to violating the Word of Wisdom.**
4. **You will be more receptive to promptings from the Holy Ghost and will receive other spiritual blessings.**

NOW that we have reviewed some of the *principles*, let's answer some of the questions regarding the *practices* connected to the Word of Wisdom:

Why shouldn't I "try" alcohol just to see what it tastes like?

One reason we shouldn't ever touch alcohol (or anything addictive) is that we don't know how our bodies will respond to it. Even one drink could create an addictive appetite for something that can kill our minds and bodies and take away our freedom. Furthermore, even if we take only one drink of alcohol, we immediately lose our ability to be led by the Spirit. There have been many people who have ruined their lives due to *one* night of drinking and the poor decisions they made on that one occasion.[15]

Why shouldn't I take something into my body if science says it's good for me?

Even *if* substances prohibited by the Word of Wisdom were *good* for our bodies, the Word of Wisdom is about more than just physical health. It is also about remaining in control of our actions and decisions and being in tune with the delicate promptings of the Holy Ghost (reasons #3 and #4). For those reasons alone, we should avoid taking anything into our body that could dull our senses, take away our agency, or lead to addiction. The Lord, who created our bodies, knows what is best for them. When he specifically states that things forbidden in the Word of Wisdom are "not for the body" (D&C 89:8), we should trust him.

Why should I avoid drinking highly caffeinated soft drinks or "energy" drinks?

Although the Church has no official position on drinking caffeinated beverages, "The leaders of the Church have advised . . . against use of any drink containing harmful habit-forming drugs."[16]

In recent years, medical research has been done on the dangers of highly caffeinated energy drinks and the results are surprising. Dr. Thomas J. Boud lists some of the side effects of caffeine-related medical conditions, which include jitteriness, agitation, insomnia, difficulty concentrating, rapid heart rate, elevated blood pressure, gastrointestinal disorders, osteoporosis, acid reflux, weight gain, and decreased blood flow. High levels of caffeine can even lead to depression and death.[17]

President Thomas S. Monson has urged us to "keep our bodies—our temples—fit and clean, free from harmful substances which destroy our physical, mental, and spiritual well-being."[19]

STRESS AND WEIGHT GAIN[18]

Risk of Heart Disease, Diabetes, and High Blood Pressure

Caffeine Introduced

Increased Cortisol Hormone Levels

Cravings for Carbs and Sugars

Increased Abdominal Fat

Further Increase in Cortisol

Cravings for Carbs and Sugars Increase

Worsening Obesity

A JOLT TO THE SYSTEM

- In 2006, 500 new brands of energy drinks were introduced.

- In 2011, the energy drink industry reached $8.1 billion in revenue.[20]

- In 2013, 1,685 people reported an energy drink overdose.[21]

Why Should I Dress Modestly?

What we wear and how we cover our bodies has been a gospel principle ever since Adam and Eve were found naked in the Garden of Eden and God made "coats of skins, and clothed them" (Genesis 3:21). Why has God always been so concerned about how his children clothe themselves? Perhaps a fishing story can help explain the answer.

FISHING FOR PIRANHAS
Anthony Says:

While in the Amazon jungle, I had the opportunity to go fishing for piranhas with some friends and a native guide. I'll never forget the moment I was handed my fishing gear for the trip as we set out in the little boat across the muddy waters of the Amazon River.

Nobody in the group was given conventional fishing poles with reels or lures to catch these mean piranhas. Instead, we were given a thick, three-foot-long stick, with roughly six feet of fishing line tied around it, and a large, finger-sized hook dangling off the end, Robinson Crusoe style.

For bait, the guide pulled out a slab of raw meat. He slapped it down on the bottom of the boat and told us to cut off a chunk, fasten it to our hooks, and simply drop the line over the side of the boat. The guide must have sensed our skepticism of the simplicity of the process. He explained that the piranhas would *come to us,* attracted by the raw meat. There was no need to cast out a line and go after them.

I dropped my hook over the side of the boat, and within seconds, there was a ripple in the water and a bite on the line. With a quick tug of the line, I pulled a piranha into the boat. Although the fish was small, the razor-sharp teeth and menacing look of the fish's mouth were enough to keep me at a distance. So, like a true man, I let the guide remove the hook from the fish's mouth.

I attached a new piece of raw meat, dropped it into the water, and caught piranha after piranha. It was amazing to see the power of attraction the raw meat had to bring in these frightening fish.

The Principle of Attraction

So what do piranhas, hooks, and raw meat have to do with hemlines, midriffs, and modesty? What does casting out bait have to do with putting on clothing? Your dress and grooming send messages to those around you; how you dress should reflect what you are on the inside.

The parable of the piranha serves to illustrate this very important point: Whatever you cast out is what you catch. It's true for fishing, and it's true for our dress standards.

Just as the meat sent a message to the piranha, our dress and appearance send messages as well, attracting and repelling different kinds of people in the world. If you don't want to be surrounded by piranhas, don't toss meat into the Amazon. Similarly, if we wanted to catch a nice trout out of a mountain lake, we wouldn't use raw meat. The trout simply wouldn't be attracted to or interested in it.

This principle of attraction is one of the primary reasons why prophets of God have always counseled us to dress modestly. Prophets understand that everything we wear and how we cover or reveal our bodies sends messages to others. If young people are constantly revealing their skin, who will they attract? They will attract "piranha" boys and girls who are primarily interested in their flesh. On the other hand, if a young person casts out righteousness, intelligence, spirituality, humor, and confidence (the "power bait"☺), that is exactly who he or she will attract: young men and women who appreciate righteousness, intelligence, spirituality, humor, and confidence.

The Lord taught, "For intelligence cleaveth unto intelligence; wisdom receiveth wisdom; truth embraceth truth; virtue loveth virtue; light cleaveth unto light" (D&C 88:40).

President Thomas S. Monson linked low *dress* standards with low *moral* standards by categorizing them together as the "Twin Demons of Immodesty and Immorality."[1]

Remember this principle of attraction: What we choose to wear directly affects the level of character of those who we attract.

Immorality   **Immodesty**

Does Your Dress Attract?

What Kind of Attention

Modesty and Men

Being modest has just as much to do with boys as it does with girls. We tend to define modesty only by tight shirts or short skirts (therefore exempting all but the boys who wear Scottish kilts), but modesty is much more than that.

The actual definition of modesty uses such words as "unassuming," "humble," and "decency,"[2] which all apply to a young man's appearance and demeanor just as much as a young woman's. Elder Robert D. Hales said that "modesty is at the core of our character" and that it "reflects who we are and what we want to be."[3] For young men, the issue with modesty usually is dressing too sloppily, too casually, too worldly, or in such a way that draws a lot of attention to themselves (such as extreme hairstyles). Dressing in this way not only violates the "humble" definition of modesty, but it also sends the message that we are a sloppy, casual, worldly, and selfish person (since how we dress is at the core of our character). For this reason, *For the Strength of Youth* teaches that "young men and young women should be neat and clean and avoid being extreme or inappropriately casual in clothing, hairstyle, and behavior."[4]

It is especially important that a young man dress neat, clean, and unassuming when administering the sacrament. Elder Dallin H. Oaks told young men to live by the "principle of non-distraction" during the sacrament. This principle suggests that young men "should not do anything that would distract any member from his or her worship and renewal of covenants."[5] Elder Jeffrey R. Holland added that, wherever possible, a white shirt should be worn by those young men who handle the sacrament.[6]

Dressing in a sloppy, casual, worldly, or distracting way causes a young man to be just as immodest as a young woman dressed in tight or revealing clothing.

The Stumbling Block of Pornography

Few Latter-day Saint women would support pornography, let alone become an active participant in that evil industry. Yet when women dress immodestly, they become a source of living pornography that can act as an immoral temptation to those around them. Elder Dallin H. Oaks said, "Young women, please understand that if you dress immodestly, you are magnifying this problem by *becoming pornography* to some of the men who see you."[7]

This truth does not justify men in their actions nor place the blame solely upon immodest women. (The Lord expects both men and women to use their agency to control their eyes and thoughts.) But we must understand

IN THE BLINK OF AN EYE . . .

"It only takes three-tenths of a second for an image to enter the eye and start a chain reaction in the body."[8]

Control your *eyes* and you can control your *thoughts!*

that when women (and men too) dress in a revealing and immodest way, they become part of the problem of pornography.

One young person said, "It's not my fault if boys can't control their eyes!" While all should control their eyes, why would faithful Saints want to create problems for their brothers or sisters? The apostle Paul spoke to some of the Saints who were following the trends of idol worship in his day, warning them to "take heed lest by any means this liberty of yours become a stumblingblock to them that are weak" (1 Corinthians 8:9). In other words, don't do anything that would cause others to falter.

No one should knowingly want to be a source of temptation to another—especially not in matters of modesty.

Physical Obsession and Spirituality

A third reason why we should dress modestly relates to the effect that revealing our bodies has on our self-esteem and spirituality. If we constantly make our physical body a source of attention and public display, then that is where our focus will be. As the Savior taught, "For where your treasure is, there will your heart be also" (Matthew 6:21).

When we become overly self-conscious about how we look and are perceived—our dress size, our waistline, our tan, our biceps, our nails, our hair, and everything else in between—then other people's opinions about our bodies begin to affect our self-confidence and self-worth. What *other* people think becomes more important than what *we* think. That can rob us of peace and happiness—and it shouldn't be that way. Elder Jeffrey R. Holland explained: "I plead with you young women to please be more accepting of yourselves, including your body shape and style, with a little less longing to look like someone else. . . . As one adviser to teenage girls said: 'You can't live your life worrying that the world is staring at you. When you let people's opinions make you self-conscious you give away your power.' . . .

"The [world's] pitch is, 'If your looks are good enough, your life will be glamorous and you will be happy and popular.' That kind of pressure is immense in the teenage years, to say nothing of later womanhood. In too many cases too much is being done to the human body to meet just such a fictional (to say nothing of superficial) standard. . . .

"[This] fixation on the physical . . . is more than social insanity; it is spiritually destructive, and it accounts for much of the unhappiness women, including young women, face in the modern world."[9]

DO TRY THIS AT HOME!

The Dove company released an incredible video that illustrates how makeup and computer software create unrealistic physical standards that truly are fictional. See for yourself by watching the clip at http://johnhiltoniii.com/qa.

CHECK OUT THE SCRIPTURAL PATTERN!

Look up these scriptures to see how the Book of Mormon teaches about the way clothing is linked to sins such as pride and selfishness.

- Jacob 2:13
- 4 Nephi 1:24–26
- Mormon 8:37

Clothed with Righteousness

With modesty able to influence our spiritual lives so dramatically, it should be obvious why the prophets of God have consistently stressed the importance to dress in such a way that we, "can show that [we] know how precious" our bodies are.[10] Notice how the scriptures speak of being "clothed with purity, yea, even with the robe of righteousness (2 Nephi 9:14), being "clothed with salvation" (D&C 109:80), and "with power and authority" (D&C 138:30), "and above all things, clothe yourselves with the bond of charity" (D&C 88:125). This type of clothing is sure to attract peace and joy to all who see it.

TELL ME ONE MORE TiME!

Why Should I Dress Modestly?

1. **How we dress affects who we attract, whether positively or negatively. (Don't go fishing for piranhas!)**
2. **Dressing in a sloppy or worldly fashion sends the message that our character is sloppy and worldly.**
3. **Those who choose to dress immodestly become "living pornography" and a source of temptation to those around them.**
4. **Wearing revealing clothing causes us to become more self-conscious about our physical appearance. This can lead us to obsess over our appearance and become increasingly self-centered, which negatively affects our pride, our charity toward others, our self-worth, our happiness, and our spirituality.**

NOW that we have reviewed some of the *principles*, let's answer some of the questions regarding the *practices* connected to dressing modestly:

Why can't I wear a strapless prom dress one night of the year?

For the Strength of Youth answers this question clearly: "Never lower your standards of dress. Do not use a special occasion as an excuse to be immodest. When you dress immodestly, you send a message that is contrary to your identity as a son or daughter of God. You also send the message that you are using your body to get attention and approval."[11] Lowering our dress standards one night of the year is similar to lowering our language standards one game of the year, or our moral standards one date of the year, or our Word of Wisdom standards one party of the year. The true tests of our conversion and commitment are those moments when it is difficult to live our standards. Holding fast to our standards of modesty, especially on prom night, is a great way to show your Heavenly Father that you are willing to do what is right when things are difficult, not just when they are easy.

Why shouldn't I let skin show between my shirt and my pants?

This has become a trend recently, and some don't see why it is a big deal. Principle #4 applies because if we are showing off our mid-section, we become self-conscious about how that mid-section looks. If we don't have rock-hard abs or zero cellulite around our belly, then we can begin to obsess about our physical appearance. Also, revealing our mid-section with low-cut pants and short shirts is a trend connected to worldly sexuality (along with showing the back of the underwear, belly piercings, and tattoos), so principle #1, the law of attraction, applies here as well. Furthermore, showing this skin can become a stumbling block to the others who are trying to avoid looking.

Why is it a big deal if boys "sag" their pants or have long hair?

The principle of attraction applies to both girls and boys. A boy who dresses sloppily, "sags" his pants, and has long, unkempt hair sends a message to others just as much as a girl who dresses in a revealing way. If a boy dresses like he uses drugs (even if he doesn't), then he will attract others who use drugs. If a boy dresses like he is in a gang, then people will treat him like a gangster. Remember, the way we dress affects how we act and behave. If we dress sloppily and according to the trends of the world, then it doesn't take long before our behavior becomes sloppy and we adopt the standards of the world.

Why Shouldn't I Date Until I'm 16?

In researching some of the reasons why we shouldn't date until we are 16 years old, we came across an interesting blog post. An inquiring person asked why Mormons can't date until they are 16. A frustrated teenager responded, "There aren't any real reasons why! They just want to control us!"

Hmmm . . . Makes us wonder if that comment was made by a bitter 15½ year old somewhere.

Do you really think that Church leaders sit around asking, "What can we do to really bug the youth?"

"I know—how about no dating until 16?"

"Great idea, let's put that in the pamphlet!"

Of course they don't! God has a purpose in all he does and all he reveals, even for things like when we should begin dating.

NOT JUST MORMONS

In a study of almost 300 parents of teens nationwide, "eighty-seven percent of parents of teens said teens should be at least 16 before they begin steady, one-on-one dating."[1]

Morally Clean and Sixteen

Perhaps the most powerful reason why we should wait until we are 16 to date has to do with keeping the law of chastity. Prophets have repeatedly warned—and statistics have shown—that the earlier we begin to date, the more likely we are to break the law of chastity. *For the Strength of Youth* says, "You should not date until you are at least 16 years old. . . . Developing serious relationships too early in life . . . can perhaps lead to immorality.."[2]

Researchers studied the connection between when a youth began dating and if they remained sexually pure through high school. Take a look at the results:

Age when students began dating and the percentage who became sexually involved before marriage.[3]

Age	Percentage
12	90%
15	60%
16	20%
17	12%

The younger a person is when he or she begins to date, the more likely he or she is to become sexually active. The most dramatic decrease in the likelihood of becoming sexually active in high school was for those students who chose to wait until they were 16 years old to start dating.

Logically, the sooner we begin to date, the quicker we will move into serious relationships before we are ready to handle them. Anytime we enter into serious relationships in our early teens, we increase the moral temptation and therefore the chances of breaking the law of chastity. President Spencer W. Kimball said: "Dating in the earlier teen-age years leads to early steady dating with its multiplicity of dangers and problems, and frequently early and disappointing marriage."[5]

Sweet Sixteen . . . Sorry Fifteen

"While about 70 percent of [LDS youth] who did not date until they were 16 had avoided immoral behavior, more than 80 percent of those who reported dating before age 16 had become sexually involved enough to require a bishop's help for repentance."—Bruce Monson[4]

In other words, you are almost *three times* more likely to commit serious sexual sin if you begin dating before age 16.

THE "MULTIPLICITY" OF DATING DANGERS

Dating in early adolescence is connected with such at-risk behaviors as poor school performance, drug use, delinquency, having poor social skills that last through the later teenage years, depression, and sexual activity.[6]

Growing Pains

The "bitter blogger" from the beginning of the chapter was right about one thing, though. One of the reasons why we should wait to date *is* about control. Not parental or Church control—but *self*-control. Just listen to most 12- to 15-year-old boys speak, and we'll quickly get a good auditory reason why we should wait to date a little bit. Boy's voices fluctuate from low to high and from high to low during these years, sometimes squeaking like a mouse and other times sounding like a tuba. If a young teenage boy finds it difficult to control his voice, how much more difficult is it to control his physical emotions?

Simply stated, we are not yet physically or emotionally stable while we are in our early teens to begin dating. Our bodies are going through massive changes. It is wise to postpone dating until we have begun to figure ourselves out. We simply don't need to get involved romantically before we form our own personal identity. Part of dating is to get to know other people, which is hard to do if we don't even know ourselves.

LET'S USE OUR BRAIN . . . WELL, THE PARTS WE CAN

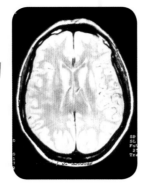

Research shows that brain development goes through a second wave of change around age 12 and isn't complete until our late teens.[7]

DUDE, I THINK YOU GREW OVER-NIGHT!

The average teenager grows between 3 to 5 inches per year during their early teens.

Paul's counsel about milk and meat is appropriate here. He taught, "I have fed you with milk, and not with meat: for hitherto ye were not able to bear it, neither yet now are ye able" (1 Corinthians 3:2).

In other words, you don't feed a baby a sizzlin' steak until they are older and ready for it.

There will come a time for the "steak" of dating, but we make a serious "mi-stake" if we start too soon.

YOU WANT TO RIDE ON BACK?

A practical reason why we should wait until we are 16 to date is that we can't drive yet. It is very hard to look cool pulling up on your tandem bike to pick up your date.

"I'll pick ya up at seven . . . you're on back!"

But I'm 15.99999 Years Old . . . Does it Really Matter?

Maybe you say that you are *almost* 16, that you are mature for your age, that you don't have any "romantic" interest in anyone, but you just want to have "fun" on a date. Can you be the exception to the rule?

You may not change a lot between the day before you turn 16 and the day after, but remember this principle: Waiting to date until you are 16 helps you develop a pattern of obedience that will bless you for the rest of your life. Sticking to this standard will help you stick to other standards when you are tempted to excuse yourself as the exception. It's not about digits . . . it's about discipleship! We extend the promise of the First Presidency to you that, "as you keep the covenants you have made and these standards [such as not dating until 16], you will be blessed with the companionship of the Holy Ghost, your faith and testimony will grow stronger, and you will enjoy increasing happiness."[8] You will never regret living this standard of waiting to date until you are 16.

ARE WE JUST "HANGING OUT" . . . OR IS IT A "DATE"?

DO TRY THIS AT HOME!

FYI: A "date" is officially defined in the dictionary as "a social engagement between two persons that often has a *romantic* character." But even staying home alone with a member of the opposite sex should be avoided. Studies have shown that the

most common time of day when teens break the law of chastity is not late at night on Friday, but after school on weekdays at home![9]

Work on developing your friendships during your teenage years. Learning how to be a good friend will help you more to have a successful marriage in the future than learning how to be in a romantic relationship will.

TELL ME ONE MORE TiME!

Why Shouldn't I Date Until I'm 16?

1. **The prophets have warned and statistics show that the earlier we begin to date, the more likely we are to break the law of chastity.**
2. **We are not sufficiently physically or emotionally ready to date while we are in our early teens.**
3. **Not being able to stick to a numerical standard (dating at age 16) threatens our ability to stick to other spiritual standards. It's not about digits . . . it's about discipleship!**

NOW that we have reviewed some of the *principles*, let's answer some of the questions regarding the *practices* connected to not dating before we are 16:

Why is 16 the magical age? Is it all that different from 15?

If you look at the studies, then the answer is, yes, 16 appears to be a magical age and very different from 15. (Somebody is 300% more likely to break the law of chastity if they begin dating at age 15 instead of age 16).[10] Principles #1 and #3 both apply here. If we can stick to our dating standards and wait until we are 16, then we will develop a pattern of obedience that will help us more easily stick to other important relationship standards, such as group dating, keeping the law of chastity, and not steady dating.

Why isn't it a good idea to hang out at the house of someone of the opposite gender who I really "like"?

Remember, the dictionary definition of a "date": "a social engagement between two persons that often has a *romantic* character." It doesn't matter where you go out to—the park, meeting at a movie theatre, attending a school game, or even "hanging out" at someone's house—it is still a romantic engagement. More importantly, being at the house of someone you really like is a seedbed of temptation, probably more so than a public setting. In a study of more than 2,000 teenagers who had had pre-marital sex, 91% reported doing so in a home setting.[11]

Why is it still considered a date if a group of my friends goes to the park to meet a group of the opposite gender whom some of us like?

Once again, it is our intent that matters. The Lord said he "knowest thy thoughts and the intents of thy heart" (D&C 6:16). If we are trying to disguise a "date," or a social engagement of romantic interest, by grouping it together with a large conglomerate of friends who are all meeting together, it is still a date. We shouldn't look for loopholes or try to deceive our parents in this way, because when it comes right down to it, the Lord knows exactly what we are doing.

Why Shouldn't I Steady Date in High School?

Did you read that title clearly? It says, "Why shouldn't I steady date *in high school.*" Let's not make the assumption that we should never steady date, or we would have a major problem in the Church in our quest for exaltation. (Can anyone say, "eternal singles ward"?) The question is not *if* we steady date, but *when.* The Lord does want us to become involved in serious relationships that will lead us to the temple—but "in *his* time" (Ecclesiastes 3:11; emphasis added). The Lord has made it clear through his prophets that steady dating in high school is not the right time.

Timing Is Everything
IS TIMING IMPORTANT? YOU BE THE JUDGE

- Try getting to the airport five minutes after your plane left.
- Try asking somebody on a date by calling at 5:30 AM.
- Try showing up to a party a half-hour early.
- Try eating cookies that are three minutes under-baked.

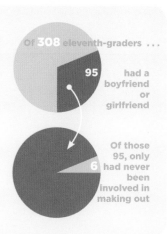

Elder Larry R. Lawrence taught, "Postpone romantic relationships until the time comes when [you] are ready for marriage. Prematurely pairing off with a boyfriend or girlfriend is dangerous. Becoming a 'couple' creates emotional intimacy, which too often leads to physical intimacy. Satan knows this sequence and uses it to his advantage. He will do whatever he can . . . to prevent temple marriages."[1]

The Familiarity Factor

A major reason why we should avoid forming serious relationships in high school is that *steady dating* leads to (*steady temptation.*)

Steady Dating and Steady Temptation

In a study of LDS teens conducted by Bruce Monson, he found that "of the 308 11th graders surveyed, 95 reported having a current boyfriend or girlfriend. Of those 95, only six had never been involved in making out (or kissing for a long time)."[2] (Remember that *For the Strength of Youth* says "Do not participate in passionate kissing."[3]) Furthermore, *more than half* of those who had steady-dated had even more seriously transgressed the law of chastity.

Of **308** eleventh-graders . . .

95 had a boyfriend or girlfriend

Of those 95, only **6** had never been involved in making out

The physical familiarity that comes from spending so much time with one person to whom you are attracted can lead to moral temptations and moral trouble. President Gordon B. Hinckley said: "Steady dating at an early age leads so often to tragedy. . . . Have a wonderful time, *but stay away from familiarity.* Keep your hands to yourself. It may not be easy, but it is possible."[4]

When we begin to feel familiar with those we date, there is a tendency to continue pushing the line of familiarity further and further. Soon holding hands isn't as fun, and a quick kiss gets old; it doesn't take long before passionate kissing (making out) becomes the norm—and deeper sin ensues. President Spencer W. Kimball taught: "A vicious, destructive, social pattern of early steady dating must be changed. . . . *The change of this one pattern of social activities of our youth would immediately eliminate a majority of the sins of our young folks.*"[5]

IF YOU THINK YOU CAN HANDLE THE TEMPTATION . . . THINK AGAIN

"Dr. Phil . . . aired a program in which he staged an experiment to demonstrate the [temptation and] danger of guns in the home. Amid a group of playing little girls and boys, a teacher placed two fake guns inside a dollhouse. *The teacher warned the kids not to play with the guns,* and then left the room. The boys promptly began playing with the guns. Dr. Phil came in, *warned the boys again,* and after eliciting a promise not to play with the guns, which he put on a table, he left the room. Again, the boys promptly began playing with the guns."[6]

One moral of the experiment is that it is better to avoid the temptation than to resist the sin. When it comes to steady dating in high school, it is better to just not start.

BUT WE'RE GOOD KIDS!

Some may think, "But we're not like that. We are both active and have high standards!" President Spencer W. Kimball taught, "The devil knows how to destroy our young girls and boys. He may not be able to tempt a person to murder or to commit adultery immediately, but he knows that if he can get a boy and a girl to sit in the car late enough after the dance, or to park long enough in the dark at the end of the lane, *the best boy and the best girl will finally succumb and fall.* He knows that all have a limit to their resistance."[7]

The Emotional Rollercoaster

Another reason why we should not steady date in high school is that we are not emotionally ready to handle serious relationships in our teens. Evidence of emotional instability in the teen years is supported by the fact that problems such as anorexia, bulimia, suicide, and self-hurting (cutting), are higher among teens than for any other group of people. Research says teenagers are the least stable with their self-identity and are the most susceptible to peer influence than any other age group.[8]

With so many social pressures, anxieties, and worries during our teenage years, we don't need the added emotional drama, stress, temptation, and worry that comes along with a serious boyfriend or girlfriend.

Early Steady Dating: An Emotional Roller Coaster

RELATIONSHIP STRESS

- "53% of teens who are involved with a boyfriend or a girlfriend say their relationship causes them stress."[9]
- "61% of teens who had been in a relationship stated they had a boyfriend/girlfriend who made them 'feel bad or embarrassed' about themselves."[10]

Most romantic relationships among 12- to 18-year-olds are short-lived. One college student said, "I got a girlfriend in junior high. That was one of the worst choices I have ever made. Because of that relationship I had my heart broken and stomped on when I was way too young to handle it. It wasn't just the girl's fault either, I know I hurt her too. We would have both been so much better off if we had just waited."

- "25% of [teens] in a 'serious' relationship were 'hit, slapped, or pushed.'"[11]

WHAT EMOTION DO YOU SEE IN THIS FACE?

"In a recent study mapping differences between the brains of adults and teens, [researcher Deborah Yurgelun-Todd] put teenage and adult volunteers through an MRI and monitored how their brains responded to a series of pictures. Volunteers were asked to discern the emotion in a series of faces like this one. The results were surprising. All the adults identified the emotion as fear, but many of the teenagers saw something different, such as shock or anger. When she examined their brain scans, Todd found that the teenagers were using a different part of the brain when reading the images."[12] In addition, researchers found that some parts of the brain do not even function in the teenage years. These studies show that teenagers process information in a manner substantially different than adults—which may be a factor in why teenage relationships often lead to heartbreak.[13]

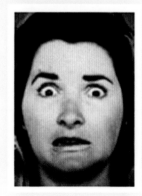

We have our entire lives to be involved in a serious relationship, so let's not rush into it during our developing teenage years. It is better to do so when we are emotionally ready to handle it.

Fish in the Sea

He's a little too puffed up for me.

For the Strength of Youth gives another reason why we should avoid steady dating in our teens. "Developing serious relationships too early in life can limit the number of other people you meet."[14] One of the purposes for dating during our teen years is to develop friendships and learn what kinds of people we enjoy being with. This takes a *variety* of dating experiences.

Steady dating is courtship, and surely the beginning of courtship ought to be delayed until you have emerged from your teens."[15]

—President Boyd K. Packer

We will be much better off by following President Gordon B. Hinckley's advice: "It is better, my friends, to date a variety of companions until you are ready to marry."[16]

Girlfriends and Missions

Some may think that it's okay for young men to steady date after high school but before their missions. But President Ezra Taft Benson taught: "*Avoid steady dating with a young man prior to the time of his mission call.* If your relationship with him is more casual, then he can make that decision to serve more easily and also can concentrate his full energies on his missionary work instead of the girlfriend back home."[17]

An Actual Dear John?

Dear John (Jim),

Yes, this is a "Dear John" letter (email). Sorry to have it start off like that, but you always said I was blunt. Well, I guess you're right.

I'm engaged to be married at the end of this month! I'm soooo excited! The same day I got the internet like you suggested (so that I could email you) I also saw a commercial on TV about [an LDS dating site]. Well, I signed up for that too and they matched me up with Desidorio, from Spain!

I thought it was interesting that I got matched up with someone living in the same country as your mission! We've been communicating ever since and we've fallen in love and will be getting married! We've never met in person, but we don't need to. We prayed over the phone and we felt the Spirit soooooo strong I think it would be wrong NOT to get married!

So, if anything, I wanted to THANK YOU for suggesting that I get the internet. If it wasn't for you listening to the Spirit to tell me that, then I would have never met Desidorio! You truly are a great friend!

You will always have a place in my heart!

Com Amor,

Valerie

P.S.—Desidorio and I want to vacation with you and your family before you leave Spain! Is that okay? Aren't you excited?[18]

Simply put, having a girlfriend back home distracts the missionary. Instead of being able to dedicate 100% of his focus on the Lord's work, part of his energy is focused on his girl back home. Remember the principle: We want to delay forming serious relationships *until the time we are ready to be married.* Young men are not ready to be married when they are called and set apart as a full-time missionary.

Being obedient to the Lord's commandments—including not steady dating in high school—will help you be happier. Depending on your personal circumstances, avoiding a serious relationship in your teens may be the toughest standard for you to live. But, for all the reasons listed in this chapter and many more, we promise you it will be worth it.

DO TRY THIS AT HOME!

Attracted to One Another

Take two magnets that are strongly attracted to each other and place one on the table. Holding the other in your hand, bring it down as slowly as possible until you are as close as you can get to the other magnet without causing them to come together. What happened? Liken the results to pushing "the line" with physical familiarity and staying morally clean.

TELL ME ONE MORE TIME!

Why Shouldn't I Steady Date in High School?

1. When we steady date we become increasingly familiar with our boyfriend/girlfriend. Steady dating leads to steady temptation to break the law of chastity.

Cont.

2. **We are not emotionally ready to handle serious, romantic relationships in our teens.**

3. **Steady dating in high school limits the number of other young people we meet.**

4. **Steady dating distracts missionaries from being able to serve the Lord with *all* their "heart, might, mind and strength" (D&C 4:2).**

NOW that we have reviewed some of the *principles*, let's answer some of the questions regarding the *practices* connected to not steady dating in high school:

Why date other people if I only like one person?

High school is not the time to be looking for a spouse but a time for building friendships. If you truly do only like one person, then dating other people until you are both at a marriageable age (translation: after the young man's mission) will only confirm that he or she is the one for you. After all, it's hard to know what your favorite ice cream is if you have tried only vanilla and chocolate. More importantly, we should date a variety of people in order to limit the emotional bond that is created when two people who care for each other spend a lot of time together. Remember, when we form an emotional bond with someone, we naturally want to express those feelings physically, which could result in breaking the law of chastity.

Why is it wrong to steady date someone in high school if we both have high standards?

Principle #1 applies best here. No matter how high your standards are, steady dating leads to steady temptation. Emotions and desires connected to physical intimacy are among the strongest human emotions we have. There is simply no good reason to subject two good LDS youth to increased moral temptation when you don't need it. It would be much better to keep the relationship at a safe distance, date other people, and then pursue a steady relationship when you reach an age when you are ready to be married.

Why is it OK to steady date after my mission, but not before?

The Church's magazine for youth, the *New Era,* answered this with, "Church leaders haven't specified an age when single dating is appropriate. When you are older and in a position to consider marriage, you most certainly should single date. Until then, talk to your parents about the decision to start single dating."[19]

Why Should I Be Sexually Pure?

Lisa was in an awkward situation. She was on a double date and didn't really know any of the people she was with. The four of them had been having a picnic at a park. It was nice, but now the sun was going down and the other couple had gone off on a walk together—she was alone with her date. She could tell that her date had some intimate expectations, so she decided she better explain her standards.

She had scarcely begun when he said, "Lisa, I know you're Mormon and that you don't believe in pre-marital sex. But I don't get it—why does your Church care about it so much? What's the big deal?"

Tips to Staying Sexually Pure: PROPHETIC PRINCIPLE #1

Avoid being alone with someone you are attracted to.

For the Strength of Youth advises that "When you begin dating, go with one or more additional couples."[1]

Don't be afraid to be like Joseph in Egypt and run away from a compromising situation! (See Genesis 39:9-12.)

Many teenagers find themselves in a situation where they have to explain to others—or perhaps they wonder to themselves—why morality is such a big deal. Before we talk about why we should stay sexually pure, think about this question: "Why would somebody *not* stay sexually pure?"

There may be lots of reasons—peer pressure, to feel accepted, to solidify a relationship, to try to show someone you "love" them, crazy hormones, and so on. President Ezra Taft Benson gave this reason when he said, "Most people fall into sexual sin in a misguided attempt to fulfill basic human

Tips to Staying Sexually Pure: PROPHETIC PRINCIPLE #2

"You should not date until you are at least 16 years old. . . . Avoid going on frequent dates with the same person. Developing serious relationships too early in life can limit the number of other people you meet and can perhaps lead to immorality."[2]

Tips to Staying Sexually Pure: #3
PROPHETIC PRINCIPLE

Only date those with high moral standards.

"Choose to date only those who have high moral standards and in whose company you can maintain your standards."[3]

If even your dad knows that other people call your date "the harlot Isabel," you probably shouldn't go out with her (see Alma 39:3).

needs. We all have a need to feel loved and worthwhile. We all seek to have joy and happiness in our lives. Knowing this, Satan often lures people into immorality by playing on their basic needs. He promises pleasure, happiness, and fulfillment.

"But this is, of course, a deception."[4]

Take a minute to think about your own or other people's experiences. Do you know of instances in which somebody violated the law of chastity so that person would feel love? Did it work?

The truth is that it doesn't. This is one reason why it is so important to stay sexually pure—so that we can experience the respectful love that we deeply desire. When we violate the law of chastity, feelings of guilt, sorrow, regret, shame, and bitterness usually result instead of the love we seek.

President Gordon B. Hinckley compared breaking the law of chastity with the implosion of a building. To see an implosion and hear President Hinckley's comparison visit http://johnhiltoniii.com/qa.

Immorality and Hate

In the Old Testament there was a guy named Amnon who was infatuated with a woman named Tamar. The scriptures say he was so "sick for [her]" that he couldn't do anything else but think about her. Unfortunately, this obsession with Tamar led Amnon to want to be immoral with her, and he "[raped] her, and lay with her" (2 Samuel 13:14).

What do you think the result of this immorality was? Do you think that Amnon fell in love with her after stealing her virtue? He did not. Second Samuel 13:15 says, "Then Amnon hated her exceedingly; so that the hatred wherewith he hated her was greater than the love wherewith he had loved her." For Amnon, immorality led to hate, not love.

Why can something that is an "expression of love between husband and wife"[5] result in guilt and hate between those who aren't married? If "physical intimacy between husband and wife is beautiful and sacred"[6] then why is it not so between boyfriend and girlfriend? It hinges on the timing, or the *order* of when the physical intimacy takes place. There is a time and a season for everything, and God has commanded that marriage must come before physical intimacy. If we do this in the wrong order, something sweet can become bitter.

DO TRY THIS AT HOME!

Think the order isn't important? Try this experiment. Pour a tall glass of orange juice and drink half of it. Tasty, isn't it? Now, brush your teeth and rinse with mouthwash. Nice and fresh! Now, drink the other half of your orange juice. How does it taste? Isn't it interesting that if we do this in the wrong order, something sweet can become bitter? Physical intimacy is no different.

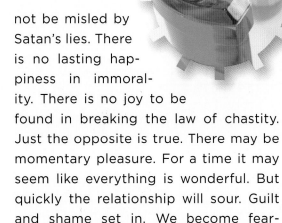

not be misled by Satan's lies. There is no lasting happiness in immorality. There is no joy to be found in breaking the law of chastity. Just the opposite is true. There may be momentary pleasure. For a time it may seem like everything is wonderful. But quickly the relationship will sour. Guilt and shame set in. We become fearful that our sins will be discovered. We must sneak and hide, lie and cheat.

Tips to Staying Sexually Pure: PROPHETIC PRINCIPLE #4

Know "the line" and stay far from it.

For the Strength of Youth says we should not participate in passionate kissing or anything that arouses powerful emotions.[7]

Just like if we were driving next to a cliff, the further we stay away from "the line," the safer we will be.

Physical intimacy is similar to orange juice and mouthwash. If physical intimacy comes *after* the marriage covenant, it is beautiful and sacred. If physical intimacy comes *before* marriage, it leads to a whole list of ugly results. Read what President Benson taught: "Do

Tips to Staying Sexually Pure: PROPHETIC PRINCIPLE #5

Don't steady date before a young man's mission.

"Avoid going on frequent dates with the same person."[8]

"When you are young, do not get involved in steady dating. When you reach an age where you think of marriage, then is the time to become so involved. But you boys who are in high school don't need this, and neither do the girls."—President Gordon B. Hinckley[9]

Tips to Staying Sexually Pure: #6
PROPHETIC PRINCIPLE

Avoid pornography like a foul disease.

If someone released a jar of mosquitoes that carried malaria or West Nile Virus in a room, what would you do? Do the same when your computer, TV, or a movie releases pornography.

"Do not attend, view, or participate in anything that is vulgar, immoral, violent, or pornographic in any way. Pornography . . . can lead to other sexual transgression."[11]

Love begins to die. Bitterness, jealousy, anger, and even hate begin to grow. All of these are the natural results of sin and transgression."[10]

One reason why we should stay sexually pure is that immorality leads to negative and bitter feelings, not love. Let's look at some other reasons why it is so important to live the law of chastity.

Making a Mockery of the Atonement

Another reason why we should avoid breaking the law of chastity is that when we do, we mock the Savior's Atonement. Elder Jeffrey R. Holland explained this concept. "In exploiting the body of another—which means exploiting his or her soul—one desecrates the Atonement of Christ, which saved that soul and which makes possible the gift of eternal life. And when one mocks the Son of Righteousness, one steps into a realm of heat hotter and holier than the noonday sun. You cannot do so and not be burned."[12]

That sounds pretty serious! Keep reading:

"'Flee fornication,' Paul cries, and flee 'anything like unto it,' the Doctrine and Covenants adds. Why? Well, for one reason because of the incalculable suffering in both body and spirit endured by the Savior so that we could flee. We owe Him something for that. Indeed, we owe Him everything for that. 'Ye are not your own,' Paul says. 'Ye [have been] bought with a price: therefore glorify God in your body, and in your spirit, which are God's.'"[14]

LOSS OF THE SPIRIT

Another major reason why we should stay sexually pure relates to the Holy Ghost. The Lord warned that "if any shall commit adultery in their hearts, they shall not have the Spirit" (D&C 63:16). If we are sexually immoral, we will lose the guidance of the Holy Ghost.

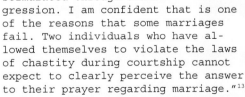

Elder Richard G. Scott said, "Recognize that an individual who is violating commandments of the Lord will find it very difficult to discern a prompting of the Spirit from the powerful emotions that can be stimulated through transgression. I am confident that is one of the reasons that some marriages fail. Two individuals who have allowed themselves to violate the laws of chastity during courtship cannot expect to clearly perceive the answer to their prayer regarding marriage."[13]

The time of dating and courtship is one time when we desperately need the Holy Ghost. Staying sexually pure will help you qualify for that divine companionship.

According to Elder Holland, our bodies are gifts that should not be tarnished by immoral activities. We must stay morally clean because our bodies are sacred. First Corinthians 3:16–17 teaches, "Know ye not that ye are the temple of God, and that the Spirit of God dwelleth in you? If any man defile the temple of God, him shall God destroy; for the temple of God is holy, which temple ye are."

The Savior purchased our

Tips to Staying Sexually Pure: PROPHETIC PRINCIPLE #7

YOUR MESSAGE HERE

Dress modestly.

"When you dress immodestly, you send a message that is contrary to your identity as a son or daughter of God."[15] When we display our body immodestly, we send a message to others that our body isn't important to us.

bodies with his blood in the Garden of Gethsemane; we owe it to him to keep them clean. If we desecrate our bodies through immorality, we desecrate the atonement of Christ that saved that body.

Hurting the Soul of the One We "Love"

Another reason why it's so important to stay morally clean is that when we are immoral, we harm the very soul of the person we are immoral with and supposedly love.

Joseph Smith taught a key doctrine about the relationship between our physical bodies and our spirits when the Lord revealed through him, "the spirit and the body are the soul of man" (D&C 88:15). In other words, our bodies and our spirits are *connected.* When we harm or abuse our physical body, we harm or abuse our spirit. Likewise, when we harm the body of another person through immorality, we not only harm our spirit, but *theirs* as well. Elder Jeffrey R. Holland warned, "We declare that one who uses the God-given body of another without divine sanction abuses the very soul of that individual."[16]

Sometimes people are physically intimate outside of marriage and rationalize it by saying that they love each other. If we truly love someone, would we ever do anything to intentionally harm them? Would we ever want to harm their *very soul*? Would we want to be the cause of someone not being able to enjoy the gift of the Holy Ghost, attend the temple, or partake of the

Tips to Staying Sexually Pure: PROPHETIC PRINCIPLE

Have a curfew and keep it.

#8

Being out late at night when we are tired and unsupervised can lead to immorality. As President Hinckley said, "Nothing really good happens after 11 o'clock at night."[17]

"When you [get enough sleep] you . . . gain the blessings of a healthy body, an alert mind, and the guidance of the Holy Ghost."[18]

Tips to Staying Sexually Pure: #9
PROPHETIC PRINCIPLE

Keep the Word of Wisdom.

Speaking of the Word of Wisdom, the modern prophets warn, "Being under the influence of alcohol weakens your judgment and self-control"[19] and could lead you to break the law of chastity.

sacrament? Do we want to be a contributing party of causing someone to lose self-respect, to feel shame and guilt? That is *not* how we show someone we love them!

Please remember, when we violate the law of chastity, we violate not only our body and soul, but the body and soul of someone we claim to love.

Tips to Staying Sexually Pure: #10
PROPHETIC PRINCIPLE

Pray daily.

President Gordon B. Hinckley said that youth should "kneel alone in prayer before they leave home on a date that they may remain in control of themselves."[20]

Some Temporal Reasons Too

We've focused on some of the doctrinal reasons why it is so important to stay morally clean. Common sense also provides several other reasons. For example, when you live the law of chastity, you avoid contracting sexually

transmitted diseases. The *New York Times* reported that in the United States alone about 19 million new cases of sexually transmitted diseases are reported each year and that 1 in 4 sexually active teenage girls in the U.S. have a sexually transmitted disease.[21]

Furthermore, by staying morally clean, you avoid the heartache and hardships that come from pregnancy outside of marriage, including dropping out of school, losing friends, missing out on the wholesome fun and freedom of youth, and taking on the financial worry and time commitment of bearing, supporting, and raising a child. The Proclamation on the Family says that "Children are entitled to birth within the bonds of matrimony, and to be reared by a father and a mother who honor marital vows with complete fidelity."[24] As you live the law of chastity, you give your future children this right.

CHILDREN OUT OF WEDLOCK

- Of all births out of wedlock, only 16% of those parents were married five years after the birth.[22]
- "80 percent of teenage mothers end up in poverty and must rely on welfare."[23]

Only 16% Still Married Five Years Later

80% of Teenage Mothers in Poverty

At the beginning of this chapter, we wrote about how immorality leads to all sorts of negative emotions, not love. The good news is that the opposite is also true: Staying sexually pure leads to increased love. Elder David A. Bednar said: "I promise that obedience to the law of chastity will increase our happiness in mortality and make possible our progress in eternity. Chastity and virtue are now, always have been, and always will be 'most dear and precious above all things' (Moroni 9:9)."[25]

Why Should I Be Sexually Pure?

1. **Immorality leads to bitterness, jealousy, anger, and even hate—not love.**
2. **Breaking the law of chastity makes a mockery of the Atonement.**
3. **Sexual transgression harms the soul of the person we claim to love.**
4. **Staying morally clean helps us avoid pre-marital pregnancy or sexually transmitted diseases.**

NOW that we have reviewed some of the *principles*, let's answer some of the questions regarding the *practices* connected to being sexually pure:

Why is it going too far to passionately kiss someone?

In the *For the Strength of Youth* pamphlet, the prophets have clearly defined "the line" of chastity by saying, "Do not participate in passionate kissing."[26] The pamphlet also says, "Before marriage, do not participate in passionate kissing, lie on top of another person, or touch the private, sacred parts of another person's body, with or without clothing. Do not do anything else that arouses sexual feelings."[27] In other words, *anything* that sexually arouses someone should be avoided before marriage. *Anything.* By the very definition of the word, passionate kissing is supposed to elicit "passion," or arousal, and should therefore be avoided. Also, when you are involved in passionate kissing before marriage, you and your partner are usually alone and in a place or situation where you might be more easily tempted to break the law of chastity. It can become difficult to control your emotions, and you can easily end up doing something more serious that will only bring sorrow and regret.

Cont.

Why are NCMOs bad?

"NCMOs" (or "non-committal make outs") are when two people have short-term connection (a weekend or a one-night romance) just for the sake of being able to kiss or make out with someone with no further expectations of a long-term relationship. A NCMO flies in the face of almost all the principles of chastity that have been emphasized in this chapter. They are selfish in nature and show a lack of respect for the sanctity of the body and of God's children. They also pervert "kissing" into a cheap act of self-pleasure; kissing should be an expression of love, not lust.

Why is it wrong to be physically intimate with someone if I love them?

For the Strength of Youth teaches that, "Physical intimacy between husband and wife is beautiful and sacred. It is ordained of God for the creation of children and for the expression of love between husband and wife."[28] One of the purposes of physical intimacy is to bring children into the world and to have a family. When we are physically intimate before marriage, we are not ready to bring children into a family (principle #4 in the chapter) because "children are entitled to birth within the bonds of matrimony, and to be reared by a father and a mother."[29] The other purpose of physical intimacy is to express love between husband and wife. If we become physically intimate outside of marriage, "moral schizophrenia" can result.[30]

Why Is Same-Sex Marriage Contrary to God's Eternal Plan?

You most likely have been or will be confronted with questions about same-sex marriage. Over the past thirty years an enormous shift has taken place in society. Where laws once prohibited same-sex marriage, it is now legal in many countries in the world, including the United States. Society's change on this issue may prompt some people to wonder why the Church hasn't changed—why same-sex marriages are not accepted by the Church and why two people of the same sex cannot be sealed to each other in the temple. These are good and timely questions. To help answer some *why* questions about same-sex marriage and the Church, let's take a look at five foundational principles.

Principle #1: God loves all and wants all to love him.

It is important to begin with this truth: GOD LOVES ALL PEOPLE (see 1 John 4:8–11). Who is the person you most recently saw? Guess what? God loves that person. Maybe it was your mom, or the person you have a crush on. God loves them too. Even if it's your annoying sibling, the smartest kid in your class, or the weirdo who sits by you in science! In all our imperfections, God loves us perfectly.

We once drove by a billboard that said, "God Loves Gays!" and we thought, "Of course he does!" God loves all his children. We must never lose sight of that.

GOD LOVES GAYS!

Because he loves everyone he invites "*all* to come unto him and partake of his goodness; and he denieth none . . . *all* are alike unto God" (2 Nephi 26:33; emphasis added). This means we all need the Lord's authorized Church and we all need the Atonement of Jesus Christ. Our Savior was a friend to all people when he was on the earth, including those the scriptures call "sinners" (Matthew 11:19). He reached out to all types of people—from traditional Jews to immoral persons to dishonest tax collectors—inviting them to be perfected in him. In fact, some of his strongest words were against those who "trusted in themselves that they were righteous, and despised others" (Luke 18:9). Too often, discussions about same-sex marriage turn into negative judgments or rude messages. There is no place in the Church for unkindness, bullying, or mocking. There is always room for extending our personal love and God's divine love.

Modern prophets have taught, "Church members are to treat all people with love and humanity. They may express genuine love and kindness toward a gay or lesbian family member, friend, or other person without condoning any redefinition of marriage."[1] As an example, while the Church doesn't approve of same-sex marriages, they do approve of and even advocate for some laws that prohibit discrimination related to housing, employment, and medical services for same-sex couples.[2]

Principle #2: Eternal truth is not relative, nor is truth made by the votes of society; truth is proclaimed by living prophets.

When society decides by vote that something should be legal, this does not mean it becomes right to the Lord. For example, in some countries it is legal to view pornography, smoke cigarettes, commit adultery, and listen to music that would make a sailor blush (apologies to righteous sailors). This doesn't mean these things are right or good, just that they have been deemed legal in a free society. But votes and laws don't decide eternal Truth.

Elder Russell M. Nelson taught, "After World War I, a rather risqué song became popular. In promoting immorality, it [the lyrics of the song] vowed that *50 million people cannot be wrong.* But in fact, 50 million people *can* be wrong—totally wrong."[3] If you don't believe that so many people can be wrong, just look at what your parents thought was cool when they were teenagers! ☺ When trying to know if something is right, we should be more concerned with what is *eternal* than what is *popular.* There are things called "absolute truths" that don't ever change—laws and facts that are correct in all times and places—and God is the source of that capital-T Truth.

Some people claim that everything is just "relative." No, they're not saying we're all related

Edward H. Adelson

DO TRY THIS AT HOME!

Take a look at the following image. Now vote: which square is darker, A or B? (See p. 140 for the correct answer.)

(hey, cousin!); what they mean is that there is no real right or wrong; society can just decide what's okay based on their collective thinking. This is called "moral relativism," and this is not new. It is a seductive lie utilized throughout the ages by Korihor and others (see Alma 30:17). As believers in an eternal God we know there are eternal Truths to live by and that everything isn't just relative. If everything *were* just relative, then as Lehi taught, that means there is no real right and no real wrong, no real good and no real evil (see 2 Nephi 2:13).

While there are many viewpoints to respectfully consider, we logically and spiritually know there is actual right and wrong and actual good and evil. God gives us prophets and apostles to reveal and proclaim God's absolute Truths and His will in our day (see Ephesians 4:11; Jeremiah 7:25; Mosiah 8:14–17; and Doctrine and Covenants 1:38). So when formulating opinions about same-sex marriage or any other issue, ultimately what counts most in the discussion is not what a particular society has voted for, or what trends currently seem popular, but the absolute, eternal truths that God has established through modern prophets. On all topics, including same-sex marriage, we can look forward to more direction and guidance from the prophets in the years ahead. We do believe in continuing revelation and we can trust the living prophets to provide us with the revelation we need.

> **✗** <u>Relative truth</u> = there is no absolute truth, and culture and society decide what is right and wrong based on what they think.
>
> **✓** <u>Absolute truth</u> = there are eternal truths given by God that do not change regardless of culture and society.

Answer to "Do Try This at Home" on page 139.

The correct answer is that squares A and B are the exact same shade of gray. Once you remove the background, it becomes clear. The only reason you may have voted that B is lighter is because your brain is being tricked by its surroundings and thinks, "This is a checkerboard and A is a dark square and B is a light square, so therefore B is lighter than A," even though B is in shadow and therefore is just as dark as A. And just because we think or vote that something is one way doesn't mean that way is correct.

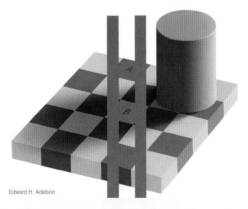

Edward H. Adelson

THE RIGHT SIDE OF ETERNITY

As we speak up on issues regarding same-sex marriage, *it is always more important to be on the right side of eternity than on the right side of history.* We should not be surprised if the teachings of God's prophets are not always popular. If we are ridiculed for our beliefs, we're in good company. Prophets such as Moses, Jeremiah, Nephi, Abinadi, Samuel the Lamanite, and many others were attacked for teaching God's truths. Because of what living prophets and seers have seen, we have been urged "to promote those measures designed to maintain and strengthen the family as the fundamental unit of society."[4] We invite you to respectfully do the same, even when it is difficult.

Principle #3: Marriage between man and woman is essential to God's eternal plan.

One of the clearest explanations of eternal Truths related to the family is found in the prophetic 1995 document, *The Family: A Proclamation to the World.* This inspired, official declaration—"given long before we experienced the challenges now facing the family"[5]—was signed by every member of the First Presidency and Quorum of the Twelve and has been repeatedly affirmed by prophets over the past decades. This proclamation states, "Marriage between man and woman is essential to His eternal plan." Part of God's eternal plan for his children is for them to be married to somebody of the opposite sex—not just for this life, but for all eternity. Although a great part of marriage is the romantic "twue wuv" part (thanks, *Princess Bride*!), marriage is not just a temporary convenience or even simply about our feelings and desires; it is about eternal purpose and progression.

Elder David A. Bednar taught, "Righteous marriage is a commandment and an essential step in the process of creating a loving family relationship that can be perpetuated beyond the grave."[6] The Church's official *Handbook of Instructions* says that "the nature of male and female spirits is such that they complete each other. Men and women are intended to progress together toward exaltation."[7] What the First Presidency seems to be saying is that in general the natures of men and women are different. The distinctive and complementary features of males and females matter so much that prophets have taught that "gender is an essential characteristic of individual premortal, mortal, and eternal identity and purpose."[8] Like the Chinese yin/yang symbol, these inherent differences in males and females, joined together in righteous marriage, can work together to make a cohesive whole. A man needs a woman, and a woman needs a man, as they complement and complete each other in a divine way (see 1 Corinthians 11:11).

Principle #4: Only a man and a woman together have procreative power to create children and eternal families.

The First Presidency has said, "From the beginning, the sacred nature of marriage was closely linked to the power of procreation. After creating Adam and Eve, God commanded them to 'be fruitful, and multiply, and replenish the earth,' and they brought forth children, forming the first family. Only a man and a woman together have the natural biological capacity to conceive

It requires a male and female to fulfill God's command to multiply and replenish the earth.

children."[9] Without going into detail (you're welcome), a same-sex marriage is not consistent with the commandment to be married and create children together.

While clearly not all couples can or will have children, this reproductive power does not only apply to this life, but also seems to apply to the next life in the celestial kingdom. The Prophet Joseph Smith taught that in heaven an eternally married man and woman "will continue to increase and have children in the celestial glory"[10] (see D&C 131:4; D&C 132:19). An official pamphlet from the Church recently confirmed this concept of creating children in heaven through marriage by a man and woman by saying, "Heaven is organized by families, which require a man and a woman, who together

exercise their creative powers within the bounds the Lord has set. Same-sex relationships are inconsistent with this plan. Without both a husband and a wife there would be no eternal family and no opportunity to become like Heavenly Father."[11]

Fulfilling the ultimate purpose of the plan of salvation—becoming like our Heavenly Father and Mother—

"If a man marry a wife by my word, which is my law . . . they shall pass by the angels . . . to their exaltation and glory in all things . . . which glory shall be a fulness and a continuation of the seeds forever and ever" (D&C 132:19).

requires a righteous male and female to be sealed for eternity.

Principle #5: Sexual relationships outside of a heterosexual marriage undermine God's divine design for families and children.

The First Presidency has declared, "Any other sexual relations [outside of a man and a woman in legal marriage], including those between persons of the same gender, undermine the divinely created institution of the family."[12] Sometimes people may claim, "This is how I am and there's nothing I can do about it." While being sympathetic to all persons' feelings and opinions, just because we have a certain sexual desire doesn't justify our acting on that desire. A married man may have desires to be with a woman who isn't his wife, but that doesn't mean he should act on those feelings. Why? Because it would harm his family and it is contrary to what God commands. A teenage girl may want to become physically passionate with her boyfriend, but

God says no, partly because unmarried sex is emotionally and spiritually damaging and can lead to children being born without a married mother and father. *Individual feelings don't determine whether acting on a sexual desire is right or wrong.* Remember that Alma taught that all of our passions, regardless of who they are directed toward, must be bridled so that we "may be filled with love" (Alma 38:12). God's divine design for families is that children be "reared by a father and a mother who honor marital vows with complete fidelity."[13]

Many people have feelings and desires that may not be consistent with what God says, but God has given us the ability to control how we act and follow his commandments. Elder Dallin H.

) ARE CHILDREN ENTITLED?

The answer is yes—but not to smartphones, late-night parties, cool teachers, or the best clothes. They are entitled to at least ONE thing: "Children are *entitled* to birth within the bonds of matrimony, and to be reared by a father and a mother who honor marital vows with complete fidelity."[14] While not every child will be raised by a married mother and father, it is an ideal that we should strive to provide whenever possible.

Oaks said, "We do not accept the fact that conditions that prevent people from attaining their eternal destiny were born into them without any ability to control. That is contrary to the Plan of Salvation, and it is contrary to the justice and mercy of God. It's contrary to the whole teaching of the Gospel of Jesus Christ, which expresses the truth that by or through the power and mercy of Jesus Christ we will have the strength to do all things. That includes resisting temptation. That includes dealing with things that we're born with."[15] Even in an area as serious and powerful as one's sexual desires, we testify of the power of Jesus Christ to help guide us through this and any other challenge we face.

Below are two pictures. Try not to look at the picture on the left and instead look only at the picture on the right. Control your actions!

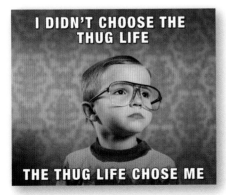

If you looked at this picture, you didn't control yourself! Remember, you have agency and can control what you do or don't do!

If you are only looking at this then you have chosen the right, literally! Way to be a good agent and control your actions!

Conclusion

These five key principles regarding same-sex marriage have been repeatedly taught by current members of the First Presidency and Quorum of the Twelve. As we strive to follow and uphold the Lord's Truths through his modern prophets regarding marriage between a man and a woman, we also must balance our stance for Truth with friendliness and fairness toward those whose opinions differ regarding same-sex marriage. On this point, Elder Dallin H. Oaks has said that we must not let "our tolerance and respect for others and their beliefs cause us to abandon our commitment to the truths we understand and the covenants we have made."[17]

If we do not struggle with same-sex attraction, let us remember that Christ loves everyone and has commanded that we should "continue to minister" to all (3 Nephi 18:32). Think of the spiritual strength and faith that it requires for a gay person to loyally worship and support the doctrines related to the traditional family in our Church! Let that empathy work inside each of us and decide today that we will be a loving friend and fellow saint to those of same-sex attraction.

To those who struggle with issues related to same-sex attraction and marriage, one of the greatest eternal, absolute Truths to remember is that because of our Savior, Jesus Christ, anything that may be unfair will one day be made right. **The central feature of the Atonement of Christ is to perfectly right any mortal wrong.** If we will follow the Lord's teachings related to the law of chastity and faithfully try to live our covenants with Him, we know He will make all things as they should be.

Following Christ takes faith in Christ and trust in His plan. We all understand that God has the power to do anything. However, if He chooses to direct His prophets to take a path different from one we want them to take, do we still trust Christ, regardless of the outcome? Or do we base our faith in Christ on whether or not particular immediate outcomes meet our own expectations?[18] He will provide opportunities for everyone to be exalted and have an eternal family, no matter what their circumstances on earth, if they will follow His eternal teachings and keep their covenants. Although we don't know all the details of how this will happen, no one who is faithful and worthy will be denied that opportunity.[19] That is what Jesus does for all God's children who love Him and keep His commandments.

AN APOSTLE ANSWERS

In a conference with young adults, Elder Jeffrey R. Holland was asked, "Those who experience same-gender attraction feel alone in the Church. If you could meet with them face to face, how would you respond to them?"

Elder Holland's response was: "We have talked altogether too much about gender and altogether too little about chastity. The issue is about chastity and not about gender. . . . We are not passing judgment on someone who has a feeling, to someone who has an attraction. . . . We're just talking about a single standard of the Lord's commandments. . . . We issue all of our love and all of our help and anything we can do to help people meet that standard."[16]

Why Is Same-Sex Marriage Contrary to God's Eternal Plan?

1. **Always remember that God loves all of his children and wants all of his children to love Him.**
2. **Eternal truth is not relative, nor is truth made by the votes of society. Truth is proclaimed by living prophets.**
3. **Marriage between man and woman is essential to God's eternal plan.**
4. **Only a man and woman together have procreative power to create children and eternal families.**
5. **Sexual relationships outside of a heterosexual marriage undermine God's divine design for families and children.**

NOW that we have understood some of the *principles*, let's answer some of the questions you might be asked regarding the *practices* connected to same-sex attraction and marriage.

Why would God allow somebody to have same-sex attraction if marriage between a man and a woman is such an important part of the plan? Do people have a choice in their sexual orientation?

Sometimes people want to know if their sexual orientation is a result of "nature" (born with it) or "nurture" (learned behavior). Elder Dallin H. Oaks stated that "the Church does not have a position on the causes of any of these susceptibilities or inclinations, including those related to same-gender attraction. Those are scientific questions—whether nature or nurture—those are things the Church doesn't have a position on."[20] See also the quotation from Elder Holland in the next question.

Is it sinful to be attracted to members of the same sex?

Elder D. Todd Christofferson said, "Same-sex attraction in and of itself is not a sin. The feeling, the desire is not classified the same as homosexual behavior itself."[21] Everyone struggles with desires that are not in harmony with God's ways. Our sexual drive is perhaps stronger than most other desires; nevertheless, there are many heterosexual and homosexual people in the Church who are single for their whole lives who still live the law of chastity. It is not easy, but they have found it is worth it.

Elder Jeffrey R. Holland said the following to a young man who was struggling with same-sex attraction: "'As for why you feel as you do, I can't answer that question. A number of factors may be involved, and they can be as different as people are different. Some things, including the cause of your feelings, we may never know in this life. *But knowing why you feel as you do isn't as important as knowing you have not transgressed.* If your life is in harmony with the commandments, then you are worthy to serve in the Church, enjoy full fellowship with the members, attend the temple, and receive all the blessings of the Savior's Atonement.'"[22]

Why should I follow the prophets if they might change the doctrine on this in the future? In the past, people of African descent could not hold the priesthood and now they can. Perhaps in the future the Church will support same-sex marriage, and so I think it is okay for me to support it now.

We believe in following the living prophets, not what other prophets might hypothetically do in the future. Doctrine and Covenants 21:4–6 states: "Thou shalt give heed unto all [the prophet's] words and commandments which he shall give unto you as he receiveth them, walking in all holiness before me; for his word ye shall receive, as if from mine own mouth, in all patience and faith. For by doing these things the gates of hell shall not prevail against you; yea, and the Lord God will disperse the powers of darkness from before you, and cause the heavens to shake for your good, and his name's glory." Those are powerful blessings that come from receiving the prophet's teachings with both patience and faith.

In terms of whether the issue of same-sex marriage will change in the future, Elder D. Todd Christofferson of the Quorum of the Twelve stated the following: "The doctrines that relate to human sexuality and gender are really central to our theology. And marriage between a man and a woman, and the families that come from those marriages—that's all central to God's plan and to the opportunities that He offers to us, here and hereafter. So homosexual behavior is contrary to those doctrines—has been, always will be."[23]

Why is marriage between a man and a woman such an important issue for the Church?

One reason why the Church continually speaks out on marriage between a man and a woman relates to the right of religious beliefs for individuals and churches. "The free exercise" of religion, as stated in the First Amendment of the United States Constitution, is a fundamental right of citizens, and freedom of religion is an acknowledged right in the constitutions of most first-world countries. But what happens if your constitutional right to exercise your religion conflicts with another person's choices? For example, should Church-owned universities like BYU be required to allow same-gender married couples to live in on-campus married student housing? Should the Church be required to allow same-gender weddings or wedding receptions to take place in their meetinghouses? These are complicated issues—and they are not simply hypothetical. For example, a CEO of a major company recently resigned when a vocal minority protested his views on same-sex marriage.[24] In another instance, "When public schools in Massachusetts began teaching students about same-sex civil marriage, a Court of Appeals ruled that parents had no right to exempt their students."[25]

The Church is interested in ensuring that religious liberty is maintained—in other words, that we all continue to have the right to act "according to the dictates of our own conscience" (Articles of Faith 1:11). Elder Dallin H. Oaks explained: "This is much bigger than just a question of whether or not society should be more tolerant of the homosexual lifestyle. . . . The Church of Jesus Christ of Latter-day Saints must take a stand on doctrine and principle. This is more than a social issue—ultimately it may be a test of our most basic religious freedoms to teach what we know our Father in Heaven wants us to teach."[26] The Church has a strong interest in maintaining religious liberty; this is an issue that each of us should learn more about.

Isn't defining marriage a societal and not a doctrinal issue?

The definition of marriage is both a doctrinal *and* a societal issue. In addition to doctrinal issues, the Church is concerned about what same-sex marriage will mean for society as a whole. As a statement from the Church says, "The legal recognition of same-sex marriage may, over time, erode the social identity, gender development, and moral character of children."[27] Traditional marriage has been in place for thousands of years and is proven to provide many social benefits—especially for children who are "reared by a father and a mother who honor marital vows with complete fidelity."[28] While not every child will be raised by a mother and a father, it is an ideal that society should strive for. In fact, prophets have warned that "the disintegration of the family will bring upon individuals, communities, and nations the calamities foretold by ancient and modern prophets."[29]

At the same time, we need to remember that "Jesus Christ, whom we follow, was clear in His condemnation of sexual immorality, but never cruel. His interest was always to lift the individual, never to tear down."[30] Elder Quentin L. Cook has stated: "As a church, nobody should be more loving and compassionate. Let us be at the forefront in terms of expressing love, compassion and outreach. Let's not have families exclude or be disrespectful of those who choose a different lifestyle as a result of their feelings about their own gender."[31]

I tried to share my beliefs about same-sex marriage and all my friends made fun of me. What should I do?

The first suggestion we have is for you to check yourself. Did you express love and kindness? Did you show regard for others' feelings? Let's assume that you respectfully expressed your point of view only to be attacked by others. What then? Well, as Elder Jeffrey R. Holland taught, "I say to all and especially the youth of the Church that if you haven't already, you will one day find yourself called upon to defend your faith or perhaps even endure some personal abuse simply because you are a member of The Church of Jesus Christ of Latter-day Saints."[32] Simply put, you are not alone. When you stand for what is right and are mocked for doing so, you stand with prophets throughout the centuries.

In general conference, Elder Neil L. Andersen shared the experience of a young woman who said: "This past year some of my friends on Facebook began posting their position on marriage.

Many favored same-sex marriage, and several LDS youth indicated they 'liked' the postings. I made no comment. I decided to declare my belief in traditional marriage in a thoughtful way. With my profile picture, I added the caption 'I believe in marriage between a man and a woman.' Almost instantly I started receiving messages. 'You are selfish.' 'You are judgmental.' One compared me to a slave owner. And I received this post from a great friend who is a strong member of the Church: 'You need to catch up with the times. Things are changing and so should you.'"[33]

Elder Andersen reported that the young woman did not fight back, but she kept her statement posted. It is not easy to stand for truth, especially if you have to stand alone. But we commend to you the advice of Elder Holland to the youth: "Be strong. Live the gospel faithfully even if others around you don't live it at all. Defend your beliefs with courtesy and with compassion, but defend them."[34] And continue to try to find ways to serve those who might struggle with this or any other gospel topic.

Additional Resources on the Subject of Same-Sex Marriage

- "The Family: A Proclamation to the World," *Ensign*, November 2010, 129.
- Gospel Topics page on same-sex attraction; see https://www.lds.org/topics/same-sex-attraction.
- First Presidency statement on same-sex marriage; see http://www.mormonnewsroom.org/article/first-presidency-statement-on-same-sex-marriage.
- Website on Mormons and gays; see http://mormonsandgays.org/.
- Interview with Elders Dallin H. Oaks and Lance B. Wickman on same-sex attraction; see http://www.mormonnewsroom.org/article/interview-oaks-wickman-same-sex-attraction.
- Elder Jeffrey R. Holland, "Helping Those Who Struggle with Same-Sex Attraction"; see https://www.lds.org/ensign/2007/10/helping-those-who-struggle-with-same-sex-attraction.
- Elder Dallin H. Oaks, "Transcript: Hope for the Years Ahead"; see http://www.mormonnewsroom.org/article/transcript-elder-dallin-oaks-constitutional-symposium-religious-freedom.
- Elder Dallin H. Oaks, "Same-Gender Attraction," *Ensign,* October 1995, 7–14.
- Elder Dallin H. Oaks, "Judging and Not Judging"; see https://www.lds.org/ensign/1999/08/judge-not-and-judging.
- Sister Julie B. Beck, "Teaching the Doctrine of the Family"; see https://www.lds.org/ensign/2011/03/teaching-the-doctrine-of-the-family.
- "The Divine Institution of Marriage"; see http://www.mormonnewsroom.org/article/the-divine-institution-of-marriage.
- "God Loveth His Children"; see https://www.lds.org/manual/god-loveth-his-children/god-loveth-his-children.
- *Voices of Hope* website; see http://www.ldsvoicesofhope.org.

22 ch Why Can't I Watch Whatever I Want?

In August of 2001, President Henry B. Eyring gave a remarkable prophecy. He said that LDS youth cannot just "go with the flow" anymore and expect to remain righteous. He then prophesied of what is to come in the future: "The flow has become a flood and soon will be a torrent. It will become a torrent of *sounds* and *sights* and *sensations* that invite temptation and offend the Spirit of God."[1]

HOW FAST IS A "TORRENT"?

A "torrent" is defined as a large amount of fast-moving or falling water. The photos to the right show the shore of Banda Aceh, Indonesia, before and after the tsunami of 2004. Tsunami waves can travel up to 600 miles an hour off-shore. Measurements show the waves that hit Banda Ache were more than 100 feet high in some points and traveled 1.24 miles inland.[2]

BEFORE

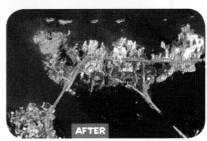

AFTER

photographs © NOAA; courtesy DigitalGlobe Inc.

Just a few short months after President Eyring prophesied of the torrent of sounds, sights, and sensations about to hit our youth, the first iPod was introduced to the general public. Two years later, the first video iPod came out. The youth of today are the first generation to be able to carry thousands of songs, images, and videos in the palm of their hand, twenty-four hours a day, seven days a week.

In the Palm of Your Hand

With multiple gigabytes of storage on even inexpensive devices, you can carry thousands of songs and hours of video and endless images everywhere you go.

Not only have iPods blossomed, but since 2001, so have cultural phenomena such as **YouTube**, **Google**, **Facebook**, **Twitter**, **Instagram**, **Snapchat**, **virtual reality gaming systems**, **Netflix**, **HD TV**, and **smartphones** and **tablets**. Truly a torrent of sounds, sights, and sensations has washed over this current generation like never before in the history of the world. If ever there was a need to understand why it matters so much what we watch, it is now.

A 2015 Pew Research study found that:
- 92% of teens (ages 13–17) go online daily and 24% are "almost constantly" online
- Three-quarters of teens have a smartphone
- 71% of teens use Facebook, 52% use Instagram, and 41% use Snapchat; 71% use multiple social media platforms[3]

A TORRENT OF SIGHTS AND SOUNDS

Category	Percentage
Multiple Social Media	71%
Snapchat	41%
Instagram	52%
Facebook	71%
Have Smartphone	75%
Always Online	24%
Online Daily	92%

Monkey See, Monkey Do

There is an old saying, "Monkey see, monkey do." That is not only true for primates, but also for people as well. *For the Strength of Youth* says, "Whatever you read . . . or look at has an effect on you."[4]

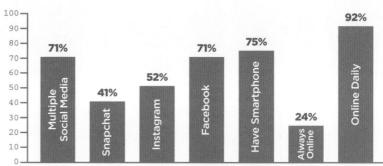

WHATEVER YOU SEE . . .

- By age 18, the average U.S. teen will have seen 16,000 simulated murders and 200,000 acts of violence.
- 64% of all TV shows surveyed in 2001–2002 included sexual content or references.
- Of those shows surveyed, there was an average of 4.4 sexually-related scenes per hour.[5]

Willingness to Have Pre-marital Sex Based on Number of R-Rated Movies Viewed During a Two-Year Period[6]

Number of "R" Movies Watched	% Willing
0–4	20%
5–15	51%
16–29	65%
30–49	73%
50+	93%

One reason why it is so important to filter what we watch is because what we *see* triggers what we *think*, what we think influences what we *desire*, what we desire affects our *actions*, our combined actions determine our *character*, and our character determines our *eternal destiny*.

Our Eyes and Our Eternity

see=> think=> desire=> actions=> character=> eternity

What We Watch Influences How We Act

The sad downfall of King David is a startling example of how what people view changes their actions. Though David was a great man, he lost everything due to a moment of weakness that began by looking at something he should not have seen.

While on the king's roof, David beheld Bathsheba "washing herself; and the woman was very beautiful to look upon" (2 Samuel 11:2). Instead of looking away and controlling what his eyes beheld, he lusted after her and "sent and inquired after the woman. . . . And she came in unto him, and he lay with her" (2 Samuel 11:3-4). What he saw from the roof created lustful and immoral desires, and those desires led to the sin of adultery, then to the tragic murder of Bathsheba's husband (see 2 Samuel 11:5-17), and eventually the loss of David's exaltation (see D&C 132:39). All because he did not control what he watched!

YO, ROCKY—MONKEY SEE, MONKEY DO

Anthony Says:

When I was a kid, the first *Rocky* movies were popular. My brother and I, with our friends, would watch Rocky train and get in shape for his upcoming fight and then take on his challenger. As Rocky would work out, we would try to do the same things. If he did push-ups and sit-ups, so did we. If he went out for a run, we would run around the family room. When the time for the fight came, one of us would be designated as Rocky and someone else as his opponent, and we would re-enact each scene, fake punch by fake punch. Without even realizing it, the movie influenced how we acted and behaved, down to the last right hook.

We are influenced not only by images we see, but also by the words we read. One scholar ran an experiment where people were divided into two groups. One group read sentences that contained aggressive words, "bold," "rude," "bother," "disturb," "intrude," and "infringe."

The other group was given sentences with the words "respect," "considerate," "appreciate," "patiently," "yield," "polite," and "courteous."

After reading the sentences, the individuals were told to return to an office for their next assignment. But the researcher made sure he was already engaged in a conversation with a co-researcher when the individual arrived. The question was, "Would the people who had read the aggressive sentences be more likely to interrupt the conversation?"

The group who had read the aggressive words interrupted after about five minutes, on average. The group who had read the words that promoted politeness *never interrupted at all!* (The researchers ended the waiting after ten minutes, though who knows how long they would have stood there!)[7]

Proverbs states, "For as [a man] thinketh in his heart, so is he" (23:7). What we see is a primary stimulus for what we think and how we act. This truth is one major reason why it is so important we only watch and view media that helps us to have "virtue garnish [our] thoughts unceasingly" (D&C 121:45).

The Skew of the View

Without our realizing it, media skews or alters our perspective of reality. Video games allow us to shoot, hit, and kill people without any blood or feeling. TV shows depict immoral lifestyles as "normal" and rarely mention the consequences. Beauty magazines and pornographic pictures display women who are so fabricated—nipped, tucked, airbrushed, and digitally manipulated—as to make the average girl wonder why she is the only one with pimples and a bit of cellulite. It is ironic that in our "reality TV" generation, most of what we see in the media is so fake that it couldn't be further from reality. If we are not careful with the media we use, we can start perceiving these false images as reality.

Does the media we watch give us mixed signals?

DIGITAL DECEPTION

Is She for Real?

To see a digitally altered before-and-after shot, visit http://johnhiltoniii.com/qa.

More than 1,000 studies attest to a causal connection between media violence and aggressive behavior in some children. Studies show that the more "real-life" the violence portrayed, the greater the likelihood that such behavior will be "learned."[8]

Addictive and Restrictive

Media such as pornography is addictive, but other types of visual media—video games, television shows, and internet blogs and chats, for example—can also be addictive. Social media sites such as Instagram, Facebook, and Pinterest have such an all-consuming nature that some of their users have deemed them "cybercrack." Users can't wait to update their personal profiles and read the posts on their personal sites. Their eyes and ears crave it, just like an addict craves another hit or high. As a matter of fact, research has shown that playing some video games raises the amount of dopamine in the brain to a level equivalent to a hit of speed.[9]

THE LAYSAN ALBATROSS

The Laysan albatross is a beautiful, but vulnerable species. The bird frequently mistakes trash for food, and birds have been found with bellies full of trash, including cigarette lighters, toothbrushes, syringes, toys, and clothespins. Because the albatross cannot digest the trash, the garbage stays in the bird's stomach until the stomach becomes so full of trash that it can no longer take in good food or nutrition. In some areas where the bird lives, forty percent of albatross chicks die from dehydration and starvation because of the trash filling their bellies.

Mmm, delicious!

Are we like the Laysan albatross? If we fill our minds with media that is destructive—or even simply a waste of time—we may miss out on the vital nutrients our spirits really need.

One of our tests here in mortality is to have our spirit gain control over our physical bodies, including our eyes and ears. Just like drugs can addict the body, media can enslave our minds. Elder Russell M. Nelson taught, "Addiction to *any substance* enslaves not only the physical body but *the spirit* as well."[10]

As we face the onslaught of sights, sounds, and sensations, we need to be selective about what we watch in order to avoid drowning spiritually in this modern-day river of filth (see 1 Nephi 12:16). What we watch matters.

DO TRY THIS AT HOME!

Are you in control of what you watch? Find out by taking a "no-media" test. Pick one of your favorite sources of media and go without it for a week. For example, no video games, no social media, no movies, no YouTube, etc. Instead, read books, do some service projects, spend time with your family, or any of the thousand other things that people did for the last 6,000 years before the visual media began to dominate our culture. Can you do it?

TELL ME ONE MORE TiME!

Why Can't I Watch Whatever I Want?

1. **Everything we see affects what we think, and therefore what we desire and how we act.**
2. **Visual media can dangerously skew our perspective of reality.**
3. **Certain forms of visual media are addictive and can take control of our life.**

NOW that we have reviewed some of the *principles*, let's answer some of the questions regarding the *practices* connected to the media we watch:

Why can't I watch a movie if it only has one or two "bad" parts?

Our minds have an amazing ability to record and remember images, and once we have seen something, it is hard to *un*-see it. Elder Dallin H. Oaks said, "The brain won't vomit back

Cont.

filth. Once recorded, it will always remain subject to recall, flashing its perverted images across your mind and drawing you away from the wholesome things in life."[11] When you think of the hundreds or thousands of movies that some people watch during their lives, one or two bad parts in a movie can equal hundreds or thousands of improper images that are recorded in

our minds for recall. The prophet Alma teaches that by small and simple things, great things come about (Alma 37:6). The reverse is also true—by a few small *bad* scenes running through our heads, really *negative* things can be the result.

Why is it wrong to watch a movie that glorifies violence or immorality if it is historically accurate?

Just because it is historical doesn't mean it is good. Seeing glorified violence—whether the violence is historically accurate or not—can dull our spiritual senses and affect our actions. The Church has produced some excellent historical films that, of necessity, contain images of war or bloodshed. But they do it in such a way that the images are not graphic or gruesome and the movies do not glorify the violence taking place. *For the Strength of Youth* says, "Do not attend, view, or participate in anything that is vulgar, immoral, violent, or pornographic in any way. Do not participate in anything that presents immorality or violence as acceptable."[12] Historical accuracy does not trump spiritual appropriateness, no matter what story is being told.

Why shouldn't I play video games where I fight and kill people if I know it's just pretend?

Even if it is pretend, the images are still seen by our eyes and recorded in our minds. As principle #1 in this chapter teaches, everything we see affects our behavior. Even if the violence is computer-generated, it is still violence and will ultimately affect how we think and act. *For the Strength of Youth* teaches that "Whatever you . . . look at has an effect on you,"[13] even if it is fake. Earlier in this chapter, we talked about people *reading* aggressive words and having it affect their actions. And remember the Laysan albatross? If you are spending your time playing video games, you may be filling your time with "empty" activities when in reality you could be putting your time to much better use.

How Can I Resist and Overcome Pornography?

Pornography. It is "one of the most damning influences on earth."[1] We could list a bunch of statistics about the prevalence of pornography, but we won't. They are too depressing and too obvious. Whether it is through the Internet, television shows, movies, advertisements, magazine covers, lyrics and music, filthy books, crude jokes, or simply by the dress and behavior of those around us, "we are exposed to [pornography] daily."[2] Pornography comes in many forms, but its purpose is always the same: to stimulate unwholesome sexual feelings. The question for this generation is not "*Will* I see pornography?" but "What will I do *when* I see pornography?" We need a generation who is keenly aware of the evil of pornography and who has the knowledge, resources, and spiritual strength to withstand it.

So how can we resist and overcome pornography?

HOW are young women being targeted by pornography?

Although we don't know exactly how the pornography industry is targeting young women, one potential source is through books that are sexually explicit or create sexual feelings. An article in the *Ensign* described a woman's perspective on this issue from someone who had struggled with addiction to such books: "Often when we hear about the evils of pornography, we think of pornographic magazines, movies, and Web sites. Because men are more visually oriented, such material seems to appeal primarily to them. Yet the sexually explicit literature targeted at women, who are more verbally oriented, can be damaging as well. Like visual pornography, such literature presents a warped view of sexuality and is arousing and addictive. It dulls our spiritual senses, which distances us from God, and it can impair our ability to have healthy, lasting relationships."[5]

Flu Virus

WHICH IS DEADLIER?

Did you know that more Americans died from the 1918 flu than died in World War I, World War II, the Korean War, and the Vietnam War combined?[4] Although we might have thought the wars were much more dangerous than the flu, we would have been wrong. In a similar way we may underestimate how deadly a disease pornography is.

Know That We Have the Divine Ability and Strength to Resist Pornography

The Prophet Joseph Smith taught an empowering truth that we can relate to pornography: "The devil has no power over us only as we permit him."[6] In other words, we have our agency, and we can choose our behavior. Lehi taught us that we were created by God with power "to act" and not just "to be acted upon" by outside influences, like pornography (see 2 Nephi 2:13–14). We can "do many things of [our] own free will, and bring to pass much righteousness; for the power is in [us]" (D&C 58:27–28). We can choose how we will respond when we are confronted with pornography. We have the power to "turn away from [pornography] immediately."[7] The adversary cannot control our eyes, our minds, or our mouse!

John Says: SPIT IT OUT!

On a trip to the Universal Orlando Resort theme park, I was chosen to participate in a game based on the television show *Fear Factor*. My job was to drink a terrible drink that included sour milk, chicken, and bugs (seriously). It was so nasty that as soon as I started drinking it, I had to spit it out.

Pornography is just as nasty. As soon as you encounter it, spit it out!

Have a Spiritual Understanding of the Sacredness of the Human Body and the Divine Power of Procreation

Two main false ideas contribute to the problem of pornography. The first is the false message that the human body is just an object, and the second is that sexual intimacy exists for selfish purposes. Both of these statements are deceptions used by the adversary to have God's children misuse their bodies and procreative power. God's prophets have taught us that our bodies are "the temple of God" (1 Corinthians 3:16) and that our physical body is directly linked with our very soul (see D&C 88:15).

Elder Jeffrey R. Holland has taught that "one who uses the God-given body of another without divine sanction abuses the very soul of that individual."[8] Using another's body through pornography abuses his or her soul. If we understand the sacredness of the human body, we will be less tempted to treat it as a common object or misuse it. We will want to reject anything that is inconsistent with the message of the sacredness of the human body, such as pornography.

In Moses' time, the ark of the covenant was a chest that was placed in the center of the holy of holies in the tabernacle or temple. On the lid of the ark was the mercy seat, where the Lord told Moses, "I will meet with thee, and I will commune with thee from above the mercy seat" (Exodus 25:22). Sacred items, such as the tables of the law, were held inside the ark. It was considered to be the "most sacred of the religious symbols of the Israelites" and "it was treated with the greatest reverence."[9] It was so sacred that only authorized Israelites could touch the ark when it needed to be moved—the unauthorized would die (see 2 Samuel 6:6-7). It was covered with the veil of the temple and a cloth of skins (see Numbers 4:5-6).

Would the Israelites have treated the ark differently if Moses had told them it was simply a nice piece of furniture? (That's right, boys, just throw it in the moving van with the rocking chair!) Without the knowledge of its sacredness, the Israelites would probably have misused and abused the ark. However, having knowledge of the sacredness of the ark shaped the Israelites' behavior so they treated it as a special item. The same can be true for us. We can honor the sacredness of our bodies and our procreative power in order to avoid pornography. Accepting the sacred aids in rejecting the profane.

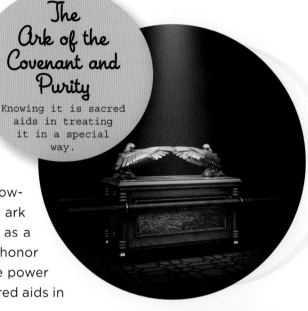

The Ark of the Covenant and Purity

Knowing it is sacred aids in treating it in a special way.

DO TRY THIS AT HOME!

WHAT DO YOU SEE IN THIS PERSON?

If you tilt your head sideways, you'll see that he is a liar (it spells liar in cursive). Now, the interesting thing is this: try *not* to see him as a liar. Can you? Or has viewing the word liar changed the way you see him? How is this like pornography?

For the Strength of Youth says, "Pornography . . . is a poison that . . . changes the way you see others."[10] If we become involved in pornography, instead of seeing a young woman as an intelligent, creative, fun, humorous, athletic, kind, daughter of God, we may only see her as a physical object to be used for lustful desires. We can lose the ability to see her for who she really is, and we miss out on her true beauty. This change in how we view others partially fulfills President Gordon B. Hinckley's warning that pornography "will rob you of a sense of the beauties of life."[11]

Know and Think About the Short- and Long-Term Consequences of Pornography

One of the tools of the adversary is to tell us to not think about the consequences of our actions, but to be selfish and enjoy the moment, to "eat, drink, and be merry" (2 Nephi 28:7). But there are consequences for purposeful involvement in pornography—they are real, and they are devastating. Here are some consequences that have been mentioned by the modern prophets:[12]

- Loss of the Holy Ghost
- Loss of priesthood power
- Loss of feeling for the beauties of life
- Unworthiness to participate in the ordinances of the gospel (such as baptism, the sacrament, and the temple)
- Negative changes about how others are viewed
- Weakened self-control
- Destructively powerful addiction that takes control of life
- Loss of energy, time, and dedication to productive things
- Distorted views about the purpose and nature of physical intimacy, including an inability to have a normal relationship with future or current spouse
- Feelings of shame, guilt, and remorse
- Loss of trust by others
- Emotional damage to loved ones
- Immoral thoughts
- Crude language or behavior
- Criminal behavior due to deviant sexual desires
- Immorality and adultery
- Destruction of marriage and family life through infidelity
- Loss of eternal salvation and exaltation

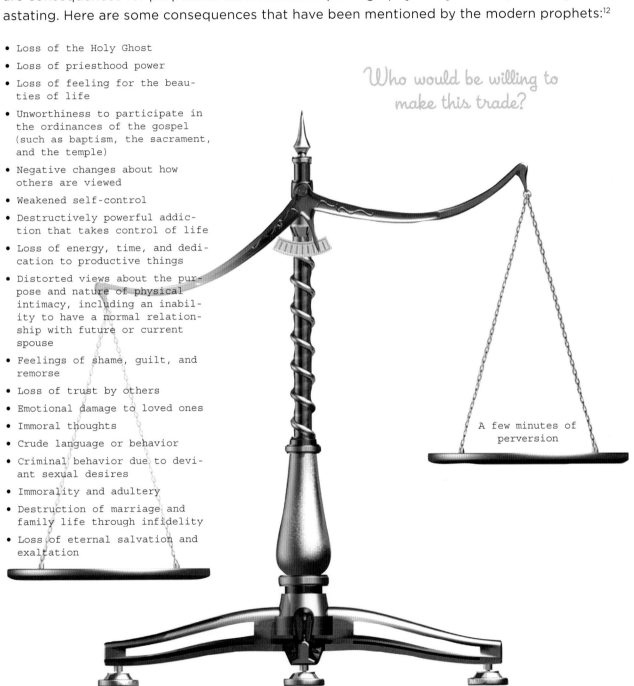

Who would be willing to make this trade?

A few minutes of perversion

THE INCREDIBLE SHRINKING BRAIN

Want another negative consequence? Research indicates that viewing pornography may shrink the size of your brain![13]

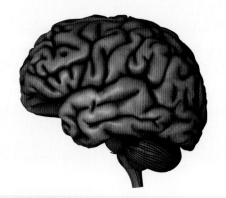

What a heavy price to pay for viewing filthy images! Do not be deceived by Satan's lies. The seemingly momentary pleasure is not worth the negative consequences that will follow in the days, months, years, and perhaps lifetime that follows. If we can remember the destructive consequences of pornography, we will have increased power to resist it.

PORNOGRAPHY AND THE BARK BEETLE

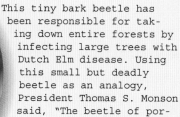

This tiny bark beetle has been responsible for taking down entire forests by infecting large trees with Dutch Elm disease. Using this small but deadly beetle as an analogy, President Thomas S. Monson said, "The beetle of pornography is doing his deadly task—undercutting our will, destroying our immunity, and stifling that upward reach within each of us."[14]

Remember That There Are No "Private" Sins

The adversary tells many lies about pornography: that it is a "private" sin, that it doesn't hurt anybody, that it is just you and the filthy image, and that nobody else knows so it's no big deal. These are all *lies!* Don't fall into the trap described by Elder Richard G. Scott. He said, "I've heard some men argue that it isn't that bad to look at things that are inappropriate on the screen because they are not hurting anyone. They are damaging their own spiritual strength and they certainly are creating harmful influences in their sacred relationship as husband and wife."[15]

If we take another look at the potential consequences of pornography on page 159 and ask, "Which of these consequences has a public consequence?" we will find that most all of them do. When we understand that there is no such thing as a private sin, it will help us overcome pornography. When the temptation to view pornography arises, imagine your father, mother, sister, brother, or current or future spouse sitting there, and ask yourself if your "private" decision will publicly and negatively affect those you love.

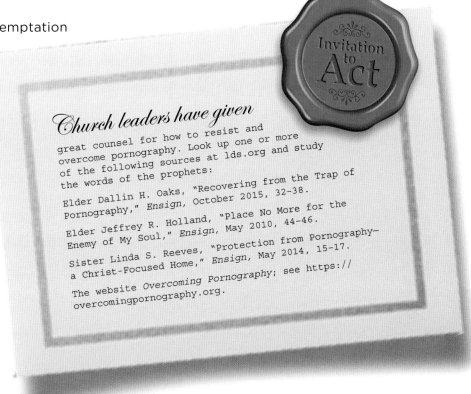

Invitation to Act

Church leaders have given great counsel for how to resist and overcome pornography. Look up one or more of the following sources at lds.org and study the words of the prophets:

Elder Dallin H. Oaks, "Recovering from the Trap of Pornography," *Ensign*, October 2015, 32–38.

Elder Jeffrey R. Holland, "Place No More for the Enemy of My Soul," *Ensign*, May 2010, 44–46.

Sister Linda S. Reeves, "Protection from Pornography— a Christ-Focused Home," *Ensign*, May 2014, 15–17.

The website *Overcoming Pornography*; see https://overcomingpornography.org.

Fill Our Lives with Light and Truth

The Lord said, "Light and truth forsake that evil one" (D&C 93:37). As we fill our lives with more and more light and truth, we will "chase darkness from among [us]" (D&C 50:25). In other words, the closer we come to the Light of the World— Jesus Christ—the further away from us the darkness of sin will go. As we fill our lives with light and truth we will receive increased power to refuse and reject pornographic images.

THE HOUSE OF LIGHT HELPS CHASE AWAY DARKNESS

President Gordon B. Hinckley said, "Make a habit of going to the house of the Lord. There is no better way to ensure proper living than temple attendance. It will crowd out the evils of pornography."[16]

Practice the Proactive and the Practical

Captain Moroni provides us a great example of the principles related to proactive self-defense. Even during a time of peace, "Moroni did not stop making preparations for war, or to defend his people against the Lamanites" (Alma 50:1). He had his people build towers, walls, and pickets, and establish mounds of earth to protect their cities (see Alma 50:1–4). His actions prepared his people and helped them defeat their enemies. Similarly, we can take practical and proactive measures to help defend ourselves against the enemy of pornography. The following are a few defensive suggestions:

- Install filters on each computer and mobile device you use in order to block offensive and pornographic content. Some Internet filtering software will provide reports of websites visited, or keywords used to search, or sites that were blocked, etc. These reports of Internet activity can be valuable to both parents and youth.

- Put computers or use your mobile device where everyone can see what you're doing. Elder M. Russell Ballard said, "Move your computer into a room where there is always the possibility of someone walking in on you. Make sure the monitor faces the room so that others can see what it is you are doing on the screen at any time. . . . Take action when you are strong so that if you are tempted you will have armed yourself and it will be much more difficult to fall."[17]

- Don't surf the Internet aimlessly. Have a specific reason for being online. We could change the proverbial saying and state that "An idle mouse is the devil's playground." The Church publication *Let Virtue Garnish Thy Thoughts* specifically states, "Limit the time you spend watching TV, playing video games, and using computers for entertainment. Set standards for your participation in these activities, such as restricting Internet use to specific purposes."[18]

- Place a picture of your family, the temple, or the Savior next to televisions, personal computers, cell phones, and media players to remind you what is important. A wise bishop once gave advice to a young father and said that each time he goes on a business trip he carries a framed picture of his wife and children and places it next to the television in his hotel room. That way, as he watches television when he is alone, he is strengthened by the image of his family and is given increased power to avoid the potential filth available to him.

Always remember Him . . . Especially on the Internet

HOW do some people become part of the pornography problem, and maybe don't even know it?

Elder Dallin H. Oaks said, "Young women, please understand that if you dress immodestly, you are magnifying this problem by becoming pornography to some of the men who see you."[19] Most young women and men would never participate in the pornography industry. However, we must understand that we can inadvertently participate in pornography through the way we dress—and in the way we choose to view others.

If Involved in Pornography, Immediately Seek the Help of Priesthood Leaders and Professionals

If you have been in contact with pornography, immediately seek help from your parents and bishop. Pornography is a dark sin, and Satan often wants us to stay in the dark. He knows the longer we stay in the dark, the harder it will be to make it back to the light. Remember that because of the atonement of Jesus Christ, we all can repent and change. What great hope! Jesus Christ will cleanse you and give you the strength to go forward. Have the courage to talk to your bishop. He will help in the process of repentance and can provide wise counsel and, if necessary, recommend professional resources in overcoming the sin of pornography.

GET HELP!

Elder Joseph B. Wirthin gave this analogy: "Pornography is much like quicksand. You can become so easily trapped and overcome as soon as you step into it that you do not realize the severe danger. Most likely you will need assistance to get out of the quicksand of pornography."[20]

We testify that through the Lord's atoning grace and power, and through the direction of his servants, the sin of pornography can be forgiven, erased, resisted, and overcome!

Seek Shelter from the Storm of Pornography

Although the temptation of pornography is everywhere in our day, we do not need to be a part of it. We have the strength to resist and overcome it. President Gordon B. Hinckley said, "The excuse is given that it is hard to avoid, that it is right at our fingertips and there is no escape. Suppose a storm is raging and the winds howl and the snow swirls about you. You find yourself unable to stop it. But you can dress properly and seek shelter, and the storm will have no effect upon you. Likewise, even though the Internet is saturated with sleazy material, you do not have to watch it. You can retreat to the shelter of the gospel and its teaching of cleanliness and virtue and purity of life."[21]

TELL ME ONE MORE TIME!

How Can I Resist and Overcome Pornography?

- **Know that we have the divine ability and strength to resist pornography.**
- **Have a spiritual understanding of the sacredness of the human body and the divine power of procreation.**
- **Know and think about the short- and long-term consequences of pornography.**
- **Remember that there are no "private" sins.**
- **Fill your life with light and truth.**
- **Practice the proactive and the practical.**
- **If involved in pornography, immediately seek the help of priesthood leaders and professionals.**

Why Should I Use Clean Language?

John had the following experience that illustrates why it is so important to watch what we say. "One of my most embarrassing moments happened on my mission. I was serving in a singles' ward, and one day at church I noticed a woman arrive late to sacrament meeting. Her clothes were mismatched and her hair was extremely messy; she looked out of place. After the meeting, she ran to get out of the building before anyone could speak to her, but I ran faster. As we talked, I learned she was less-active and hadn't been to church for several years. I set up an appointment for my companion and I to meet with her the next week.

"I have to go to the bathroom."

"The day of our appointment, my companion and I went to the church to meet with the girl. When we arrived, the girl wasn't there yet, but I saw the Relief Society president and thought I should talk with her so that she could help fellowship the young woman we were going to meet with.

"'She's a little bit shy,' I said to the Relief Society president. 'She doesn't really have any friends here and doesn't fit in. Her clothes weren't that nice and her hair is kind of ratty. She was late for church and—'

"From behind me, I heard a female voice say, 'I was *not* late.' I turned around, and sure enough there was the girl. She had been there the whole time, but this time she was wearing nice clothes and her hair was combed. I didn't even recognize her.

"Time froze as I looked at her. Finally I said, 'I have to go to the bathroom,' and took off!

"I didn't mean to do anything wrong, but I realized that because I didn't watch what I said, I really hurt somebody's feelings."

We Will Be Judged by the Things We Say

In his great discourse to the Nephites, King Benjamin taught this truth: "If ye do not watch yourselves, and your thoughts, *and your words,* and your deeds . . . ye must perish. And now, O man, remember, and perish not" (Mosiah 4:30; emphasis added).

One reason why we should use good language is that part of our final judgment will include not only the things we have done, but also the things we have *said.* In Matthew 12:36, the Savior says, "Every idle word that men shall speak, they shall give account thereof in the day of judgment."

"Every idle word" means that we'll be held accountable for not only swear words, but also for words we say in joking or that we don't really mean. Sarcastic comments to younger siblings, a cruel text message, a prideful comment—they are all part of our final judgment.

On the positive side, every compliment given, every verbal expression of love, and every testimony of the gospel we share will also be part of our eternal evaluation. We should use good, clean language so that at judgment day the angels won't have to ask for earplugs as they review what we've said.

MIKED FOR ETERNITY

One of the latest trends in professional sports is to attach a small microphone to players and coaches so everyone can hear what they are saying during the game. We would do well to remember that we are all already "miked" for eternity.

Vocabulary and Intelligence

What we say not only affects our final judgment in the eternities, it also affects how other people judge us here and now. For better or worse, the words we use make an impression on others. Therefore, another reason why we should use good language is that our language reflects our character and intelligence. President Gordon B. Hinckley taught, "Failure to express yourself in language that is clean marks you as one whose vocabulary is extremely limited."[1]

YOU'RE NOT HIRED!

The following people were judged by the words they used on their job applications. Who would you hire?

- "Instrumental in ruining entire operation for a Midwest chain operation."

- "Physical disabilities include minor allergies to house cats and Mongolian sheep."

- "Please call me after five-thirty because I am self-employed and my employer does not know I am looking for another job."[2]

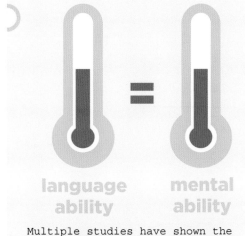

language ability = mental ability

Multiple studies have shown the relationship between language ability and mental ability.[3]

For the Strength of Youth says, "How you communicate should reflect who you are as a son or daughter of God. Clean and intelligent language is evidence of a bright and wholesome mind."[4] People who tell racist or sexist jokes only reveal their own ignorant prejudices and bigotry. Those who put down others demonstrate disloyalty. On the other hand, people who compliment and congratulate others show that they are kind and thoughtful.

What We Say Affects Our Ability to Feel the Holy Ghost

President Henry B. Eyring taught, "We cannot hope to speak for the Lord unless we are careful with our speech. Vulgarity and profanity offend the Spirit. . . . You can decide—and you must—to change what you say even when you can't control what others say."[5]

For example, one morning Joseph Smith was translating the plates, and he got in an argument with his wife. When he went to translate the plates later that day, he found that he could not do it—the angry words he had spoken to his wife had robbed him of his ability to feel the Spirit. If we are not careful, the same thing can happen to us.[6]

The modern prophets have taught that our language will affect our spirituality:

"When you use good language, you invite the Spirit to be with you.

"Always use the names of God and Jesus Christ with reverence and respect. Misusing the names of Deity is a sin. . . . Do not use profane, vulgar, or crude language or gestures, and do not tell jokes or stories about immoral actions. These are offensive to God and to others."[7]

Encourage Others to Use Good Language: The Example of President Kimball

"In the hospital one day I was wheeled out of the operating room by an attendant who stumbled, and there issued from his angry lips vicious cursing with a combination of the names of the Savior. Even half-conscious, I recoiled and implored: 'Please! Please! That is my Lord whose names you revile.'

"There was a deathly silence; then a subdued voice whispered, 'I am sorry.'"—President Spencer W. Kimball[8]

CAN YOU CONTROL YOUR TONGUE?

Try to say "toy boat" ten times fast. Can you do it? What about saying "knapsack straps" ten times fast? Or the kicker, "Santa's short suit shrunk." James knew that it is hard to control the tongue. He wrote, "If any man offend not in word, the same is a perfect man. . . . The tongue is a fire. . . . Out of the same mouth proceedeth blessing and cursing. My brethren, these things ought not so to be" (James 3:2, 6, 10).

Sticks and Stones May Break Bones, But Words Will Always Hurt

The saying "Sticks and stones may break my bones, but words will never hurt me" isn't true. Broken bones heal over time, but words can continue to hurt throughout our lives.

Perhaps that is why the scriptures frequently warn us to not speak unkindly about each other. Consider the following:

- "Let all . . . evil speaking, be put away from you." (Ephesians 4:31)
- "Speak evil of no man." (Titus 3:2)
- "Thou shalt not speak evil of thy neighbor." (D&C 42:27)
- "Cease to speak evil one of another." (D&C 136:23)

You have probably seen firsthand the effect words can have. An experience John had when he was fifteen is still etched in his memory. He says:

"We were having a teachers' quorum activity—driving around the city to make a movie. There were about seven teachers at the activity, and we were split up between two cars. One of the teachers who was there that night was Chris, a young man who had recently joined the Church. Chris was very nice, and also shy and significantly overweight.

"As we drove back to the Church, the car I was in went over a speed bump. The car bounced up and down, and it felt like it nearly smacked the ground. One of my friends said, 'It's a lucky thing Chris is in the other car. We would have smashed the ground for sure if he was in here!'

"And then we heard Chris's voice from the back seat, 'But I am in the car.'

"My heart ached for Chris that night. But the unkind words could not be unspoken. Maybe that comment was part of the reason Chris stopped coming to Church. I wish those words had never been said."

How many of us can still vividly remember something negative that somebody said to us? Let us never forget that what we say can hurt much more than any stick or any stone.

Have you noticed how babies learn to talk? They listen to everything around them and mimic what they hear. If you are having a problem with swearing, maybe you are hearing it too much in your music and media. Get rid of any CD or DVD and delete any file that "uses vulgar or offensive language."[9]

Kind Words Lift Spirits

It's amazing how kind words can help others. Have you ever felt sad or discouraged and then heard a compliment from somebody else? It feels great!

At the conclusion of Elder Neal A. Maxwell's mission, his mission president wrote a short note at the bottom of a letter to Elder Maxwell's bishop, complimenting the young missionary on his work. Elder Maxwell said, "It took President Eyre thirty seconds to write [the note], but it gave me encouragement for fifty years."[10]

Elder Maxwell also said, "We sometimes give needed physical cloaks to warm people and to cover them, and it is good that we do. How often do you and I also give what the scriptures call the 'garment of praise' (Isa. 61:3)? The 'garment of praise' is often more desperately needed than the physical cloak. In any case, as we all know, these needs are all around us, every day. There are so many ways we can 'lift up the hands which hang down, and strengthen the feeble knees' (D&C 81:5)."[11] One way to strengthen others is to speak kind words to them.

As in all things, our Savior is the supreme example of controlling the tongue. Often people justify using bad language when they are frustrated, upset, hurt, or being treated unkindly. None of these excuses held true for the Savior. After suffering unspeakable pain in the Garden of Gethsemane, he was captured by soldiers and mocked by the leaders of the people. Despite his suffering, we read that the Savior "held his peace" (Matthew 26:63), or as the footnote explains, "kept silent."

When we feel like lashing out at somebody in anger, swearing, taking the Lord's name in vain, or using any sort of foul language, remembering that majestic moment of our Savior's self-control should inspire us to follow his example.

WHICH AM I?

I watched them tearing a building down,
A gang of men in a busy town.
With a ho-heave-ho and a lusty yell,
They swung the beams and the sidewalls fell.

I asked the foreman, "Are these men skilled,
The kind you'd hire were you to build?"
He laughed and said, "Why, no indeed!
Just common laborers are all I need.
They can easily wreck in a day or two
What builders have taken years to do."

And I thought to myself as I went on my way:
"What part in the game of life do I play?
Am I a builder who works with care,
Measuring life by the rule and square?

Am I shaping my deeds to a well-made plan,
Patiently doing the best I can?
Or am I a wrecker who walks the town,
Content with the labor of tearing down?"[12]

WISE ADVICE

In a scene from the movie *Bambi,* the rabbit Thumper makes fun of Bambi. His mother says, "Thumper, what did your father tell you this morning?"

Thumper hesitates and then says, "If you can't say something nice, don't say nothing at all." As cheesy at that sounds, it's still good advice!

DO TRY THIS AT HOME!

Read the following words out loud as fast as you can. Can you finish the list in five seconds? One trick though—don't say the color that the words spell, read the *color of ink* that the word is written in. Ready, set, go!

Red	Green
Yellow	Green
Red	Black
Blue	Yellow

Could you do it without making any mistakes? This activity shows that we tend to say the first thing that comes to mind—and that isn't always the right thing to say. The old saying "Think before you speak" is good counsel.

TELL ME ONE MORE TIME!

Why Should I Use Clean Language?

1. **God will judge us by the things we say.**
2. **How we speak reveals our intelligence and character.**
3. **What we say affects our ability to feel the Holy Ghost.**
4. **Sticks and stones may break bones, but words will hurt forever.**
5. **Kind words lift spirits.**

Cont.

NOW that we have reviewed some of the *principles*, let's answer some of the questions regarding the *practices* connected to clean language:

Why shouldn't I gossip or talk behind people's backs?

Gossiping is a negative example of each of the five principles we discussed in this chapter. God will judge us for speaking ill of others. The scriptures teach we will be judged by "every *idle word,*" which footnote 36b suggests is "gossip" (Matthew 12:36; emphasis added). Gossiping reveals shallowness of character and will lessen our ability to feel the Spirit. By gossiping, we hurt others when we could be lifting them up. At a minimum, never say anything behind someone's back that you wouldn't say in front of them.

Why shouldn't I make fun of people, even if I'm joking?

Sometimes it can be hard to know when a joke is a joke. One young woman said, "This one guy would always rip on me and then say he was joking. I didn't say anything but his words really hurt." Perhaps that is why *For the Strength of Youth* says, "Choose not to insult others or put them down, even in joking."[13]

Why should I watch my tongue, even when playing sports?

It might seem like everybody swears playing sports, but in some ways that is the most important time to watch what we say. High-pressure situations in our life reveal our character. It is in those moments that we reveal who we really are. Also, you never know who can hear you, or who is reading your lips (such as your family or friends), and when your choice of language might disappoint them. When you control your mouth during intense situations (like sports), you show that you are truly in control of yourself and understand why you should use good language.

VIDEO BONUS

Watch a video of John teaching about the importance of our words at http://johnhiltoniii.com/qa.

Write some "appreciation notes" that compliment friends or family members. Secretly put them in a place where you know they will be found.

DO TRY THIS AT HOME!

Why Does the Music I Listen to Matter?

How many times have you heard music today? Think about it. Did you wake up to music from your alarm clock? Was the radio on during your drive to work or school this morning? Did you hear it in the hallways before class? Did you hear it *in* class at some point? (Was your iPod playing when you should have been *listening* in class? ☺) Is the ringtone of your cell phone the tune of a song? Did you pay attention when you walked into a store or a restaurant—because music was probably playing there, too. What about in the background of a TV show?

The fact is that in our culture, music is everywhere. The invention of digital music has only increased the constant availability of music to the masses. Most of our digital devices, with gigabytes of storage and ever-growing streaming capabilities, give us access to virtually unlimited hours of listening. Never more in the history of the world have God's children needed to understand why the music they listen to matters.

Musicians Say the WACKIEST THINGS

"Smoking, drinking, sex—why is it such a big deal with me?"
—Britney Spears[1]

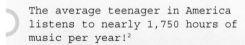

The average teenager in America listens to nearly 1,750 hours of music per year![2]

Music and the Holy Ghost

Stephen D. Richardson, a stake president, wanted to teach the youth in his stake about the effects of music, so he decided to do a little experiment. He put plants in different parts of his house and made sure they received equal amounts of light and water. The only difference between the plants was the music they listened to. Plants listening to music? Yes! One group of plants listened 24/7 to a station that played alternative rock. The other group listened to classical music. The results? Interestingly enough, the plants that listened to classical music grew better and appeared healthier than those that listened to harder music.

Classical   Alternative

If music can affect plants, imagine how much more it can affect people. Have you noticed how music can affect how you feel? Maybe you have heard a patriotic song and had a feeling of national pride. Or perhaps you have been hurt emotionally and listened to loud, angry music to make the pain go away. Hopefully you have had the experience of listening to sacred music and feeling the presence of the Spirit.

One reason why the music we listen to is important is that music can and does affect how we feel; therefore, music affects our ability to recognize the Holy Ghost. *For the Strength of Youth* teaches, "Some music can carry evil and destructive messages. . . . Such music can dull your spiritual sensitivity."[3] The prophets specifically tell us to "pay attention to how you *feel* when you are listening" to music.[4]

If you don't think music affects how you feel, ask yourself why movie producers spend so much time and money on the musical score. How different would the movie *Jaws* be if the theme song for *Mr. Rogers Neighborhood* pops on when the shark fin pops up?

> *It's a beautiful day in this neighborhood,*
> *A beautiful day for a neighbor . . .*
> *Hello, neighbor . . .* (as the shark opens his mouth on the unsuspecting victim)

That simple difference in music changes the moment from nail-biting suspense to laugh-out-loud comedy.

COUNT THE "VERY"S

"You are very, very, very, very, very, very foolish when you like to participate in music that is dark and noisy. Worthy inspiration cannot get through to you where you are. No matter how popular it may be or how much you want to belong, just remember that there are those angels of the devil using you."

—President Boyd K. Packer[5]

DO TRY THIS AT HOME!

Remember those *Choose Your Own Adventure* books where you jumped to different pages in the book depending on what choice you made? Well, here's your chance to make some choices. You have a choice between turning to page 175 *or* 176 and reading a list of words. Choose just one, and then turn to page 178.

Musicians Say the WACKIEST THINGS

"So what if I'm smokin' weed onstage?" —Snoop Dogg[6]

A seminary student was asked, "Do you think the music you listen to affects you?"

"No," the seminary student responded. "It doesn't. For example, I was listening to some new music. When I first started listening to it, I had a really bad feeling inside. But I kept listening, and after a while, the bad feeling went away."

WHOOPS!

The student had missed the point—the music he was listening to *did* affect him. He didn't realize it, but the bad feeling he had as the music was playing was the Spirit not dwelling with him. Over time, the student grew desensitized and did not even notice the loss of the Spirit.

BOUNDLESS POWER

"Music has boundless powers for moving families toward greater spirituality and devotion to the gospel. Latter-day Saints should fill their homes with the sound of worthy music."

—The First Presidency[8]

On the positive side, if you listen to good music, it *increases* your ability to respond to the Spirit. An example is found in the Old Testament, in 1 Samuel 16. King Saul was being afflicted by an evil spirit that was not from God. The scriptures record that "David took an harp, and played with his hand: so Saul was refreshed, and was well, and the evil spirit departed from him" (JST 1 Samuel 16:23). The effect on our feelings and on the Spirit is the first reason why the music we choose to listen to matters so much.

Music Affects Our Actions

A second reason why the music you listen to matters is that music can affect your actions. Elder Gene R. Cook of the Quorum of the Seventy shared an experience that illustrates the power of music. He was on an airplane and happened to sit next to a world-famous rock star—Mick Jagger of the Rolling Stones.

After introducing himself, Elder Cook had a question for Mick Jagger. He said, "I have had the opportunity over the years to be with many young people all over the world. . . . Some of the young people I'm with tell me that rock music, the kind of music you and others are involved in has no real impact on them. . . . You've been in this thing for twenty years, I'd like to know—what's your opinion?"

Mick Jagger responded (and these were his exact words): "Our music is calculated to drive the kids to sex."

Elder Cook was shocked. But there it was, as plain as could be. This popular rock star said that the whole purpose of his music was to get people to be unchaste.[10]

"Our music is calculated to drive the kids to sex." —Mick Jagger

SURVEY SAYS

The *New York Times* reported on researchers who did a two-year study observing teenagers and music. The study showed that teenagers who were "exposed to the highest levels of sexually degrading lyrics were twice as likely to have had sex by the end of the study" as other teens.[11]

Musicians Say the WACKIEST THINGS

"I hurt myself today to see if I still feel." —Trent Reznor[12]

I (DON'T) WANT MY MTV

Researchers found that in 171 hours of MTV programming (that's less than 30 minutes a day for one year), there were:

1,548 sexual scenes

3,056 depictions of sex or various forms of nudity

2,881 verbal sexual references

1,518 uses of unedited profanities

3,127 bleeped profanities[13]

Music and Memory

A third reason why the music you listen to matters is that the lyrics you listen to affect how you think, whether you realize it or not. Can you fill in the blanks?

Oh come, all ye _____, joyful and triumphant.
(Christmas hymn)
Everything I do, I do it _____ _____. (Bryan Adams)
I wish they all could be _____ girls.
(The Beach Boys)
I still haven't found what ____ _____ for. (U2)

True Story!

Sadly, we have seen friends who have listened to music that encouraged negative behavior act on the teachings of those songs. One friend loved a song that was about shoplifting. He would always sing the chorus, which talked about walking right through the door with the stolen item. Before this young man was seventeen years old, he had already been in court for shoplifting. Did the music he listened to have an influence on his actions? There can be no doubt.

DO TRY THIS AT HOME!

religious | Catholic | leader (now turn to page 178)

Even though some of these songs are older than you are (and some are even older than we are!), you probably knew the missing lyrics, didn't you? Isn't it amazing how the words just popped into your mind, as if they had been filed away from hearing the songs sung over and over? Numerous studies have shown that the human brain has an incredible ability to easily memorize words when they are put to music.[15]

Musicians Say the WACKIEST THINGS

"I have the same goal I've had ever since I was a girl. I want to rule the world." —Madonna[14]

HAVING TROUBLE MEMORIZING YOUR SCRIPTURE MASTERY VERSES?

Many teachers have put scripture mastery verses to music to help aid their students with memorization. If you want to download the songs to help you memorize the scriptures, go to http://johnhiltoniii.com/qa.

Music can easily get stuck in your head and stay there all day. This can be good or bad. One of John's children had been practicing a Christmas hymn each morning. One evening the child reported, "At school, I just sang that song in my heart and felt so happy."

Think of the impact of memorizing Primary songs or Church hymns and singing them to yourself every day:

"I Am a Child of God"
"We Thank Thee, O God, for a Prophet"
"I Love to See the Temple"
"I Believe in Christ"
"Teach Me to Walk in the Light"
"Love One Another"
"I Hope They Call Me on a Mission"
"Count Your Blessings"

DO YOU NEED A SLAP?

"Anyone who thinks there isn't a direct link between gangster rap, thug behavior and the problems that exist in inner city neighborhoods across this nation needs to be slapped!"—70s disco musician Gary "The G-man" Toms[16]

Musicians Say the WACKIEST THINGS

"I'm the type to swallow my blood 'fore I swallow my pride."

—50 Cent[17]

Compare that with singing lyrics from some of the popular songs on the radio! (We wanted to include the lyrics of a recent #1 song but they were too suggestive.)

When we listen to good music, our thoughts and spirits will be uplifted throughout the day.

  thin | metal | round (now turn to page 178)

STOP DOWNLOADING IT AND START PLAYING IT

Music is better at enhancing early childhood development than computer use. Music training, specifically piano instruction, is far superior to computer instruction in dramatically enhancing children's abstract reasoning skills necessary for learning math and science.[18]

DO TRY THIS AT HOME!

Fill your digital device with free music! You can download hymns, EFY music, or seminary music at http:// youth.lds.org. You can also fill your iPod with talks from Church leaders or popular LDS speakers. Download the talks for free at lds.org; speeches.byu.edu; or byuradio.org.

TELL ME ONE MORE TiME!

Why Does the Music I Listen to Matter?

1. Music affects our emotions and our ability to feel the Holy Ghost.

2. Music affects our actions.

3. Song lyrics are easily memorized, and their message can influence us.

NOW that we have reviewed some of the *principles*, let's answer some of the questions regarding the *practices* connected to music:

Why can't I listen to a song that only has a couple of swear words if I hear worse than that every day at school?

Although you may *accidentally* hear foul or offensive language at school, there is a big difference between overhearing a swear word and deliberately joining in the conversation. Consider the following analogy: You are walking home when a bully comes along and beats you up. Although this would be sad, you may not be able to stop it from happening. But that doesn't mean you should start approaching bullies and picking fights with them.

Voluntarily listening to music with swearing in it is like picking fights with bullies. *For the Strength of Youth* tells us to "politely walk away"[19] if we are around people who use bad language. If we are seeking out music that contains swear words, we are not "walking away" from the foul language but actively choosing to make it a part of our life. Choosing to listen to songs with offensive swear words goes directly against the thirteenth Article of Faith, which tells us to "seek" out things that are "virtuous, lovely, or of good report or praiseworthy" (Article of Faith 1:13).

Why does it matter how loud my music is?

You mean besides the danger of hearing loss?☺ Well, principle #1 in this chapter teaches that music affects our ability to feel the Holy Ghost. The Spirit is described many times as a "still small voice" that "whispereth" (D&C 85:6). If our music is too loud, it can affect our ability to be in tune to those subtle whisperings of the Holy Spirit. Sister Sharon G. Larsen, a former member of the Young Women general presidency, said in a general conference address, "There may be times the Spirit finds it difficult to help you because . . . maybe the message can't get through the loud music."[20] In fact, sometimes it is best to have no music on at all so that you can more easily listen to what the Spirit is teaching you.

Why should I listen to or sing the Church hymns?

Sometimes we focus on not doing bad things. As we look at the three main points in this chapter, listening to and singing the hymns provides a positive alternative for each point: Hymns will increase our ability to feel the Holy Ghost, inspiring music can improve our actions, and we can be uplifted by memorizing lyrics that teach eternal truths.

DO TRY THIS AT HOME!

(Continued from page 173) Look at the following word and say the first thing that comes to your mind: P _ PE

If you chose page 175, you probably said "Pope." If you chose 176, you probably said "Pipe." What made the difference? The list of words you read primed your mind to think of something specific. If a few printed words affected your response, it should be obvious that music and lyrics will really affect your choices.

How Can I Smartly Use My Digital Device?

Back when we walked uphill both ways in the snow to and from junior high school, the Internet didn't exist. Yep. No Google. No email. No memes. No social media. The only photos we "pinned" were actual photos with real pins—we really did that! There was no way for us to "like" something our friend was wearing until we actually saw our friend at school. Oh, the inhumanity! We used this awesome, handheld music device called a "Walkman"—a fascinating technology that let you listen to a music cassette tape with headphones *while you walked.* That bad boy could play 16 songs. Man, we sound old.

But just so you don't think we're too old, keep in mind that all this technology that has flooded the earth is really, really new to all of us, including you. Look at the following dates when these technologies that have altered our everyday lives were introduced:

- First iPod, 2001
- Facebook, 2004
- YouTube, 2005
- Twitter, 2006
- First iPhone, 2007
- First iPad, 2010
- Instagram, 2010
- Pinterest, 2011
- Snapchat, 2012

This bad boy could play about 16 songs, autoreversing the cassette tape. Boo-yah!

67% of teens own a smartphone.
53% of "tweens" have a tablet.[1]

This truly is the first generation in the history of humanity that has had to learn how to be good disciples of Christ in a digital-centered world. While people used to worry about how much TV kids watched, now the worry is over how much "screen time" someone has, a question that is quickly becoming as relevant as how much "breathing time" someone has. A recent stat indicated that the average person now spends more time on their smartphone or other electronic device than SLEEPING each day,[2] with teenagers spending nine hours per day using digital media.[3]

Some people have learned really well how to navigate this new digital world, while others have struggled and stumbled. Some have harnessed the power of technology to make life better, create wonderful things, connect better with family and friends, further the work of the

Lord, and learn and grow, while others have distractedly wasted countless hours, become negatively obsessed with "likes," "reposts," and "followers," accessed media and images degrading to the mind, body, and soul, and have become legitimately addicted to their devices.

Many young teens look forward to receiving a smartphone or digital device more than getting a driver's license. But to quote Brother Randall L. Ridd, second counselor in the Young Men's general presidency, "Owning a smartphone does not make you smart. . . . Don't do dumb things with your smartphone."[4] So as technology continues to become more of a part of our everyday lives, *how* do we learn to be smart with our digital devices and social media? Although technology will continue to change and evolve with new apps and tools and abilities (by the time we print this chapter the new iPhone 82.4 will be out!), we want to look at some timeless doctrinal truths and principles that we hope can guide our behavior to be smart, no matter what technology comes in the future. To do so, let's understand truths related to the following SMART acrostic:

THE NEW BALL AND CHAIN: TECHNOLOGY

A 2015 study found that 87% of young adults between 18 and 34 reported that their smartphone "never leaves my side, night or day," and 75% of them report that the first thing they do each morning is "reach for my smartphone."[5]

Spirit
Missionary
Agency
Relationships
True Identity

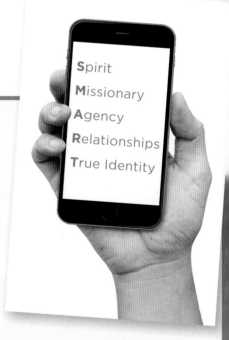

Spirit
Missionary
Agency
Relationships
True Identity

SMART PHONES CAN MAKE YOU DUMB

Two-thirds of teenagers feel that watching TV or texting makes no difference during homework and doesn't affect their ability to learn. 50% feel the same about using social media. However, researchers at Stanford found that heavy media multitaskers performed worse on memory and were slower on other learning tests, concluding that "multitaskers are distracted by the multiple streams of media they are consuming" and can't focus as well as non-multitaskers because their attention was divided.[6] The truth is there's no such thing as multitasking; it's simply called "not paying full attention to anything."

Spirit Principle

The S in SMART stands for the Spirit principle. This is based on the doctrine that God, our Heavenly Father, and His Son, Jesus Christ, have physical bodies of flesh and bone, but the Spirit doesn't. This makes the Holy Ghost able to "dwell with us" (D&C 130:22) always. However, if we don't live our lives in harmony with God's will and we do things that are offensive to Him, then we can minimize or lose the influence of the Holy Ghost. With the influence of the Holy Ghost, we can have access to the blessings of the Atonement of Jesus Christ. With the Spirit: "The Lord will make much more out of your life than you can by yourself. He will increase your opportunities, expand your vision, and strengthen you. He will give you the help you need to meet your trials and challenges. You will gain a stronger testimony and find true joy as you come to know your Father in Heaven and His Son, Jesus Christ, and feel Their love for you."[7] Without the Holy Ghost we are left to ourselves. These doctrinal truths lead us to the following principle:

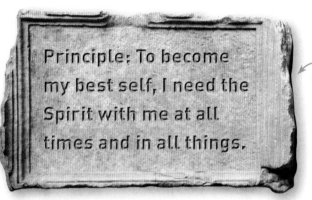

Principle: To become my best self, I need the Spirit with me at all times and in all things.

With this principle, a major question arises: *Is my device inviting or offending the Spirit?* If we are being smart, our device will help invite the Spirit. Some not-so-smart ways in which people violate the Spirit principle with their devices may be:

- When we use our digital device to view anything that is pornographic, crude, includes foul or offensive language, or promotes immoral behavior as acceptable.
- When we use our device for entertainment when we should be respectfully listening and/or actively participating in school classes or church meetings.
- When we use social media to post or send messages that are mean and hurtful about others.
- When we use our digital device to do anything contrary to the *For the Strength of Youth* standards.
- When we use our digital device to disconnect and remove ourselves from those who are around us, love us, and can uplift us.

CONNECTING TO OUR PHONES DURING THE SACRAMENT CAN DISCONNECT US FROM THE SPIRIT

Elder M. Russell Ballard said: "You cannot connect to the Spirit during the presentation of the sacrament while looking at or sending a message on your smartphone or your tablet. This connection requires the Light of Christ, settling from your minds into your hearts with burning love and devotion."[8]

Some smart ways to use your digital device to invite the Spirit might include:

- Using it to watch edifying and uplifting media at the right time and place.
- Using it to access Church materials and apps, such as the Gospel Library App (if that app isn't installed on your device, do it now! No, seriously. Put this book down and download it. Good job 👍).
- Using your device to plan your day better and be more organized, as God's house is a house of order.
- Using your device to create better relationships with family, friends, and others.
- Putting inspiring material, such as a picture of the temple or a scripture you are pondering, as your wallpaper or lock screen.

Never forget that sometimes the best way to use a digital device to invite the Spirit is to turn it off. Sure, you should use it to watch edifying media, send good messages, connect with loved ones, or read and mark scriptures—but then shut it off, put it away, and "lift up your eyes" (John 4:35). Take in the beauties of the earth around you, look someone in the eyes and smile at them, do something active, or do something quiet, such as praying out loud to connect with God.

GOD CAN'T BE GOOGLED

Only the Holy Ghost can give us eternal truths.

Remember, the Lord said, "Be still, and know that I am God" (D&C 101:16). Speaking of this, Elder M. Russell Ballard said, "As an Apostle, I now ask you a question: Do you have any personal quiet time? I have wondered if those who lived in the past had more opportunity than we do now to see, feel, and experience the presence of the Spirit in their lives."[9] Or as Elder José A. Teixeira of the Seventy said, "The habit of setting aside your mobile device for a time will enrich and broaden your view of life, for life is not confined to a four-inch (10-cm) screen."[10] As good as our digital devices are in potentially helping us, let us never forget that God cannot be googled. Siri can't help me truly know the Savior. The Maps app can tell you how to get to your friend's house, but only the Holy Ghost can tell you whether you should stay at your friend's house. Having the Spirit is what matters most, so be smart and use your smartphone to invite and not offend the Holy Ghost.

Missionary Principle

The M in SMART stands for the Missionary principle. This comes from the doctrine that each person on earth "is a beloved spirit son or daughter of heavenly parents."[11] Because God loves each of His children, He wants them to have the blessings of the fulness of the gospel. However, not everyone on earth has the restored truth. As Joseph Smith said, there are many "who are only kept from the truth because they know not where to find it" (D&C 123:12). These truths lead us to the following principle:

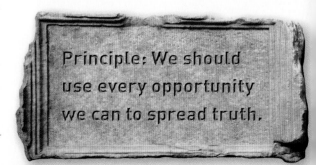

Principle: We should use every opportunity we can to spread truth.

This principle leads us to the following question: *How can/should I use technology and digital devices to help share gospel truths with people?* Our generation has a unique opportunity that no other in history has had: With a few touches, we can send and post messages and images to thousands, even millions, of people instantly. Our social networks enable us to immediately have our voices heard across the world in ways previous generations could not have imagined. (Think of how much good King Benjamin could have done with a smartphone!)

It doesn't matter if we have 100 followers or 10,000—together we can quickly send truth across the digital universe to cumulative masses.

Elder David A. Bednar gave a landmark address on this topic of using social media to spread truth. He cited a prophecy in Moses 7:62 that says that "righteousness and truth will I [the Lord] cause to sweep the earth as with a flood." Elder Bednar explained, "The Lord is hastening His work, and it is no coincidence that these powerful communication innovations and inventions are occurring in the dispensation of the fulness of times. Social media channels are global tools that can personally and positively impact large numbers of individuals and families. And I believe the time has come for us as disciples of Christ to use these inspired tools appropriately and more effectively to testify of God the Eternal Father, His plan of happiness for His children, and His Son, Jesus Christ, as the Savior of the world; to proclaim the reality of the Restoration of the gospel in the latter days; and to accomplish the Lord's work. . . . Beginning at this place on this day, I exhort you to sweep the earth with messages filled with righteousness and truth—messages that are authentic, edifying, and praiseworthy—and literally to sweep the earth as with a flood."[12]

FOLLOW, FOLLOW ME

We try to use social media for good and to spread truth. Follow Anthony and John on Instagram @brotheranthonysweat and @johnhiltoniii as we post gospel-centered images from our families, lives, teaching, and experiences. Yes, you can see pictures of our beautiful wives, teenagers (no, you can't date them), and little ones and get uplifting posts centered on the gospel, scriptures, family, and life.

Thousands of good people across the world have used their social media presence to testify of the blessings of the gospel by sharing images and thoughts about their family, a scripture, the Savior, the Restoration, living prophets, general conference, and others. Each of us should ask, "When is the last time I posted something on social media that shared my beliefs in Heavenly Father; His Son, Jesus Christ; the restored gospel; the Book of Mormon; living prophets; temples; or the blessings of eternal families?" Digital media gives an interesting application to the Lord's words in 1832 when He said, "Therefore, go ye into all the world; and unto *whatsoever place ye cannot go ye shall send,* that the testimony may go from you into all the world unto every creature" (D&C 84:62; emphasis added). One of the smartest things we can do with our smartphones is to take advantage of the missionary opportunity that is ours and use our devices to help send gospel truths through our digital networks and sweep the earth with a flood.

In addition to mass communication with social media, you can also use your smartphone to have gospel conversations with friends. When a friend texts you about a difficult issue he or she is facing, that might be the perfect time for you to share a scripture or a testimony. Sometimes gospel conversations that might feel awkward if they took place in person can seem effortless via texting.

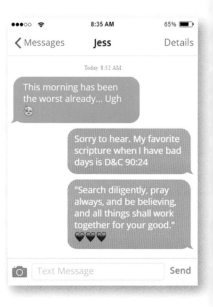

CAN WE CONTROL IT? DAVID O. MCKAY'S TECHNOLOGY PROPHECY

In 1966, President David O. McKay prophesied about scientific discoveries that would "stagger the imagination. . . . Discoveries latent with such potent power either for the blessing or the destruction of human beings as to make man's responsibility in controlling them the most gigantic ever placed in human hands. . . . This age is fraught with limitless perils, as well as untold possibilities."[13]

Agency Principle

If we are to be SMART with our digital devices, the next truth we can apply has to do with what we call the Agency principle. This is based on the doctrine that there are two divisions of God's creations: "things to act and things to be acted upon" (2 Nephi 2:14). Things that get *acted upon* are those things that cannot control their own actions, such as this book or your

family car or your lunch. Things that *act* are those that have self-will and can control what they do, such as us. God's children are "to act for [themselves]" (2 Nephi 2:16) and not to be acted upon. This ability to act, to choose for ourselves, and to control our own behavior is called agency. Being a good agent means being in control of our actions. Having our agency taken away and being acted upon is what Satan desires for us (see Moses 4:3). At the heart of the war on agency is the issue of whether we are in control—*are we acting, or being acted upon?*

These doctrinal teachings lead us to the following (principle:)

The application of this principle related to our digital devices is easily seen: Handheld devices are to be our servants, not our masters. A new addiction has arisen in our digital generation that can be just as powerful as other addictive

Principle: Good agents act and are in control of their behavior; poor agents are acted upon and aren't in control.

behaviors—smartphone addiction. Some people literally cannot leave their smartphone alone. They impulsively need to check it, look at it, and be on it. They think about their posts and likes and followers like drug addicts think about their next high. In social situations, even when they know they shouldn't be on their device or check it, they can't help but pull it out. Even while they are living an exciting moment, they can't help but fantasize about posting a picture of it on social media. They are losing control of their will, and their device is controlling them. They cannot be without their device, and to lose it causes real pain, withdrawal, and panic, like an addict. Experts even have a name for it: *nomophobia*, "the fear of being without your smartphone [which] affects as much as 40% of the population."[14]

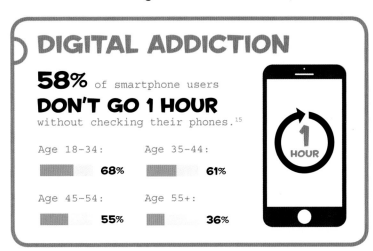

DIGITAL ADDICTION

58% of smartphone users **DON'T GO 1 HOUR** without checking their phones.[15]

Age 18-34:	Age 35-44:
68%	61%
Age 45-54:	Age 55+:
55%	36%

We're not saying that everyone who checks or uses their smartphone consistently is addicted to it. We know digital technology has become a necessary part of many of our daily lives. What we *are* saying is that we need to check ourselves to see if we are actually in control of our digital device or whether *it* is controlling *us*. Based on some scholarly expertise,[16] and in line with the agency principle, try the following:

- Set a time each night when you will turn your device completely off (like an hour before you go to bed). Shut it down, power it off, put it away, and don't reach for it again until the next day. Seriously! Did you know that "teens who wake up in the middle of the night to check their phones are more likely to suffer from depression and anxiety issues"?[17] Put that phone away for the night!
- Set a time when you will turn your phone on in the morning; don't reach for it first thing. Get dressed, pray, pack your lunch, and so forth. Don't let checking your device be the first thing you need to do!
- Set rules for yourself when you will NOT pull out your phone at all. For example, don't use your phone during a meal or in a class where the teacher hasn't given permission. Don't use your phone during sacrament meeting. Don't use your phone anytime you owe another person your full attention.
- Choose some apps that you know will help you. These could be gospel-related apps or apps that will help you in school (there's an app to help you study for nearly every class or big test you will take—think ACT prep). Use your agency to spend as much or more time on these apps than those that are less meaningful.
- Take the advice of Sandra Bond Chapman, author of the book *Make Your Brain Smarter*. She suggests spending 30 minutes working on homework while you're not using any other media. Then try working on homework for 30 minutes and allow

yourself to check your phone or use another device. Do you notice a difference between the two conditions?[18]

- Because it's hard to force yourself to make good choices, use your agency now to ask your parents to help you set limits on your phone use. Tell them that if you break the rules you set for yourself (such as the above-mentioned suggestions), they can take away your phone for a couple of days.

- Set a mental time limit. This may sound scary or weird, but according to addiction expert Dr. Paul Hokemeyer, to help control your smartphone usage and not become addicted, you should "track the amount of time you spend on your phone or tablet to help you face reality."[19] If we can't proactively limit the amount of time we are using them, what does that say?

Remember, if something is beginning to take control of our lives, we need to take control of it and put it in its place, both literally and figuratively. Our Savior taught, "If thy right eye offend thee, pluck it out, and cast it from thee. . . . And if thy right hand offend thee, cut if off, and cast it from thee" (Matthew 5:29–30). The agency principle with our digital devices means that if we ask Siri, "Who's your master?" she should answer, "You are" (go on, ask her!). If Siri says, "I am," we need to work on it.

Relationships Principle

Next we turn to being SMART with the Relationships principle. This is based on the doctrine that exaltation and eternal life depend upon our relationships with others. Specifically, we must have a relationship with God our Father and his Son, Jesus Christ (see John 17:3). The Lord also revealed that to be exalted a man and a woman must be sealed together for time and all eternity and be faithful to the "new and everlasting covenant of marriage" (D&C 131:2). To be with God and like God, we must also "love one another" (John 15:12; see also 1 John 4:7). We too must particularly love and give attention and honor to our parents, grandparents, and ancestors if we are to be saved (see D&C 128:15; Exodus 20:12).

DO TRY THIS AT HOME!

TAKE THE DISCONNECT CHALLENGE

A group of teenagers at a school in London chose to take the "disconnect" challenge. They traded in their smartphones for a week, exchanging them for phones that could only call or text. At first the teens went through withdrawals, but as the week progressed they found that it was invigorating not to be continually tied to their phones. One participant said, "It's cheered me up for some reason, I don't know why, I feel different. I can concentrate more." Another said, "You have a weird feeling inside yourself that makes you feel happy."[20] Maybe that "weird feeling" is the Spirit whispering that it's good to take an extended break from your phone every once in a while!

Heaven requires relationships; we cannot get there alone. These doctrinal truths lead us to the following (principle:)

Principle: All that I do should strengthen relationships with God, my family, friends, and others.

This principle helps guide us in our use of and behavior with our digital devices. *Do our devices and how we use them strengthen relationships or weaken them?* We should never use our digital devices to hurt our relationship with God or His Son by looking at spiritually offensive material. Similarly, we should never use our devices to hurt God's children by texting or posting negative and hurtful comments, spreading gossip and rumors, or using foul language. The First Presidency has reminded us that our standards for clean language not only apply to what we say but "apply to all forms of communication, including texting on a cell phone or communicating on the Internet."[21] And also, "Do not communicate anything over the Internet or through texting that would be inappropriate to share in person."[22]

When we're with people, let's be *with* them. There is nothing more comical than to look at a group of teens "hanging out" with nobody but their phones, staring at their mobile device and stroking the screen like Sméagol with his ring saying, "My preciousss." A phone can be a crutch for some in an uncomfortable social situation. But we need to work through discomfort and form real, meaningful relationships. So put the phone down, look someone in the eye, say hello, talk to them, give them a hug—and then take a selfie! But let us always keep our focus on the people in the room, not the individuals on the Internet. It is an offensive thing to say with our actions, "I would rather engage with my device or with someone hundreds (or thousands) of miles away than with you."

The Relationships principle also applies to fostering positive relationships, especially eternal ones. Use your digital device to not just follow your friends on Instagram and Twitter and Facebook, but also use it to follow your parents' Instagram, your mom's Pinterest, and your

grandma's blog. Post comments to let them know you aren't just interested in yourself, but that you care about what they care about too. Text your parents often, and not just to say, "Hey, pick me up now" but also to randomly text them messages like, "I love you, Mom" or, "Dad, you're a rockin' taco."

Let's follow the Relationships principle and always use these wonderful devices to *strengthen*, not weaken, our relationships—especially the ones that are necessary for exaltation.

True-Identity Principle

The last part of being SMART has to do with our True Identity. This is based on the doctrine that what is most central to each of us is the truth that we are children of God, created in His image, and beloved by Him. Before we ever came to this earth we sat by our Heavenly Parents' premortal fireside, learning from Them and loving Them. We were there with Them when the earth was created, and we learned the purpose of life (see Proverbs 8:22–30; Abraham 3:22–23). We had a testimony of the plan of salvation and of Jesus Christ's central role as Savior and Redeemer (see Revelation 12:11). Being a son or daughter of God who has faith in Jesus Christ is the central, defining characteristic of our premortal spirits that were sent to this earth. These doctrinal truths lead to the following principle:

> Principle: A believing child of God is my true identity. All things inconsistent with this are a deviation from my true self, and thus hypocrisy.

How this principle applies to our mobile devices and social media comes in the form of a question: *If a stranger picked up your digital device, what would it reflect of you?* If someone scrolled through your text messages, Instagram posts, tweets, Facebook likes, and social media comments, what would they think you value? If they thumbed through the photos on your device, went to your music library, or pulled up your "recently watched" programs on your Netflix app, what would those things say you love, are interested in, and are central to the thoughts and intents of your heart (see Mosiah 5:15)? Some have called this the "Bonnie Oscarson" test. Sister Oscarson's Pinterest followers doubled immediately after she was called as the general president of the Young Women organization. What if you were suddenly called to represent the Lord and His Church? One blogger wrote, "Would your Pinterest page pass the Bonnie Oscarson test? . . . Who will people decide you are if all they know is what is on your social media page?"[23]

The reality of these questions is that all of us have been called to represent the Lord and His Church, because we are the children of God and His Saints in the latter days. That is our truest identity. Thus, the True-Identity principle helps guide our behavior regarding all our social media use. Everything we post, say, comment, pin, tweet, blog, upload, and watch should be consistent with and reflect our true identity as sons and daughters of God and believers in Christ. We shouldn't stress so much about whether what we are posting (or not) creates a *popular* image. The question we should ask ourselves is whether what we are doing on our digital device reflects *God's image.*

Let us be mindful that digital media creates a form of the "book of life" (Revelation 20:12) out of which we are judged. Despite what Snapchat claims, what we post never truly disappears. Elder David A. Bednar has said: "Anything you communicate through a social media channel indeed will live forever—even if the app or program may promise otherwise. Only say it or post it if you want the entire world to have access to your message or picture for all time."[24] Some people's digital copies of the "book of life" are consistent with their true identity as children of God, and other people's digital book of life is a deviation from their true identity, a mask pretending they are something fashioned after the ideals of the world, and therefore a form of hypocrisy.

THE NEW BOOK OF LIFE

If our device isn't consistent with our true identity as children of God and believers in Christ, make it repent! Delete that video, song, picture, post, pin, or comment. Change your digital book of life into a mirror of your true, divine inner self.

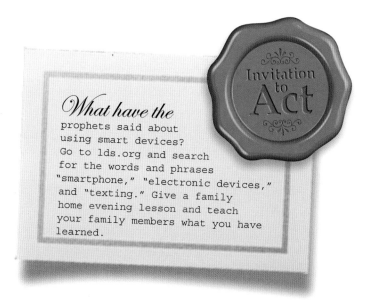

What have the prophets said about using smart devices? Go to lds.org and search for the words and phrases "smartphone," "electronic devices," and "texting." Give a family home evening lesson and teach your family members what you have learned.

Invitation to Act

DO YOU HAVE "TEXT NECK"?

A headline from a recent media outlet newspaper proclaims, "The shocking 'text neck' X-rays that show how children as young as SEVEN are becoming hunchbacks because of their addiction to smart phones."[25] *The Washington Post* proclaims, "'Text neck' is becoming an 'epidemic' and could wreck your spine."[26] One more reason to control your texting!

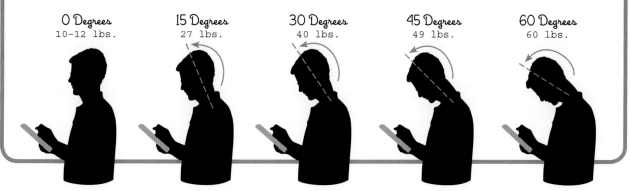

0 Degrees	15 Degrees	30 Degrees	45 Degrees	60 Degrees
10-12 lbs.	27 lbs.	40 lbs.	49 lbs.	60 lbs.

TELL ME ONE MORE TiME!

How Can I Use Social Media Effectively?

Follow the principles and practices of being SMART with your smartphone:

Spirit: Use your smartphone to invite and not offend the Holy Ghost.

Missionary: Use your smartphone to spread messages of goodness and truth.

Agency: Be in control of your smartphone usage, and don't let it control you.

Relationships: Use your smartphone to build and not hurt your most important relationships.

True Identity: Use your smartphone to reflect your identity as a child of God.

NOW that we've discussed the principles, let's look at a few additional questions related to using smart devices.

How can I use my smartphone to help keep the Sabbath day holy?

We've already talked about the importance of not using your smartphone during sacrament meeting, and using it appropriately during other church meetings. But what about the thirteen waking hours that you're not in church on the Sabbath? You could try memorizing scripture mastery verses using the LDS Scripture Mastery app. Or you could go to the LDS Youth app and check out the latest talks to youth or Mormon Messages videos. The Mormon Channel app has literally hundreds of awesome episodes you can listen to, many of which are geared toward youth. One fun way to check your Sabbath phone usage is to look at the apps you've most frequently used on Sunday. Does it seem like your phone is helping or harming your Sabbath day worship?

How can I convince my parents to get me a smartphone? Will you write to them?

Ha ha—nice try! Parents usually know best, and in many cases it may be that having a smartphone is *not* the best thing for a teenager. We suggest you go give your parents a big hug and say, "Thanks for loving me enough to set rules that you think will help me." Who knows, maybe they will be so impressed with your maturity that they *will* give you a phone! ☺

Why Does It Matter Who My Friends Are?

Which of these photos do you think is an arctic fox? Actually, they both are! During the winter, the arctic fox's coat is white to blend in with the surrounding snow. But when the seasons change, so does the fox. With the coming of summer and its attendant browns and yellows, the fox's coat changes to match its environment.

Are we different? Depending on who we surround ourselves with, we may tend to change just like the arctic fox does. In order to understand why it matters so much who our friends are, we must accept this universal truth: Our friends affect who we are.

The Influence of Friends

For the Strength of Youth says, "Everyone needs good and true friends. They will be a great strength and blessing to you. They will influence how you think and act, and even help determine the person you will become."[1]

The prophets say friends *will* influence how we think and act, not "friends *might* influence," or "*perhaps* friends will influence how we think and act." Rather, friends *will* influence us.

Friends influence us in different ways. Some influences are obvious, like friends who directly try to pressure us to do things we wouldn't normally do. But friends also can influence us subtly. Just being with a person increases the likelihood that we will become more like that person. For example, have you ever caught yourself unconsciously using the same slang phrases that your friends use?

MERRY GRINCHMAS!

John Says:

A few years ago, my wife and I went to Universal Studios in Orlando, Florida. It was December, and we were able to see a holiday show called "Grinchmas" (like Christmas—get it?). As part of the show, you could stand in a line to meet the Grinch instead of Santa.

The Grinch looked unbelievably real, and he was unbelievably mean. When it was time for a child to take a picture with the Grinch, the child began to cry. "Fine," said the Grinch. "I don't like you either."

When two giggling teenage girls came to take their picture with him, he burped in their faces! Later, I saw one of the attendants come in and ask the Grinch to go outside to get his picture taken with somebody who could not come in. The Grinch stormed outside to find a person in a wheelchair. Do you think he showed compassion? Nope! He looked at her and said, "Well, what makes you so special?"

I thought the Grinch was so funny that I watched him for an hour. Later that day, I found myself talking like the Grinch—and my wife didn't like it! Just hanging around the Grinch for a short period of time had affected how I acted.

Have you ever started liking a certain music group, or TV show, or style of clothing because a friend introduced it to you? If you don't think that friends influence each other, pay attention the next time you are with a group of teenagers. Odds are they will dress the same way, have similar hairstyles, have common interests, and talk the same way.

WHAT DO YOUR FRIENDS BRING OUT IN YOU?

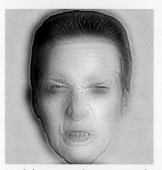 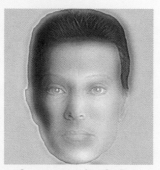

Looking at these two faces close-up, the left face appears to be an angry man, and the right face appears to be a woman with a neutral emotion. Have somebody hold the book and step back from it (perhaps several feet). Squint, blink, or let your eyes become unfocused, and watch the faces change expression—even genders! The angry man should change into the face of the woman, and the neutral woman should change into an angry man.[2] Our friends have the same ability to bring out different sides in us, positive or negative.

Simply being around people has an influence on how we think and act. The proverb says, "Make no friendship with an angry man; and with a furious man thou shalt not go: *Lest thou learn his ways, and get a snare to thy soul*" (Proverbs 22:24–25; emphasis added).

One young woman wrote, "When I was a teenager I never would admit it, but now I can see that my friends had a negative influence on me more than I thought. I thought I was strong and that my 'wild' friends wouldn't affect me. I was strong and stood up against their teasings and temptings, but in my efforts to 'save' them I can see that over time I started to compromise my standards and accept things that weren't right.

Hanging out with bad friends will affect you even if you think it won't."[3]

To illustrate the power of peer pressure, the television show *Candid Camera* did an experiment with people entering an elevator. When the elevator doors opened, an unsuspecting person saw that everyone inside the elevator (all actors) were facing the back wall of the elevator. What did each person do as they got on the elevator? In succession, they all turned around and faced backward as well.

Why would grown adults stand backwards in an elevator? It is simply because they were influenced by what they saw and heard around them. If we are influenced by complete strangers, what happens to us when we are with our friends? This is the first reason why it is so important that we choose friends carefully: They will influence us and help determine the kind of person we become.

DO TRY THIS AT HOME!

Now . . . Which Way Do I Face?

Check out the video of the *Candid Camera* elevator experiment at http://john hiltoniii.com/qa.

Positive Peer Pressure

Now let's look on the bright side of things. Peer pressure isn't always used for *bad;* in fact, it can often be used for *good.* Friends can be an incredibly positive influence in your life. If you are down and discouraged, or tempted and wavering, good friends can encourage you to do the right thing.

As if That Weren't Enough . . .

Researchers have found that the number one reason LDS youth do bad things is pressure from their friends.[4]

CAUTION: PEER PRESSURE

A powerful example of this appears in the Old Testament. David (the same one who killed Goliath) was going through a difficult time. He was alone in the woods and feeling extremely discouraged. Notice what his friend Jonathan did: "And Jonathan Saul's son arose, and went to David into the wood, *and strengthened his hand in God*" (1 Samuel 23:16; emphasis added). True friends will "strengthen [your] hand in God" and influence you for good in difficult times.

Speaking of the strengthening effect that good friends can have, President Thomas S. Monson cited an interesting Church study: "In a survey made in selected wards and stakes of the Church, we learned a most significant fact: those persons whose friends married in the temple usually married in the temple, while those persons whose friends did not marry in the temple usually did not marry in the temple. The influence of one's friends appeared to be a highly dominant factor—even more so than parental urging, classroom instruction, or proximity to a temple."[5]

> "Teenage years are often years of insecurity, of feeling as though you don't measure up, of trying to find your place with your peers, and of trying to fit in. You may be tempted to lower your standards and to follow the crowd in order to be accepted by those you desire to have as friends. Please be strong, and be alert to *anything* that would rob you of the blessings of eternity. The choices you make here and now are forever important.—President Thomas S. Monson[6]

A TRUE BFF

Would a *real* friend ever tell on you, or scold you, or set you straight? They should! Does a *real* friend let you do whatever you want? They shouldn't! Sometimes we think our BFFs (best friend forever!) are good friends because they "like me for me" and don't care how we act. A true friend *does* care how you act. *For the Strength of Youth* says we should "strengthen and encourage each other in living high standards."[7]

Influence Your Friends for Good

This study leads to a second reason why our choice of friends matters so much: We can help lift up those around us. The Savior taught, "Ye are the light of the world. A city that is set on an hill cannot be hid" (Matthew 5:14). As we are a light to others, we have the potential to have an eternal influence on them.

Many people are lonely—and we can lift them up. *For the Strength of Youth* says, "Make a special effort to reach out to new converts and to those who are less active."[8] Sharing your testimony and setting a good example will strengthen them and help them feel welcome among your group of friends. To our friends of other faiths, we can invite them "to [our] Church meetings and activities,"[9] where they can learn about the gospel. We should also continue to be their friend even if they aren't interested in the Church.

> "More than half the members of the Church today chose to be baptized after the age of eight."—President Henry B. Eyring[10]

The Doctrine and Covenants tells us that we should "succor the weak, lift up the hands which hang down, and strengthen the feeble knees" (D&C 81:5). Strengthening others and setting a positive example is another reason why it is so important who we choose as our friends.

TELL ME ONE MORE TiME!

Why Does It Matter Who My Friends Are?

1. **Friends influence how we think and act—for good or bad—and help determine the kind of person we become.**
2. **You can be a positive influence in the lives of others who need strengthening.**

NOW that we have reviewed some of the *principles*, let's answer some questions regarding the *practices* connected to friendship:

Why is it OK to still be friends with people if they aren't LDS?

For the Strength of Youth tells us to "choose friends who share your values so you can strengthen and encourage each other in living high standards."[11] Millions of people of other faiths have high standards. The question is not whether they are LDS, but whether they help you live your LDS standards. Also, as the second principle in the chapter emphasizes, by sincerely befriending those who are not LDS, we may find ways to share the gospel with them.

Why can a friend still be bad if they aren't pressuring me to break the commandments?

We need to pay attention to how we *feel* when we are with certain friends. Do they physically or verbally harm us? Does their influence make us feel bad about ourselves, or encourage us to adopt a negative or bad attitude when we are around them? A true friend doesn't ask you to adopt bad habits or attitudes with them; a true friend encourages you to be better than you are. Even if they don't encourage us to do wrong, some friends may indirectly *discourage* you from being your best self.

Why is it wrong for me to "cover" for my friends and not tell on them? Isn't that what good friends do?

A good friend should be a positive influence and strengthen their friends in living the gospel. When we cover for our friend's mistakes or wickedness, we act like Kishkumen who "was upheld by his band, who had entered into a covenant that *no one should know his wickedness*" (Helaman 2:3; emphasis added). A true friend will have the courage to stand up to friends who are doing things wrong, set a positive example for them, and try to persuade them to be righteous.

How Can I Help Friends and Family Who Are Struggling with Serious Problems?

What should we do when someone we care for is in trouble?

Michelle opened her mouth to speak to her best friend Jessica, but no words came. Silent tears began flowing down her cheeks.

"What on earth could have happened?" Jessica thought to herself as she waited for Michelle to speak.

It took a couple of minutes, but Michelle was finally able to speak. "I have an eating disorder," she said over her tears.

"What?" Jessica cried.

"You're the only one I've told, and I don't want you to tell anyone. I feel like I'm dying, and I can't keep this secret inside me anymore. Everyone thinks I'm perfect, but I'm not. Nobody knows except you. I don't know what to do, Jessica, you've got to help me."

Although the previous dialogue is fictional, the challenge presented is all too real. We frequently hear youth ask how they can help friends or family members who are in trouble. Here are some of those questions:

- How can I help an inactive family member come back to church?
- How can I help my friend whose parents are getting divorced?
- How can I help my sister who is starting to do bad things with her boyfriend?
- How can I help my friend who is harming her body by self-cutting?
- How do I help a friend with a pornography problem?
- How can I help my friend who talks about taking his life?

While these are only a few of the many different scenarios our friends might be in, we've found that one question youth desperately want an answer to is: *How can I help friends and family who are struggling with serious problems?*

Strengthen Their Hand in God

As we discussed in the previous chapter, an Old Testament account of friendship provides an insight of how to help friends and family in trouble. David (as in David and Goliath) was in serious trouble. Although he was living righteously, the king was trying to kill him. When David was hiding in the forest his friend Jonathan "went to David into the wood, and strengthened his hand in God" (1 Samuel 23:16). Think about that phrase: he "strengthened his hand in God."

Whatever problem our loved ones may have, it is likely that they will need to be strengthened spiritually. We can encourage our friends and family to study the scriptures, to pray, and to attend church. Also, we can teach, remind, and testify to them of eternal gospel truths they may be forgetting or need to hear—truths from the plan of salvation.

One young man shared the following experience. "My friend was going through a really hard time. When she told me about it, she said, 'I just don't know what to do!'

"I asked, 'Have you prayed about it?'

"She said, 'No, I hadn't thought about that.' The next day she sent me a text and told me that after she prayed she had received the answer she needed."

Strengthening our loved ones in God means that we uplift them spiritually and help them turn to the Lord for guidance. We pray with them. We invite them to study the scriptures. We study with them! We invite them to seminary, institute, Young Men or Young Women, and to church. And we can go to all those places with them. All of this will strengthen their hand in God.

Stay on the High Ground

One thing to keep in mind, particularly if the problem our family or friend is struggling with has to do with sin, is that we need to be careful that we stay on the high spiritual ground. A young man who has a friend who is struggling with alcohol might say, "I need to help my friend out, so I'll go with him to the party to keep him out of trouble." He is asking for trouble himself. Remember this truth: The Lord will never require us to break a commandment to save someone else! It would be like trying to pick someone up off the floor when we are lying down right next to them.

President Harold B. Lee said, "You cannot lift another soul until you are standing on higher ground than he is."[1] Staying on higher ground and providing an example will do more for our struggling friends than lowering our standards and getting stuck in sin with them just to try to help them out.

HOW should I respond if my friends want me to "cover" for them?

Satan wants us to hide our sins and participate in "secret works of darkness" (2 Nephi 9:9). If your friends are asking you to help them hide what they are doing, just say no. You should not help your friends make bad choices.

DO TRY THIS AT HOME!

Sometimes people think maybe they can just have some good friends and some bad friends. To see how this doesn't work, try this: With your leg straight, lift up your right foot in the air and swing it in a clockwise direction. Now, with your foot rotating in a clockwise direction, point your right arm straight in front of you and try to draw the number 6 in the air.

Did you notice what happened? Either your foot or your hand changed directions! Similarly, we can't make the mistake of thinking we can be good and go in one direction, yet still hang out with bad friends who are going the other direction. We eventually will change directions with them. (To check out a video clip of John and Anthony doing this activity in a fireside, visit http://johnhiltoniii.com/qa.)

LIFE SAVING 101

If someone is drowning in a swimming pool, do you jump in the water with them, or do you throw them a rope or extend a pole to them?

We hope you chose to throw them something or give them something to grab onto to pull them in, and not to jump in the pool after them. This is because it is much safer and more effective to *be on firm ground yourself* to save a drowning victim than to be in the water with them. Unfortunately, sometimes those who jump in the water to save a panicking victim simply get pulled under themselves, sadly resulting in two drowning victims. Saving a swimmer and saving a soul are very similar: Staying on firm ground is the best way.

Lovingly Correct When Needed

Sometimes, we mistakenly think that being a good friend means that we accept our friends as they are—that we let them do whatever they want. We may hear misinformed statements like, "My friends just accept me for me."

This is opposite of what *For the Strength of Youth* teaches us: "True friends . . . will help you be a better person and will make it easier for you to live the gospel of Jesus Christ."[2]

Similarly, Elder Richard G. Scott said, "A true friend is not one that always encourages you to do what you want to do, but one who helps you do what you know you ought to do."[3]

Sometimes we hold back on correcting a family member or friend when they are doing wrong because we don't want to offend them or make them feel badly. However, we would do well to ask ourselves in this situation: Who am I *really* concerned about? Most often we will find that we are just trying to protect ourselves from a potentially uncomfortable conversation and are not really trying to help our loved one. Elder Neal A. Maxwell taught that "our capacity to grow and to assist each other depends very much upon our being 'willing to communicate.' (1 Timothy 6:18.) Communication includes proper measures of *counsel, correction, and commendation.* . . . We worry (and understandably so) that some [corrective] communications will only produce more distance. But silence is very risky, too."[4]

Withholding correction when needed is often a sign of selfishness. While we should be as sensitive as possible—and our comments should be uplifting, edifying, and inspired—we can still tell our family and friends we don't approve of inappropriate behavior. Remember, "whom the Lord loveth he correcteth" (Proverbs 3:12). If we love our family and friends and desire to help them, we will do the same.

HOW can I know if I should tell on my friend?

There are some extreme situations in which you might want to seek outside help even if your friend refuses to do so. A young man named Michael was faced with a difficult situation when one of his friends started doing drugs. Michael talked to his friend and encouraged him to make different choices. He tried to help his friend in every way he could. However, his friend continued to use drugs. After praying about it, Michael decided to talk to his friend's parents.

It was a difficult conversation, but at the end his friend's parents said, "Michael, we are so grateful you had the courage to talk to us. We've known something was wrong with our son, but we haven't known exactly what it was. Just today we had a special fast to know what we could do to help our son—you have been an answer to our prayers."

Michael's friend was able to get professional help and get his life back on track. Michael later said, "I'm so glad I had the courage to really help my friend." If you are wondering if you should tell on your friend, seek guidance from your parents (see also the conclusion of this book).

"The world today tells you to leave your friend alone. He has the right to come and go as he pleases. The world tells you that persuasion to attend church or priesthood meeting or to discard a bad habit might lead to frustration and undue pressures; but again I repeat the word of the Lord: You are your brother's keeper, and when you are converted, you have an obligation to strengthen your brother."
—Elder Robert L. Simpson[5]

Encourage Them to Seek Help from Others

A lot of times the problems our friends and family are having are serious—they need outside help and quite possibly the help of an adult. For example, suppose we are talking to a friend of ours and she tells that she is struggling with depression. Of course it's good to talk to our friend and to pray for her; however, in this situation she probably needs more help than we can provide alone. The ideal would be to encourage our friend to seek help from a capable adult or professional.

Depending on the situation our friend or family member is in, there are lots of things we could do to encourage them to seek help, such as offering to go with them to talk with the bishop. Perhaps we could invite them to talk with our parents, or even a school counselor. This is especially true if someone's behavior is spiritually or physically self-destructive.

Pray for Our Struggling Friends and Family Members

Perhaps the simplest, yet most effective thing we can do for a struggling loved one is to pray for them. Remember, the prophet Alma had a son known as Alma the Younger. Alma the Younger was struggling spiritually and was making sinful choices. Then an angel of the Lord appeared to him and called on him to repent. Listen to what the angel said about why he came: "Behold, the Lord hath heard the prayers of his people, and also the prayers of his servant, Alma, who is thy father; for he has prayed with much faith concerning thee that thou mightest be brought to the knowledge of the truth; therefore, for this purpose have I come to convince thee of the power and authority of God, *that the prayers of his servants might be answered according to their faith*" (Mosiah 27:14; emphasis added). Our prayers for loved ones make a difference.

Do you have a friend or family member who is going through some serious problems? We invite you to pray and ask the Lord what he would have you do to help your friend. Act on the promptings and direction you receive.

Invitation to Act

HOW can I help friends or family members who don't attend church?

As members of the Church, many of us have parents, siblings, or other relatives who don't attend church. Did you know that many members of the First Presidency and Quorum of the Twelve have come from homes where family members were not active in the Church? For example, Elder Richard G. Scott's mother was less active, and his father was not a member of the Church.[6] Elder Russell M. Nelson's parents were not very active in the Church,[7] and Elder David A. Bednar's father was not a member of the Church while he was growing up.[8]

Perhaps one of the best things we can do for less-active family members is to pray for them (see the example of Alma in Mosiah 27). In some cases that may mean sincerely praying daily for years. As we work to help loved ones come to church, remember this counsel from Elder Richard G. Scott: "Never give up on a loved one, never!"[9]

SURVEY SAYS

We asked 1,000 teenagers the question: "How can I help friends who are making bad choices?" Here are the top ten answers.

1. Be a good example.
2. Tell your friends that you don't approve of what they're doing.
3. Pray for them.
4. Invite them to do good things.
5. Help them see how their choices affect them and others.
6. Ask them to talk to their parents or a bishop.
7. Talk to an adult about the problem.
8. Fast, either with your friends or by yourself.
9. Compliment them when they make right choices.
10. Listen to your friends and then give them advice.

TELL ME ONE MORE TIME!

How Can I Help Friends and Family Who Are Struggling with Serious Problems?

- **Strengthen their hand in God.**
- **Stay on the high ground.**
- **Lovingly correct when needed.**
- **Encourage them to seek help from others.**
- **Pray for our struggling friends and family members.**

How Can I Stay Faithful When Life Is Hard?

On a summer day in 2002, our good friends Peter and Michelle lost their only daughter, Alex, in a tragic accident. This kind of trial is among the most difficult tests of faith that anyone can face in mortality. It can bring grief, sorrow, despair, pain, regret, frustration, anger, bitterness, and darkness. Peter and Michelle were faced with those feelings and more in the moments and subsequent days after the accident. Peter says, "That evening when my wife and I were left to mourn and to cry, we began to pray for strength and peace. Then a very real choice came to us: we could right then choose darkness and hate and hurt, or choose light, peace, and love. That night we chose to trust in God and to lean on His power and grace. We felt such comfort and peace—no answers to our 'why's' came, but we felt peace."

When hard times come our way, we, like Peter and Michelle, have a choice. We can become bitter and angry and lose faith and the peace of the Spirit in our lives, or we can choose light and truth and remain faithful. We've asked hundreds of teenagers what hard things they face in their lives. Here are some things we've heard.

- I come from an extended family that is all involved in street gangs. They want me to become a part of it. It's really hard to avoid gang life and still be part of my family.

- I want to earn enough money for college and a mission, but it's hard because my parents need help paying the bills.

- My brother didn't go on a mission and is not active in the Church. It really hurts to see how his bad choices affect our family.

- Last year an older boy took advantage of me. I have talked to my bishop about it, but I still feel so bad.

- I have cancer and it is not curable. I have to live with it every single day.

- My dad just cheated on my mom and was excommunicated from the Church. My parents argue all the time and my younger sisters all depend on me for support. It is hard to even want to be at home.

"Though faced with struggles, you can overcome."
—Nick Vujicic, born with no arms or legs.[1]

HOW can God love us if he lets bad things happen to us?

This is perhaps one of the most often asked questions regarding trials. If God loves us so much, then why does he let bad things happen? President Spencer W. Kimball answered this question by saying: "Could the Lord have prevented [all] tragedies? The answer is yes. The Lord is omnipotent, with all power to control our lives, save us pain, prevent all accidents, drive all planes and cars, feed us, protect us, save us from labor, effort, sickness, even from death. . . . But . . . the basic gospel law is free agency. To force us to be careful or righteous would be to nullify that fundamental law, and growth would be impossible. . . . Is there not wisdom in his giving us trials that we might rise above them, responsibilities that we might achieve, work to harden our muscles, sorrows to try our souls? Are we not permitted temptations to test our strength, sickness that we might learn patience, death that we might be immortalized and glorified? . . . *We* know so little. *Our* judgment is so limited."[2]

YOU CAN HANDLE IT!

One of the great promises in the scriptures is that God "will not suffer you to be tempted [or tried] above that ye are able" (1 Corinthians 10:13).

WHO IS GOING THROUGH THE HARDER TRIAL?

It is easy to think that the good-looking, active person probably isn't going through as hard of a trial as the sick person, but consider this quote from President Boyd K. Packer: "Some are tested by poor health, some by a body that is deformed or homely. Others are tested by handsome and healthy bodies. . . . *All are part of the test, and there is more equality in this testing than sometimes we suspect.*"[3]

How might someone with a handsome, healthy body be tried? Perhaps with increased tests of immorality and pride. Keep in mind that a trial is anything that tests us spiritually, and those spiritual tests come in many forms and ways. Don't mistakenly think that trials always come in the form of misfortune or tragedy.

Staying faithful when life is difficult is no easy task. But it *is* possible. When we asked Peter and Michelle what they did to remain faithful during their trials, they said for them there was one main key: *They did things that invited the Spirit of God.* This is because the Spirit brings peace (see D&C 19:23), eternal perspective (see Jacob 4:13), and comfort (see John 14:16). The following are some keys to inviting the Spirit during hard times so we can come through our trials faithfully.

Ask "What" and Not "Why"

In hard times it's tempting to question God and ask "Why?" "Why me?" "Why now?" "Why didn't you stop this?" Elder Richard G. Scott said, "When you face adversity, you can be led to ask many questions. Some serve a useful purpose; others do not. To ask, Why does this have to happen to me? Why do I have to suffer this, now? What have I done to cause this? will lead you into blind alleys. It really does no good to ask questions that reflect opposition to the will of God."[4] This is what our friends Peter and Michelle said about asking "why," and about what questions we *should* ask:

Peter: "'Why's do not carry comfort with them—they only carry bitterness and anger. You are not trying to understand God when asking 'why'? It's when you can accept and say, 'Thy will be done' that the comfort comes. 'Thy will be done' is the opposite of 'why'? One brings darkness, the other brings light."

Michelle: "'Why' made me feel horrible. We need to ask, 'What do I have to learn from this?' When you take that question to the Lord, he is willing to give you an answer. At the beginning I was having a really hard time with 'why'—'Why is this little girl alive and ours isn't?' But when we focus on 'thy will be done' and not the 'why,' we learn more about God's timing and how to deal with it."

DO TRY THIS AT HOME!

Get a bucket of ice water, a bucket of hot water, and a bucket of lukewarm water. Place your left hand in the bucket of cold water, and your right hand in the bucket of hot water, and leave them there for a minute. After your hands have gotten used to the feel of the water, pull out each hand and instantly place them both into the bucket of lukewarm water. You will have an interesting experience. The hand that was in the cold water will feel like the lukewarm water is hot, and the hand that was in the hot water will feel cold. How is that possible? How can the same water be felt as two different temperatures? It is because of the environment the hand was originally placed in.

Similarly, what we surround ourselves with during times of trial will greatly affect how we feel during our trial. Depending on whether we surround ourselves with angry "why" questions or faithful "thy will be done" statements will greatly change how we feel about the hard time we are going through.

HOT   LUKE WARM   COLD

Elder Richard G. Scott gives us some questions we *should* ask during hard times: "What am I to do? What am I to learn from this experience? What am I to change? Whom am I to help? How can I remember my many blessings in times of trial? . . . When you pray with real conviction, 'Please let me know Thy will' and 'May Thy will be done,' you are in the strongest position to receive the maximum help from your loving Father."[5]

REMEMBER, TRIALS CAN BLESS YOU

"No pain that we suffer, no trial that we experience is wasted. It ministers to our education, to the development of such qualities as patience, faith, fortitude and humility. All that we suffer and all that we endure, especially when we endure it patiently, builds up our characters, purifies our hearts, expands our souls and makes us more tender and charitable, more worthy to be called the children of God."—Elder Orson F. Whitney[6]

Search, Ponder, and Pray

One of the blessings of scripture study, pondering, and prayer is that it opens us up to receive direction, comfort, and peace from the Holy Ghost. It also helps us understand God's purposes, and gives us hope.

Our friend Peter said, "When I would doubt I would go back to the scriptures. It literally was a continual return to God's word that gave us hope. The only thing that relieved the suffering was the promises and the assurances in the scriptures and words of the prophets."

Peter and Michelle also said that they began to listen to less worldly music during car rides so that they could ponder and think and have some quiet time to reflect. This is also why temple attendance is recommended during hard times—so we can ponder and help ourselves be in tune with the Spirit.

Elder Joseph B. Wirthlin taught, "Some are distracted by the things of the world that block out the influence of the Holy Ghost, preventing them from recognizing spiritual promptings. This is a noisy and busy world that we live in. . . . If we are not careful, the things of this world can crowd out the things of the Spirit."[8]

Elder Richard G. Scott taught, "Challenges often come in multiple doses applied simultaneously. When those trials are not consequences of your disobedience, they are evidence that the Lord feels you are prepared to grow more."[7]

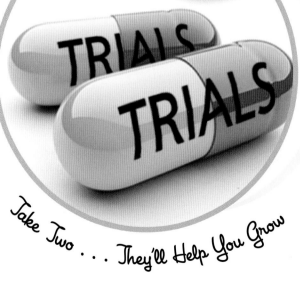

Take Two . . . They'll Help You Grow

Serve Others

Some might read that heading and think, "Serve others? When I'm having a hard time I want people to serve *me.* I'm the one who needs help and support." Those are natural thoughts, but remember, the way of the Savior is often different than our natural desires. For example, when the Savior's relative and friend John the Baptist was murdered, Jesus wanted to be alone, and he went "into a desert place apart" (Matthew 14:13). The Savior probably wanted some private time to grieve. But when the people found out that Christ had left them, they followed after him. When the Savior saw them, he "was moved with compassion toward them, and he healed their sick" (Matthew 14:14).

In the next
twenty-four hours you will come across somebody who needs service. Maybe it's a formal service project, or perhaps it will simply be smiling at somebody or having a conversation with somebody who is lonely. Whether or not you are going through a hard time, try to make somebody else's life better by serving them.

One great blessing of doing service during hard times is that we are able to feel charity—the pure love of God—for others. As we do so, we also feel the love God has for us.

Michelle was a great example of thinking of others during her time of trial. In the weeks and months after their daughter passed away, she volunteered to help with a special-needs class. Michelle said, "Through serving others I could feel the Spirit. The small acts of service are how I felt peace. When you are helping others you are always feeling more comfort and you can forget about yourself. Because of serving others I was able to feel the love of God."

On February 3, 1993, President Howard W. Hunter was giving a talk to students at Brigham Young University. As he stood to speak, a man rushed to the podium, saying he had a bomb. The man threatened to detonate the bomb unless President Hunter read a message to the crowd.

President Hunter refused. The BYU students began singing, "We Thank Thee, O God, for a Prophet," and the man became distracted. Members of the congregation then tackled the man. President Hunter "resumed his speech by saying, 'Life has a fair number of challenges in it.' He stopped, looked over the audience, and added, 'As demonstrated.'"[9] What a great example of staying faithful in a trying time!

A BOMB AT BYU?

Remember the Blessings We *Do* Have

An important key for staying faithful even when life is hard is to remember the blessings that we *do* have. We're reminded of a favorite saying by an unidentified author:

"I thought I was abused because I had no shoes until I met a man who had no feet."[10]

Show Gratitude

Scientific research has shown that people who express gratitude

- Are more optimistic
- Are healthier
- Sleep better
- Progress better on personal goals
- Serve others more
- Are less likely to say they are "bitter"[12]

There are several ways that we can be more grateful during times of trial. Consider doing these as you go through hard times:

1. Keep a "gratitude journal" and make a list of everything you are grateful for.
2. Specifically look for positive things in the world and attempt to really enjoy these things.
3. Write a letter of gratitude to an important person in your life.

One woman reported that a psychological expert told her that if she did these things she would feel happier, which is what happened.[13]

HOW can I overcome feelings of ingratitude?

When we feel ungrateful we should pause and counter those feelings by thinking of things we are grateful for. It's easy to overlook simple things that we should be thankful for. For example, do we send text messages? If so, think of how much we use our thumbs to send text messages, among other things (try buttoning your shirt without using your thumbs)! But when was the last time we thanked Heavenly Father for our thumbs? When we pause to think of the many things we *have* been given, it helps us overcome ungrateful feelings for the few things we may not have.

NO NEED TO WHINE

Sometimes there is a temptation to complain when life is hard. But remember, although some things are difficult we still have much to be grateful for. Elder Jeffrey R. Holland said, "No misfortune is so bad that whining about it won't make it worse."[14] When we are tempted to complain about the hard things we face, counting the blessings that we do have will help us through hard times.

We know that there are and will be hard things that happen to each of us in life. Some of us may have experienced some severe trials already. Some things we cannot change. We cannot change what has happened in the past. We cannot control the actions of others. But we can choose to focus on those things that are in our control. We can choose to seek help from trusted parents or friends. We can choose to serve others. We can choose to go to the scriptures and find direction and assurance. We can choose to remember the blessings we do have. We can say "thy will be done" and choose light rather than darkness. Like Peter, Michelle, and thousands of other faithful Saints, we can choose to remain faithful during hard times.

In All Conditions

President Henry B. Eyring taught, "If we have faith in Jesus Christ, the hardest as well as the easiest times in life can be a blessing. In all conditions, we can choose the right with the guidance of the Spirit. We have the gospel of Jesus Christ to shape and guide our lives if we choose it. And with prophets revealing to us our place in the plan of salvation, we can live with perfect hope and a feeling of peace. We never need to feel that we are alone or unloved in the Lord's service because we never are. We can feel the love of God. The Savior has promised angels on our left and our right to bear us up. And He always keeps His word."[15]

TELL ME ONE MORE TIME!

How Can I Stay Faithful When Life Is Hard?

- **Ask "What" and not "Why."**
- **Search, ponder, and pray.**
- **Serve others.**
- **Remember the blessings you *do* have.**

How Can I Set Meaningful Personal Goals?

"In order to accomplish the things we desire . . . we must have positive and definite goals in mind. Success in life, school, marriage, business, or any other pursuit doesn't come by accident, but as the result of a well-defined plan and a concentrated effort to bring about a realization of the plan."
—President Howard W. Hunter[1]

When we were children, we would sometimes make up our own recipes. Sometimes they went well, other times they didn't. Anthony once made a potato chip sandwich, and John created "cornflake cookies"—they were pretty disgusting. Some things were just not meant to be combined.

When you create and cook from a recipe, you actually create the food twice. There is the recipe, where it's created on paper, and then the actual food that is cooked. In a similar way when God created the earth he created everything twice—spiritually and then physically. In Moses 3:5 we read, "For I, the Lord God, created all things, of which I have spoken, spiritually, before they were naturally upon the face of the earth."

In other words, before the animals or plants were put on earth they were spiritually created. Before humans were made physically, we were created spiritually. All things were spiritually created first. A recipe is sort of a "spiritual creation"; the dish, when prepared, becomes the second, physical creation. Similarly, before a house is physically built, there are blueprints drawn up. Before a dress is made there is a sewing pattern.

How does this relate to our lives? Setting goals is a form of pre-planning and life direction. As we make plans for what we want to become in our lives we are creating a blueprint of what we desire to happen. We shouldn't passively let life happen to us; rather, we should be proactive in setting and achieving goals.

Are We DRIVING or Being DRIVEN by Conditions?

Oliver Wendell Holmes said, "To reach the port of heaven, we must sail sometimes with the wind and sometimes against it, but we must sail, and not drift, nor lie at anchor."[2]

President Ezra Taft Benson said, "Every accountable child of God needs to set goals, short- and long-range goals."[3] Even our Heavenly Father has the overall goal, "to bring to pass the immortality and eternal life of man" (Moses 1:39). So how do we set meaningful personal goals to plan and give direction to our lives?

Involve God in Your Goals

As we set goals we should remember to include our Father in Heaven. He has a plan for each of us individually that he will reveal line upon line if we ask him. Elder Richard G. Scott said, "The Lord has a purpose for you. . . . Discover it and fulfill it."[4]

We should talk directly to God and ask him what goals he wants us to set. As we tap into the vision of what he wants us to become we will be better able to set goals that will help us fulfill our potential. Elder Jeffrey R. Holland explained, "I believe that in our own individual ways, God takes us to the grove . . . and there shows us the wonder of what his plan is for us."[5] Elder M. Russell Ballard simply said, "Pray for divine guidance in your goal setting."[6] When you know you are working on a goal that God wants you to accomplish, it is easier to achieve it.

? HOW can I know where to begin setting goals?

Elder M. Russell Ballard quoted Benjamin N. Woodson as saying: "'All you need to do is this: Beginning this very day, stop doing one thing you know you should not do.' After you have written this one thing down, stop doing it! . . . Write down one thing that you are going to start doing that you have been meaning to do for a long time but that you just haven't got-

ten around to. I don't know what it might be, but place into your life, beginning tonight, one thing that you are going to do that is going to make you a better person. I believe if you make this a regular practice, you will start to fulfill the Savior's teaching when He asked us, 'Be ye therefore perfect, even as your Father which is in heaven is perfect.'"[7]

ANYBODY WANT A MARSHMALLOW?

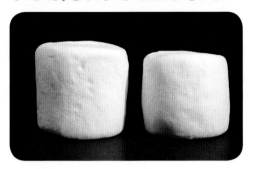

An academic study at Stanford University in the late 1960s tested young children on their ability to delay gratification. These children were told that they could have either a marshmallow at that moment or, if they would wait a few minutes while the professor left the room, two marshmallows when the professor returned. When the professor left the room, some kids ate the marshmallow. Other kids made themselves wait (sometimes for as long as fifteen minutes) and eventually got two marshmallows. About ten years passed and the researchers again contacted the parents of the same children (now teenagers) and discovered that the children who didn't wait to eat the marshmallows "seemed more likely to have behavioral problems, both in school and at home. They got lower S.A.T. scores. They struggled in stressful situations, often had trouble paying attention, and found it difficult to maintain friendships. The child who could wait fifteen minutes had an S.A.T. score that was, on average, two hundred and ten points higher than that of the kid who could wait only thirty seconds."[9]

One lesson we learn from this study is that the ability to put off what you want right now for a more worthy future goal says a lot about your ability to succeed. When you have a goal, do not be distracted from achieving it. If your goal is to write in your journal every day, and one day you want to stay on Facebook for a few more minutes instead of writing in your journal, say no to that Facebook marshmallow. Don't trade the goals you have set for something that only gratifies you in the moment.

Set Well-Rounded Goals

We would be wise to set goals and strive to be well-rounded in our lives. A good pattern to begin with is the only verse about the Savior's teenage years: "And Jesus increased in wisdom and stature, and in favour with God and man" (Luke 2:52). Notice that this verse describes four primary areas of focus to live a balanced life: wisdom (intellectual), stature (physical), favour with God (spiritual), and favour with man (social).

Set goals related to intellectual development. These goals can be anything that stimulates, expands, or enlarges your mind. In other words, do things that make you smarter. Goals in this area might include getting better grades, doing homework, reading books, going to college, learning a new skill, playing an instrument, writing, painting, building, or creating things.

Set goals related to physical development. Losing weight is the most common New Year's resolution, but physical development involves much more than dropping pounds. Physical development concerns caring for the overall gift of your physical body, not necessarily how toned or ripped your right bicep is. Goals in this area might include obeying the Word of Wisdom; exercising daily; participating in sports; learning to play a new sport; completing a 10K, marathon, or triathlon; hiking; biking; eating more nutritious meals; packing a healthier lunch (a candy bar and a soft drink doesn't cut it!); or eliminating caffeine, excess sugar, or energy drinks from your diet.

Set goals related to spiritual development. Goals in this area can include doing better at daily scripture study, having more meaningful personal prayer, attending family home evenings, partaking of the sacrament each week, serving in our callings, participating in Sunday School and seminary, fasting, attending the temple, repenting of our sins, developing faith in Jesus Christ, sharing the gospel with others, or preparing for missions.

Set goals related to social development. To move the kingdom of God forward, we need to develop our social skills and abilities as best as possible. Goals in this area could be connected to doing service projects; being involved in school government or community leadership; being part of formal school groups, teams, or clubs; having a job and contributing to society through meaningful employment; going on dates (if you are older than sixteen); keeping yourself well groomed and modestly dressed; attending performances and uplifting concerts; and limiting the time you spend texting and social networking so that you can actually talk and socialize with living human beings face to face!

Setting goals in all these areas will help us create and maintain a well-balanced life.

ARE YOUR GOALS ON TARGET?

Ready for a challenge? Stand up over this book, hold a pen or pencil, point down, over the target and try to drop it in the bull's-eye. Do it five times. How accurate were you? How consistent were you? It is important to realize that to truly be "on target" we need to be both accurate and consistent. If we are consistent in achieving our goals, but our goals are on the periphery (like constantly hitting the edge of the target, not the middle) then consistency may not be a good thing. For example, if your goal is to watch twenty hours of television each week, and you consistently meet your goal, that may not be good! Make sure your goals are on target with righteous living and what the Lord desires for you—and then consistently hit them!

Invitation to Act

Set one personal goal in each of the four areas (intellectual, physical, spiritual, and social). Keep in mind that setting and meeting goals in all of these areas can count toward Personal Progress and Duty to God awards.

Set SMART'R Goals

To reach our goals in these four areas of our lives, it is important that we set *S.M.A.R.T.* goals.[9]

Specific: Goals that are specific give us focus and direction. It is the difference between saying "I think I'll go visit Europe" and "I'm going to go to Europe in January to snowboard the Swiss Alps." In spiritual terms, "I'll study my scriptures" could more specifically be stated as "I'll study from the Book of Mormon each day for fifteen minutes and finish the book by the end of the year." Answer these questions about your goals: who will be involved, what will be accomplished, where it will take place, when it will be finished, and how will I make it happen.

*M*easurable: President Thomas S. Monson has said, "When performance is measured, performance improves."[10] How can we know if we reached a goal, or know our progress, if it isn't measurable—if we can't see the results? Measuring a goal helps us stay focused and evaluate our success in the specified goal. For example, if our goal is to study the scriptures daily, we can measure it by checking off a box on a calendar.

*A*chievable: A goal that is achievable or attainable is one that is realistically in the realm of reaching. It would be silly to set a goal to walk from your house to your mailbox this year, but it would also be unrealistic to think "I'm going to walk to the moon." Elder M. Russell Ballard said, "Set short-term goals that you can reach. Set goals that are well balanced—not too many nor too few, and not too high nor too low. Write down your attainable goals and work on them according to their importance."[11]

*R*elevant: Set goals based on their order of importance to you in your life. Pick the top few in each of the four categories that are most relevant to the overall direction you want your life to go and that have the most important areas to progress in. *Most importantly, make sure the goal is relevant to what you can control!* Setting goals based on other people's performance is not in harmony with the principle of agency. For example, don't set a goal that Jennifer will go to prom with you—you cannot control what Jennifer does. Instead, set a goal that you can control, such as, "I will ask Jennifer to prom."

Elder Dallin H. Oaks taught that this same principle applies to missionaries who are setting goals. He said, "Some of our most important plans cannot be brought to pass without the agency and actions of others. A missionary cannot baptize five persons this month without the agency and action of five other persons. A missionary can plan and work and do all within his or her power, but the desired result will depend upon the additional agency and action of others. Consequently a missionary's goals ought to be based upon the missionary's personal agency and action, not upon the agency or action of others."[12]

*T*ime-bound: A goal must have a definitive time frame to be accomplished by to provide motivation and goal completion. A great example of this was when President Gordon B. Hinckley challenged the members of the Church in August of 2005 to read the entire Book of Mormon by the end of the year.[13] That time frame gave people

DO TRY THIS AT HOME!

Get up and count how many steps it takes you to walk across the room. Got it? Now, try to beat your normal stride by taking two fewer steps. Now, try to beat that by two fewer steps. See how far you can lengthen your stride and stretch yourself. . . . It's probably a lot farther than you think.

We can all try a little harder, and do a little better, than we are now doing. We can all improve in some area. Let's set some goals and push ourselves in some areas in life that we could stretch a little more in.

motivation and context to evaluate how well they did, and many people upped their scripture study performance because of it. If President Hinckley had simply said, "Read the Book of Mormon," it might not have had the same effect or outcome.

HOW *often should I set goals?*

As often as you feel you want to improve in an area of your life. You don't need to wait until New Year's Day, that is for sure. Speaking of New Year's resolutions, Elder Jeffrey R. Holland said we should

"take stock of our lives and see where we are going" but that we should have our "eye toward *any* time of transition and change in our lives—and those moments come virtually every day."[14]

We could even add an "R" and make "SMART'R" goals by adding in "Reportable."

Reportable: President Thomas S. Monson said, "Where performance is measured, performance improves. Where performance is measured and reported the rate of improvement accelerates."[15] You can probably see how this would be the case. If you have to report to somebody else on how you are doing with your goal, you're more likely to want to achieve it so that you can give a good report. Suppose you have a goal to read your scriptures every day. You could tell your parents about your goal and give them a report every week on how many days you read.

THE COOKIE MONSTER!

Elder Bruce C. Hafen and Sister Marie K. Hafen wrote, "Our family once watched a segment of the children's television program *Sesame Street* in which the Cookie Monster won a quiz show. . . . After Mrs. Monster joined her spouse on the stage, the emcee congratulated the couple and offered them their choice among three big prizes—a $200,000 dream home next month, a $20,000 new car next week, or a cookie right now. . . . As the timer buzzed, a big smile broke across Mr. Monster's face, and he greedily announced his choice: 'Cookie!'"[16] The cookie monster wasn't able to delay gratification to pursue more important goals. Are we?

We should take the time to study out what our goals should be and then talk with the Lord about them. Additionally, we should write our goals down and post them where we can see them to constantly be reminded of our intentions. We hope the principles in this chapter will help us act on and accomplish our goals so that we can progress in our ultimate goal of becoming like God and obtaining eternal life through the Atonement of Jesus Christ.

PUT YOUR GOALS WHERE YOU CAN SEE THEM

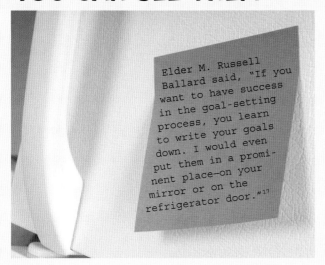

Elder M. Russell Ballard said, "If you want to have success in the goal-setting process, you learn to write your goals down. I would even put them in a prominent place—on your mirror or on the refrigerator door."[17]

"This time is a precious window of opportunity to prepare for your future. Do not waste this time away. Get out a paper and pencil and write down the things that matter most to you. List the goals that you hope to accomplish in life and what things are required if they are to become a reality for you. Plan and prepare and then do."—Elder M. Russell Ballard[18]

GOOD, BETTER, BEST GOALS

Good: "I'm going to get better grades."

Better: "I'm going to pull my math grade up from a B to an A."

Best: "By the end of the first semester I will earn an A in math. I will accomplish this by doing my math homework each afternoon from 3:00 p.m.–4:00 p.m., turning all homework assignments in on time, not intentionally missing any class, taking notes each day, and forming a study group to prepare for tests."

Memorize This Poem!

The heights by great men reached and kept were not obtained by sudden flight, but they, while their companions slept, were toiling upward in the night.
—Henry Wadsworth Longfellow[19]

WHICH PATH?

Don't think you need to set goals? Listen to President Thomas S. Monson's analogy: "Let us not find ourselves as indecisive as is Alice in Lewis Carroll's classic *Alice's Adventures in Wonderland*. You will remember that she comes to a crossroads with two paths before her, each stretching onward but in opposite directions. She is confronted by the Cheshire cat, of whom Alice asks, 'Which path shall I follow?'

"The cat answers: 'That depends where you want to go. If you do not know where you want to go, it doesn't matter which path you take.'"[20]

TELL ME ONE MORE TiME!

How Can I Set Meaningful Personal Goals?

- **Involve God in your goals.**
- **Set well-rounded goals—intellectual, physical, social, and spiritual.**
- **Set SMART'R goals—specific, measurable, achievable, relevant, time-bound, and reportable.**

How Can I Make the Temple a More Important Part of My Life?

Sister Anne C. Pingree shared the following story that illustrates how strongly some Latter-day Saints felt about the temple. She said:

Guess that **TEMPLE!**

Albuquerque, New Mexico

"I will never forget a sauna-hot day in the lush rain forest of south-eastern Nigeria. My husband and I had traveled to one of the most remote locations in our mission so he could conduct temple recommend interviews with members in the Ikot Eyo district. Some in this growing district had been Church members less than two years. All the members lived 3,000 miles away from the nearest temple in Johannesburg, South Africa. None had received their temple endowment.

"These members knew the appointed day each month we would come to their district, but even we didn't know the exact hour we would arrive; nor could we call, for telephones were rare in that part of West Africa. So these committed African Saints gathered early in the morning to wait all day if necessary for their temple recommend interviews . . .

Ikot Eyo to Johannesburg: 3,000 miles

"Many hours later, after all the interviews were completed, as my husband and I drove back along that sandy jungle trail, we were stunned when we saw . . . two sisters still walking. We realized they had trekked from their village—a distance of eighteen miles round-trip—just to obtain a temple recommend they knew they would never have the privilege of using."[1]

It is clear that those two women felt strongly about the importance of the temple. Even though they probably knew they would never have the opportunity to use their temple recommend, they wanted to be worthy of it. How can we be more like these Saints and have the temple become a more important part of our lives?

What
does this
address mean?

800 East 7400 South
Midvale, Utah

If you were in downtown Salt Lake City, and you told me your address was 800 East and 7400 South, what are you 8 blocks east and 74 blocks south of?

Read Mosiah 2:5-6 or Numbers 2 to figure it out.

Answer: Most addresses in the Salt Lake Valley are based on their location relative to the Salt Lake Temple. In other words, the address above is 8 blocks east and 74 blocks south of the Salt Lake Temple. Every time someone writes a Salt Lake City address it shows the temple is the center of the city!

Guess that TEMPLE!

Calgary, Alberta

Be Worthy of a Temple Recommend

One of the first things we can do to make the temple more important in our lives is to be worthy of a temple recommend. President Howard W. Hunter said, "It would be the deepest desire of my heart to have every member of the Church temple worthy. I would hope that every adult member would be worthy of—and carry—a current temple recommend, even if proximity to a temple does not allow immediate or frequent use of it."[2]

What Does It Take to Be Worthy of a Temple Recommend?

The *Gospel Principles* manual says we are asked questions like the following in an interview for a temple recommend:

"1. Do you have faith in and a testimony of God the Eternal Father; His Son Jesus Christ; and the Holy Ghost? Do you have a firm testimony of the restored gospel?

"2. Do you sustain the President of The Church of Jesus Christ of Latter-day Saints as the prophet, seer, and revelator? Do you recognize him as the only person on earth authorized to exercise all priesthood keys?

"3. Do you live the law of chastity?

"4. Are you a full-tithe payer?

"5. Do you keep the Word of Wisdom?

"6. Are you honest in your dealings with others?

"7. Do you strive to keep the covenants you have made, to attend your sacrament and priesthood meetings, and to keep your life in harmony with the laws and commandments of the gospel?"[3]

In addition, President Dieter F. Uchtdorf has pointed out, "The standards set by the Lord in the temple recommend questions are very similar to the standards found in *For the Strength of Youth*."[4]

If the temple is an important part of our lives, we should be worthy to be there. President Howard W. Hunter also taught, "The things that we must do and not do to be worthy of a temple recommend are the very things that ensure we will be happy as individuals and as families."[5]

SET THE PRISONERS FREE!

Joseph Smith taught, "Every man that has been baptized and belongs to the kingdom has a right to be baptized for those who have gone before; and *as soon as the law of the Gospel is obeyed here by their friends who act as proxy for them, the Lord has administrators there to set them free.*"[11] When you go to the temple to perform temple ordinances for the dead you may be literally setting people free from bondage.

HOW can the temple give me increased power?

Here are a few ways the temple can endow (or give) us power:

1. "The power of enlightenment, of testimony, and of understanding."[6]
2. "Power [to] thwart the forces of evil."[7]
3. "Power which enables us to use our gifts and capabilities with greater intelligence and increased effectiveness."[8]
4. "Power to overcome the sins of the world and 'stand in holy places' (D&C 45:32)."[9]
5. "Greater powers that [we] might be better qualified to teach."[10]
6. "Power with which to strengthen [our] earthly families."[12]
7. "The promised personal revelation that may bless [our] life with power, knowledge, light, beauty, and truth from on high."[13]

Go to the Temple More Often

One of the most obvious things we can do to make the temple a more important part of our lives is to go to the temple. President Howard W. Hunter said, "We should hasten to the temple as frequently, yet prudently, as our personal circumstances allow."[14]

On March 11, 2003, the First Presidency issued a letter saying, "Where time and circumstances permit, members are encouraged to replace some leisure activities with temple service. . . . We particularly encourage newer members and youth of the Church who are 12 years of age and older to live worthy to assist in this great work by serving as proxies for baptisms and confirmations."[15]

Guess that **TEMPLE!**

Atlanta, Georgia

John Says:

I grew up in Seattle and lived about twenty minutes from the Seattle Temple. I went to the temple on trips with my ward, but never went by myself. Honestly, the idea never even occurred to me. When I started teaching seminary in Spanish Fork, Utah (about twenty minutes from the Provo Utah Temple), I was really surprised when some of my students told me that they had gone to the temple early that morning. "Did you have a ward temple trip?" I asked.

"No," they told me. "We just go to the temple before school sometimes." I was so impressed with their dedication, and I realized that I could have gone to the temple more frequently as a youth.

Not all temples allow you to just walk in and do baptisms for the dead any time you want. But the temple closest to you might. Ask your parents or church leaders what the rules of your closest temple are. It's almost certain they will let you schedule a personal or family appointment to do baptisms for the dead if you bring the names of your own ancestors! (Keep reading to learn more about that.)

Our actions speak louder than our words. When we sacrifice some of our casual or free entertainment time to go to the temple, we are showing the Lord how important the temple is in our lives. After Abraham showed the Lord through his actions that God was the most important thing in his life, even above the life of his own precious son Isaac, the Lord said, "Now I know that thou fearest God, seeing thou hast not withheld thy son, thine only son from me" (Genesis 22:12). Similarly, if we give of some more of our free time to attend the temple, we will show the Lord through our actions that we love his holy house more than other things.

MAKE A TEMPLE GROUP WITH YOUR FRIENDS

Many youth are part of a temple group that attends the temple on a set day each week or month. This picture is from a group of teenagers who gather together after school each Wednesday to go do baptisms for the dead.

These youth said that having a temple group to go with has made the temple more important in their lives because they go more often: "It's easier to go when you have a group and everyone's there encouraging you to go."

Guess that TEMPLE!

St. George, Utah

Search Out Your Ancestors and Perform Temple Work for Them

President Howard W. Hunter wrote, "The dead are anxiously waiting for the Latter-day Saints to search out their names and then go into the temples to officiate in their behalf, that they may be liberated from their prison house in the spirit world. *All* of us should find joy in this magnificent labor of love."[16]

Notice the word *all* in that quote. Sometimes we think that doing family history is a work for old people—but it is a work for everyone. Especially now that the Church has created http://familysearch.org it may be that family history becomes a work for tech-savvy teenagers. This website allows you to more easily figure out who your ancestors are, and which ones need to have their baptisms performed by proxy (that's you!).

Powerful Promises to You

"I invite the young people of the Church to learn about and experience the Spirit of Elijah. I encourage you to study, to search out your ancestors, and to prepare yourselves to perform proxy baptisms in the house of the Lord. . . .

"As you respond in faith to this invitation, your hearts shall turn to the fathers. The promises made to Abraham, Isaac, and Jacob will be implanted in your hearts. . . . Your testimony of and conversion to the Savior will become deep and abiding. And I promise you will be protected against the intensifying influence of the adversary."—Elder David A. Bednar[17]

"Let us prepare every missionary to go to the temple worthily and to make that experience an even greater highlight than receiving the mission call."—President Howard W. Hunter[18]

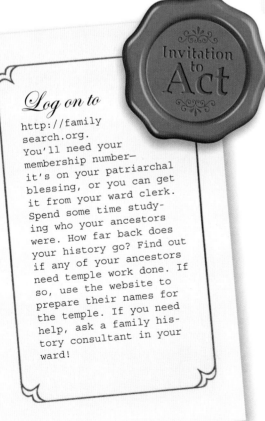

Invitation to Act

Log on to http://family search.org. You'll need your membership number—it's on your patriarchal blessing, or you can get it from your ward clerk. Spend some time studying who your ancestors were. How far back does your history go? Find out if any of your ancestors need temple work done. If so, use the website to prepare their names for the temple. If you need help, ask a family history consultant in your ward!

Learn All You Can about Temples

One factor to increasing our desire to attend the temple is to better understand its meaning and purposes. We highly recommend reading a short booklet printed by the Church entitled *Preparing to Enter the Holy Temple*.[19] Also, study the promises made about temple worship in Doctrine and Covenants 109.

PREPARING TO ENTER THE HOLY TEMPLE

President Thomas S. Monson taught, "My brothers and sisters, in our lives we will have temptations; we will have trials and challenges. As we go to the temple, as we remember the covenants we make there, we will be better able to overcome those temptations and to bear our trials. In the temple we can find peace."[20] Go to the temple with questions—you will find answers.

CASTLES AND TEMPLES

Have you ever noticed that some of the early temples look like castles? The Salt Lake Temple even has "battlements" on its roof (the place where archers would hide behind to shoot their bows and arrows). Now, why would they design it like that? Did Brigham Young really intend for archers to sit on top of the temple and shoot arrows? Probably not. Think of all the possible meanings about how a temple is similar to a castle:

_____

_____

Here are a few of many possible analogies to temples and castles:
• They both are places of protection
• Inside them are found royalty—future kings and queens

When You Are in the Temple, Focus on the Work You Are Doing

We can do small things while in the temple that will help us focus and gain more from the experience, and thus make the temple a more important part of our lives.

For example, as you are being baptized or confirmed for another person, try to imagine that this person was a close friend. Don't just go through the motions of being baptized for a bunch of people—consider each one as an individual child of God with infinite worth—for that is who they are. If possible, learn the names of the people for whom you are being baptized. Take the time to look at the year in which they lived and where they are from. Getting to know these people as best you can will make the temple experience more powerful. As Elder Richard G.

Scott suggested, "Be mindful of the individual for whom you are performing the vicarious ordinance. At times pray that he or she will recognize the vital importance of the ordinances and be worthy or prepare to be worthy to benefit from them."[21]

Consider this—when the person baptizing you states the name of the person you are being baptized for, it might be the first time in hundreds of years that that person's name has been said out loud on the earth. It is a sacred moment for that person, who may, in fact, be present for the ordinance. Do everything you can to make it sacred for him or her.

WATCH YOUR WATCH

Follow Elder Richard G. Scott's counsel to "remove your watch when you enter a house of the Lord."[22] Doing so can help you stay focused on the temple ordinances and forget the world a little more.

REMEMBER: THOSE IN THE SPIRIT WORLD ARE ALIVE!

Elder W. Grant Bangerter of the Seventy said, "May we always remember that we perform the temple ordinances for people and not for names. Those we call 'the dead' are alive in the spirit and are present in the temple."[23]

Won't it be neat to perhaps meet the people we performed temple ordinances for in the next life?

Put the Temple Where You Can See It!

A great way to have the temple be a more important part of your life is to look at temples more often. You could put a picture of the temple in your bedroom, car, or locker—even on your cell phone!

Guess that TEMPLE!

Mesa, Arizona

At the beginning of this chapter we shared an experience from Sister Pingree that illustrated the dedication some African Saints had to the temple. We conclude with an account of Elder Jeffrey R. Holland where he describes how some faithful Saints in South America showed their dedication to the temple. He said,

"The Punta Arenas Chile Stake is the Church's southernmost stake anywhere on this planet, its outermost borders stretching toward Antarctica. Any stake farther south would have to be staffed by penguins. For the Punta Arenas Saints it is a 4,200-mile round-trip bus ride to the Santiago temple. For a husband and wife it can take up to 20 percent of an annual local income just for the transportation alone. Only 50 people can be accommodated on the bus, but for every excursion 250 others come out to hold a brief service with them the morning of their departure.

"Pause for a minute and ask yourself when was the last time you stood on a cold, windswept parking lot adjacent to the Strait of Magellan just to sing with, pray for, and cheer on their way those who were going to the temple, hoping your savings would allow you to go next time? One hundred ten hours, 70 of those on dusty, bumpy, unfinished roads looping out through Argentina's wild Patagonia."[24]

We may not need to walk eighteen miles to get a temple recommend, or take a 110-hour bus ride to get to the temple—but the Lord still expects us to give the temple the high importance that it deserves. May we follow the counsel of President Howard W. Hunter and make the temple "our ultimate earthly goal and the supreme mortal experience."[25]

How Can I Make the Temple a More Important Part of My Life?

- **Be worthy of a temple recommend.**
- **Go to the temple more often.**
- **Search out your ancestors and perform temple work for them.**
- **When you are in the temple, focus on the work you are doing.**

32 ch Why Should I Serve a Mission?

When a baby boy is born to faithful members of the Church, there is the hope he will eventually serve a mission. There are even little missionary name tags that some young boys wear to Church.

FUTURE MISSIONARY

WE'LL BRING THE WORLD HIS TRUTH

As a matter of fact, it is not just *hoped* that a young man will serve a mission, he is *commanded* to serve a mission. President Spencer W. Kimball said: "A mission is not just a casual thing. . . . Neither is a mission a matter of choice any more than tithing is a choice, any more than sacrament meeting is a choice, any more than the World of Wisdom is a choice. Of course, we have our agency, and the Lord has given us choices. . . . We can go on a mission or we can remain home. But every normal young man is as much obligated to go on a mission as he is to pay his tithing, attend his meetings, keep the Sabbath day holy, and keep his life spotless and clean."[1]

Understanding why young men are commanded to serve a mission and why they should fulfill that divine obligation is instrumental in persuading a greater number of young men to become known as "Elder."

WHAT ABOUT YOUNG WOMEN AND MISSIONS?

Since the October 2012 general conference, when President Thomas S. Monson announced the change in missionary age to 19 years old for young women, sisters have joined the missionary ranks in increasing numbers. As of 2014, 28% of all full-time missionaries are young women.[2]

While the age change is exciting, a mission is not a priesthood obligation for young women as it is for LDS young men. After announcing the age change, President Monson reminded, "We affirm that missionary work is a priesthood duty. . . . Many young women also serve, but they are not under the same mandate to serve as are the young men. We assure the young sisters of the Church, however, that they make a valuable contribution as missionaries, and we welcome their service."[3]

"We need more missionaries. The message to raise the bar on missionary qualifications was not a signal to send fewer missionaries but rather a call for parents and leaders to work with young men earlier to better prepare them for missionary service and to keep them worthy of such service. All young men who are worthy and who are physically and emotionally able should prepare to serve in this most important work."—President Gordon B. Hinckley[4]

As of December 2015, there were 85,147 full-time missionaries serving in the world[5]—but many more could be serving. The Lord needs all worthy young men to serve a mission and all young women who feel to serve as well. Will you be number **85,148**?

The Best Investment

A few young men worry about serving a mission because they are afraid of missing out on some things. Some ask, "What if I fall behind in school? What about all the social opportunities I'll miss? What about the money I could make? What if the girl I like marries someone else?" (Oh, that would *never* happen! ☺) Those are all legitimate concerns, but the blessings of serving a mission far outweigh the sacrifices asked of you. President Gordon B. Hinckley gave the following promises to those who faithfully served missions. See how many you can count: "I promise you that the time you spend in the mission field, if those years are spent in dedicated service, *will yield a greater return on investment than any other two years of your lives.* You will come to know what dedication and consecration mean. You will develop powers of persuasion which will bless your entire life. Your timidity, your fears, your shyness will gradually disappear as you go forth with boldness and conviction. You will learn to work with others, to develop a spirit of teamwork. The cankering evil of selfishness will be supplanted by a sense of service to others. You will draw nearer to the Lord than you likely will in any other set of circumstances. You will come to know that without His help you are indeed weak and simple, but that with His help you can accomplish miracles.

"You will establish habits of industry. You will develop a talent for the establishment of goals of effort. You will learn to work with singleness of purpose. What a tremendous

WANT TO GET RICH?

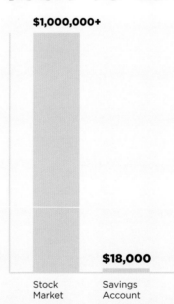

$1,000,000+

$18,000

Stock Market

Savings Account

If you invest $10,000 today in the stock market, and you earn an average of 8% interest per year, in 60 years you'll have more than a million dollars. If you take that same $10,000 and put it in a savings account earning 1% interest, in 60 years you'll have about $18,000. Which seems like a better investment to you? In a similar way, serving a mission is *by far* the best investment on your time that you can make!

foundation all of this will become for you in your later educational efforts and your life's work. Two years will not be time lost. It will be skills gained.

"You will bless the lives of those you teach, and their posterity after them. You will bless your own life. You will bless the lives of your family, who will sustain you and pray for you.

"And above and beyond all of this will come that sweet peace in your heart that you have served your Lord faithfully and well. Your service will become an expression of gratitude to your Heavenly Father.

"You will come to know your Redeemer as your greatest friend in time or eternity. You will realize that through His atoning sacrifice He has opened the way for eternal life and an exaltation above and beyond your greatest dreams.

"If you serve a mission faithfully and well, you will be a better husband, you will be a better father, you will be a better student, a better worker in your chosen vocation."[6]

We counted *twenty-two* incredible blessings! There can be no doubt about the blessings available to us as we serve a mission.

AN HUNDREDFOLD *Anthony Says:*

When I was about to leave for my mission, I had four things that I cared deeply about that I was afraid to leave behind: A girl that I hoped to marry, an opportunity to play college basketball, my own black Labrador dog that I loved, and I had a new black Jeep Wrangler. I decided to take a picture of all four of those things together to take with me. So I parked my Jeep in front of my basketball hoop, had my girlfriend and my dog climb in the front seats, and I snapped a photo.

In the MTC, I put the picture right above my bed. One day, our branch president came into our room and asked me about the picture. I explained it was of the four things I cared about the most, to which he responded, "You know what's funny, Elder Sweat? You're going to lose all four of those things on your mission." Needless to say . . . I didn't think it was funny. I thought to myself, "Why would God make me *lose* what I love if I am serving him?"

It didn't take long before the branch president's prophecy began to come true. Five months into my mission I learned my dog had died of a sudden seizure. Six months into my mission things ended with the girl at home. The basketball skills and recruiting letters quickly left me. And to top it off, my Jeep was eventually sold to my best friend. Luckily, I came across this promise from the Savior: "Verily I say unto you, There is no man that hath left house, or brethren, or sisters, or father, or mother, or wife, or children, or lands, for my sake, and the gospel's, but he shall receive an *hundredfold* now in this time, houses, and brethren, and sisters, and mothers, and children, and lands, with persecutions; and in the world to come eternal life" (Mark 10:29–30; emphasis added).

Upon returning home from my mission, I was led to and married my wife, Cindy, whom I love with all my heart. Instead of playing basketball, I get to teach for a living, which has brought me more joy and opportunities than hoops ever did. I have seven beautiful children (can't even compare that one). And instead of a beautiful Jeep Wrangler . . . for 10 years I drove a minivan! Yeah, baby! (OK, so I am still waiting for that promise to be fulfilled . . . but it will be.

I found the Savior's promise to bless those who sacrifice for the gospel "an hundredfold" to be true, and so will you.

Elder Richard G. Scott made his decision to serve a mission after he graduated from college. One of his professors told him that if he went on a mission it would be a waste of his education—that everything he had learned would be obsolete by the time he returned. Nevertheless, Elder Scott served a mission. When he returned, he was hired to work in the Naval Nuclear Program. A few months after he began his new job, he was given a list of people he was responsible for. On that list was the same professor who had discouraged him years before. The professor was now working *three levels below* Elder Scott.

In summarizing his mission, Elder Scott said: "All that I now hold dear in life began to mature in the mission field. Had I not been encouraged to be a missionary, I would not have the eternal companion or precious family I dearly love. I am confident that I would not have had the exceptional professional opportunities that stretched my every capacity. I am certain that I would not have received the sacred callings with opportunities to serve for which I will be eternally grateful. My life has been richly blessed beyond measure because I served a mission."[8]

There can be no doubt that serving a mission *helped* not *hindered* Elder Scott. A mission is an investment that pays over and over.

Start now to prepare for your missionary service by studying the Book of Mormon, *Preach My Gospel,* and saving money so that you can serve.

DO TRY THIS AT HOME!

A MISSION WILL MAKE YOU A MAN

Before the Mission	After the Mission
You can shave with two tweezer plucks.	You have a 5 o'clock shadow by 4 o'clock.
You can wear a size 14 collared shirt (that's still too big).	You're at least a 16 because you actually have an Adam's apple.
Your suit is pressed and your shoes are shined.	Your suit is worn at the elbows and too small. Your shoes are considered "holy."
Some scripture pages are still stuck together because that page has never been read. (There's a book called Habbakuk?)	Each page is marked and underlined. The binding is broken, and you have empanada juice stains on the book of Habbakuk because you read it so much at lunch.
Letters from your mom at home.	Text messages from your companion's girlfriend now that you are home.

The Seed of Abraham—It Is Who You Are

Anciently God made a covenant with Abraham and his descendants. They were given posterity, priesthood, and a promised land. In return, the descendants of Abraham accepted certain responsibilities. The Lord said to Abraham, "Thou shalt be a blessing unto thy seed after thee, that in their hands *they shall bear this ministry and Priesthood unto all nations*" (Abraham 2:9; emphasis added).

Elder David A. Bednar explained, "The phrase 'bear this ministry and Priesthood unto all nations' refers to the responsibility to proclaim the gospel of Jesus Christ and to invite all to receive by proper priesthood authority the ordinances of salvation."[9] In other words, those who are the seed of Abraham have the duty to teach the gospel to others.

> WE ARE THE SEED OF ABRAHAM.
>
> **ELDER DAVID A. BEDNAR**[10]

Elder David A. Bednar further explained, "Missionary work is a manifestation of our spiritual identity and heritage. . . .

"You may enjoy music, athletics, or be mechanically inclined, and someday you may work in a trade or a profession or in the arts. As important as such activities and occupations can be, they do not define who we are. First and foremost, we are spiritual beings. *We are sons of God and the seed of Abraham.*"[11]

> EVERY WORTHY YOUNG MAN SHOULD FILL A MISSION.
>
> **PRESIDENT SPENCER W. KIMBALL**[12]

President Joseph F. Smith had a vision in which he saw the "noble and great ones who were chosen in the beginning to be rulers in the Church of God. *Even before they were born,* they, with many others, received their first lessons in the world of spirits and were prepared to come forth in the due time of the Lord *to labor in his vineyard for the salvation of the souls of men*" (D&C 138:55–56; emphasis added).

So no matter who you are, if you hold the priesthood, your foremost commitment and duty is to share the gospel with others. It is what you were born to do.

Did you know the scriptures talk about having beautiful feet? In Mosiah 15:16 it says, "How beautiful upon the mountains are the feet of those that are still publishing peace!" That verse doesn't necessarily mean that missionaries have beautiful feet, but it does mean that those who teach the gospel (those who publish peace) are blessed!

Do you have beautiful feet?

You Can Bless Others Eternally

Perhaps the most important reason why we should serve a mission is that a mission gives us the opportunity to share the life-changing message of the gospel of Jesus Christ. Think how many blessings are ours because we enjoy the privilege of having the restored gospel of Jesus Christ in our lives! Our efforts in serving as missionaries can be eternal—and they can spread throughout generations.

President Gordon B. Hinckley told the story of a missionary who left his mission discouraged. This missionary felt he had accomplished nothing. "I baptized one man in the backwoods of Tennessee," the missionary said. "He didn't know enough or have enough sense to wear shoes. And that's all I've done. I have wasted my time and my father's money."

THE RIPPLE EFFECT

Have you ever seen what happens to a still pond when a drop of water hits it? From that one spot, ripples flow in all directions until they cover the entire area. Similarly, by touching one person's life through missionary work, unknown thousands can end up being blessed by the gospel.

The mission president later checked on that man and found that he had been ordained a deacon. Later he received the Melchezidek Priesthood and was made branch president. Eventually the man moved to Idaho and had many children, and his children eventually served missions. The mission president said, "I have just completed a survey which indicates, according to the best information I can find, that over 1,100 people have come into the Church as a result of the baptism of that one man by a missionary who thought he had failed."[14]

A great scriptural example of this same ripple effect is the Book of Mormon prophet Abinadi. From what we know in the scriptures, Abinadi did not baptize anyone before he was put to death by King Noah. But he was able to change the life of one of Noah's priests, Alma. Abinadi's one convert, Alma, became one of the great Nephite prophets (see Mosiah 17–18). And the rest of the Book of Mormon deals primarily with Alma's descendants and their effect upon the Nephite and Lamanite civilizations. Think of all that happened from one man—Abinadi—bearing his testimony and teaching the gospel!

Similarly, we may never know the monumental effect our missionary work may have. But by changing even one person's life with the blessings of the gospel, we can have a large impact in moving the kingdom of God forward.

No Greater Joy

The Lord promised, "And if it so be that you should labor all your days in crying repentance unto this people, and bring, save it be one soul unto me, how great shall be your joy with him in the kingdom of my Father! And now, if your joy will be great with one soul that you have brought unto me into the kingdom of my Father, how great will be your joy if you should bring many souls unto me!" (D&C 18:15–16).

PREPARE TO CONSECRATE TWO YEARS OF YOUR LIVES TO THIS SACRED SERVICE. THAT WILL IN EFFECT CONSTITUTE A TITHE ON THE FIRST TWENTY YEARS OF YOUR LIVES.

PRESIDENT GORDON B. HINCKLEY[15]

President Brigham Young taught, "When men enjoy the spirit of their missions and realize their calling and standing before the Lord and the people, it constitutes the happiest portions of their lives."[16] Elder Orson F. Whitney promised, "There is no joy that can compare with that of a missionary who has been made the instrument for the salvation of a soul."[17] And President Ezra Taft Benson testified, "I have tasted the joy of missionary work. There is no work in all the world that can bring an individual greater joy and happiness."[18]

As returned missionaries, we both testify that there is an incomparable and indescribable joy that comes to the souls of those who have faithfully consecrated part of their life to serving the Lord as a full-time missionary. The only way you'll know is when you go.

And We Thought 18 or 24 Months Was a Long Time . . .

In August of 1852, a special conference was held in the old tabernacle on Temple Square. President Heber C. Kimball opened the conference by announcing that brethren would be called on missions.

"The missions we will call for during this conference are, generally, not to be very long ones; probably from *three to seven years* will be as long as any man will be absent from his family." Ninety-eight names were then read of men who were to leave as soon as possible.[19]

TELL ME ONE MORE TiME!

Why Should I Serve a Mission?

1. It's the best investment you can make during the early years of your life.

2. For young men, as part of the seed of Abraham, you have a priesthood responsibility to serve. Additionally, you covenanted to serve before you were born.
3. You can change a person's life eternally by sharing the blessings of the gospel.
4. There is no greater joy than in helping others come unto Christ.

NOW that we have reviewed some of the *principles*, let's answer some of the questions regarding the *practices* connected to serving missions:

Why do we need a raised bar for missionary standards?

The world in which we live is increasingly more complex and demanding. Missionaries need to be prepared in order to meet the intellectual, physical, and spiritual challenges a mission brings. Equally important, we need stronger missionaries with deeper testimonies so that they can carry the gospel to many more people.

Why can't I just serve a mission when I am older with my spouse instead of when I am 18 or 19?

Serving a mission later with your spouse is a great idea. But what about all the opportunities you will have to serve in the Church between the ages of 20 and 60? It is estimated that a missionary gains the equivalent of 30 years of Church service experience during a full-time, two-year mission. Think of how much more qualified you will be to serve the Lord for the rest of your life when you are a returned missionary in your early twenties!

Also, if you choose not to follow the prophet by serving a mission now, that decision might put your life on a different track so that by the time you are 60, you *won't* actually serve a mission, even though you think it's a good idea now.

Why do boys have to serve a mission and girls don't?

The answer is that missionary work is an assignment that belongs primarily to priesthood holders. President Gordon B. Hinckley stated, "Missionary work is essentially a priesthood responsibility. As such, our young men must carry the major burden. This is their responsibility and their obligation.

"We do not ask the young women to consider a mission as an essential part of their life's program. . . . To the sisters I say that you will be as highly respected, you will be considered as being as much in the line of duty, your efforts will be as acceptable to the Lord and to the Church whether you go on a mission or do not go on a mission."[20]

What Happens at the Second Coming?

Imagine it's a bright and sunny afternoon, and as you drive down the road with your parents you look up and notice that the sky looks different. The clouds are luminescent, bright, and heavenly. Suddenly, without warning, the sky seemingly bursts open and the veil between heaven and earth is split. Trumpets start sounding from the sky, and you see above you the most glorious being your mind could ever conceive of descending out of heaven and touching down on earth—Jesus Christ in all His glory has just returned to earth to rule and reign as King of kings and Lord of lords. The power of His resurrected glory—like fire—is transfiguring some people and consuming others.

Do you get out of your car and run toward the event, or away from it? Do you step forward in joy at Christ's appearance, or run and seek to "enter into the rock, and hide . . . in the dust, for the fear of the Lord and the glory of his majesty shall smite thee" (2 Nephi 12:10)? In essence, are you prepared for the Second Coming of Jesus Christ?

What Is the Second Coming of Christ?

After His death and resurrection in Jerusalem, Jesus reappeared to His disciples there and taught them for a short time. Then, while in the midst of His disciples, "[Jesus] was taken up; and a cloud received him out of their sight" (Acts 1:9). As the disciples looked up into heaven, two angels appeared and said, "Ye men of Galilee, why stand ye gazing up into heaven? this same Jesus, which is taken up from you into heaven, *shall so come in like manner as ye have seen him go into heaven*" (Acts 1:11; emphasis added). Since that day, the Saints have anxiously waited for the Lord to return to the earth to rule and reign in power over the whole earth. This is known as the "second coming" of Jesus Christ.

The Second Coming of Christ will be very different from the first coming of Christ. At His first coming, Jesus was "born of Mary" and came to earth as a child (Alma 7:10), with the purpose of teaching God's children and fulfilling the Atonement. At the Second Coming, the Lord will come "in the clouds of heaven with power and great glory" (Matthew 24:30) to "take vengeance upon the wicked" (Doctrine and Covenants 29:17) and to cleanse the earth from sin. The

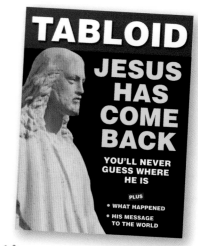

You see these sometimes at the grocery store.

Lord told Joseph Smith: "For behold, verily, verily, I say unto you, the time is soon at hand that I shall come in a cloud with power and great glory. And it shall be a great day at the time of my coming" (Doctrine and Covenants 34:7–8). Indeed it will be a great day. In fact, for the righteous, the return of Jesus Christ will be one of the best days on earth.

What Will Happen at the Second Coming?

The prophet Joel described the Second Coming as both "the *great* and the *terrible* day of the Lord" (Joel 2:31; emphasis added). How can a day be great for some but terrible for others? Well, it is because of what will happen when Jesus comes—for the righteous it will be the greatest day, but for the wicked and rebellious it won't be so great (that could be the understatement of the century). The scriptures teach us that, at the Second Coming, "among the wicked, men shall lift up their voices and curse God and die" (Doctrine and Covenants 45:32) and that the rebellious sinners' "faces shall be as flames" (2 Nephi 23:8). The Lord said, "For behold, the day cometh that shall burn as an oven; and all the proud, yea, and all that do wickedly, shall be stubble; and the day that cometh shall burn them up" (3 Nephi 25:1).

However, the Lord also says that at the Second Coming, "unto you that fear my name, shall the Son of Righteousness arise with healing in his wings" (3 Nephi 25:2). "The Lord shall be in their midst, and his glory shall be upon them, and he will be their king and their lawgiver" (Doctrine and Covenants 45:59), and "the righteous shall be gathered out from among all nations, and shall come to Zion, singing with songs of everlasting joy" (Doctrine and Covenants 45:71). Sin will cease, because when Jesus comes again, "Satan shall be bound, that he shall have no place in the hearts of the children of men" (Doctrine and Covenants 45:55). Perhaps best of all, all our righteous loved ones who have died will be resurrected at the Second Coming of Christ (see Doctrine and Covenants 45:45) and we will be with them again. Healing, singing, joy, sinlessness, and seeing our past loved ones—that doesn't sound too bad, does it? Yes, for the righteous the Second Coming will be a joyous day indeed. It will be the best day.

As we think about the Second Coming, we should be encouraged and joyful. If we are prepared, it will be a marvelous day.

What Are the Signs of the Second Coming?

"And it shall come to pass that he that feareth me shall be looking forth for the great day of the Lord to come, even for the signs of the coming of the Son of Man" (Doctrine and Covenants 45:39). In His mercy, the Lord wants us to be ready and righteous for His coming, so He has given us signs to help us prepare and anticipate His glorious return.

DO TRY THIS AT HOME!

If you know these signs, do you know the signs of the Second Coming? (Answers are at the bottom of the page.)

(Answers: Stop Sign, No Parking, State Highway, Railroad Crossing, No U-Turn, Yield, School Crossing, One Way/Detour, Circular Intersection, Reserved Handicapped Parking, Do Not Enter, Side Road, Interstate, Food, Workers Ahead)

The following are *some* of the signs of the Second Coming listed in the scriptures, in no particular order. Some have been fulfilled, some are being fulfilled now, and some have yet to happen. As you go through the list, check off whether you think these signs are fulfilled, in process, or have yet to begin.

FULFILLED	IN PROCESS	NOT STARTED	
❐	❐	❐	The Book of Mormon will come forth (see Isaiah 29; Ezekiel 37; 2 Nephi 3, 27, 29)
❐	❐	❐	Israel will be gathered (see Isaiah 11:11–12; Doctrine and Covenants 45:25, 43)
❐	❐	❐	There will be wars and rumors of wars (see Matthew 24:6–7; Doctrine and Covenants 45:26)
❐	❐	❐	The whole earth will be in commotion (see Doctrine and Covenants 45:26)
❐	❐	❐	People will despair in their hearts (see Doctrine and Covenants 45:26)
❐	❐	❐	Love of men will "wax cold" (see Matthew 24:12; Doctrine and Covenants 45:27)
❐	❐	❐	The Church will progress and fill the earth (see Daniel 2:34–35; 1 Nephi 14:12)
❐	❐	❐	The Lord will pour out His spirit upon all flesh. People will begin to have visions and dreams and prophesy (see Joel 2:28–32)
❐	❐	❐	False Christs and false prophets will appear and deceive people, including some members of the Church (see JS–Matthew 1:22; Matthew 24:24)
❐	❐	❐	People will reject the truth because of the philosophies of men (see Doctrine and Covenants 45:29)
❐	❐	❐	Wickedness will spread across the world (see Doctrine and Covenants 45:27; Matthew 24:37)
❐	❐	❐	The Gentiles will have great power and influence in the world (see Doctrine and Covenants 45:30; 1 Nephi 13:13–19)
❐	❐	❐	An overflowing scourge or desolating sickness shall cover the land (see Doctrine and Covenants 45:31)
❐	❐	❐	The righteous will be persecuted (see Matthew 24:9)
❐	❐	❐	The righteous will stand in holy places and come unto Zion for protection (see Doctrine and Covenants 45:32)
❐	❐	❐	People will curse God (see Doctrine and Covenants 45:32)
❐	❐	❐	There will be earthquakes in many places (see Isaiah 24:20; Matthew 24:7; Revelation 16:18–20; Doctrine and Covenants 45:33)
❐	❐	❐	There will be famines and pestilences (see Matthew 24:7)
❐	❐	❐	People will harden their hearts against God (see Doctrine and Covenants 45:33)
❐	❐	❐	Violence and murder will abound (see Doctrine and Covenants 45:33)
❐	❐	❐	Latter-day temples of the Lord will be built (see Isaiah 2:2; Isaiah 19:19–20; Micah 4:1–7)

FULFILLED	IN PROCESS	NOT STARTED	
❐	❐	❐	The sun will be darkened (see Joel 2:31; 3:15; Matthew 24:29; Doctrine and Covenants 45:42; 133:49)
❐	❐	❐	The moon will have the color of blood (see Matthew 24:29; Doctrine and Covenants 45:42; 133:49)
❐	❐	❐	Stars will fall from heaven (see Matthew 24:29; Doctrine and Covenants 45:42; 133:49)
❐	❐	❐	A great war called Armageddon will erupt in the Middle East (see Joel 3:14; Zechariah 12:11; Revelation 16:14–21)
❐	❐	❐	The righteous Saints who have died will be resurrected and be caught up to meet Christ (see Doctrine and Covenants 45:45)
❐	❐	❐	Christ's foot will touch down on the Mount of Olives and split it (see Zechariah 14:4–7; Doctrine and Covenants 45:48)
❐	❐	❐	The gospel will be preached to every nation (see Matthew 24:14; Doctrine and Covenants 133:37)
❐	❐	❐	The Jews will return to Jerusalem and receive their promised land (see Amos 9:14; Zechariah 2:4–12; 2 Nephi 9:2)
❐	❐	❐	Christ will suddenly come to His temple (see Malachi 3:1)
❐	❐	❐	Two prophets will minister in Jerusalem for more than three years, then be killed, lie dead in the streets for three days, and then be taken up into heaven (see Revelation 11:3–11)
❐	❐	❐	Elijah the prophet will appear to turn the hearts of the fathers to the children and the children to the fathers (see Malachi 4:5–6)
❐	❐	❐	Water will flow from under the temple at Jerusalem and heal the waters of the Dead Sea (see Ezekiel 47:1–12; Zechariah 14:8)
❐	❐	❐	Pools of living water will spring up in the barren deserts (see Doctrine and Covenants 133:29)
❐	❐	❐	A great latter-day meeting with Christ, Adam, and other Saints will take place in the valley of Adam-ondi-Ahman (see Daniel 7:13–14; Doctrine and Covenants 27:5–14; 107:53–57; 116:1)
❐	❐	❐	The Lamanites will blossom as a rose (see Doctrine and Covenants 49:24–25; 2 Nephi 30:6)
❐	❐	❐	The lost ten tribes will return from the north countries (see Doctrine and Covenants 133:26–34)
❐	❐	❐	God will send angels to preach the gospel (see Revelation 14:6–7)
❐	❐	❐	People will say that Christ delays His coming (see Doctrine and Covenants 45:26)
❐	❐	❐	The city of Zion, the New Jerusalem, will be built upon the American continent (see Articles of Faith 1:10; Isaiah 4:5–6; Ether 13:8)
❐	❐	❐	A great sign will be given in heaven that all the earth shall see together (see Doctrine and Covenants 88:93)
❐	❐	❐	Christ will appear in power and glory to rule and reign over the earth (see Isaiah 63:1–4; Matthew 24:27; Doctrine and Covenants 45:44; 133:46–48)

Remember, the purposes of these signs aren't to scare us; they are to help us recognize the signs of and become more prepared for the Second Coming. As the Lord said, "If ye are prepared ye shall not fear" (Doctrine and Covenants 38:30). When the Lord told some of these signs of the Second Coming to His disciples in Jerusalem, they "were troubled. And I said unto them: Be not troubled, for, when all these things shall come to pass, *ye may know that the promises which have been made unto you shall be fulfilled*" (Doctrine and Covenants 45:34–35; emphasis added). Seeing these signs fulfilled should help us see that God is in control, that soon evil will be defeated, and that we will have the privilege of living in the Millennium with the Lord and our loved ones.

When Will the Second Coming Be?

Would you believe us if we answered, "Tomorrow"? President Joseph Fielding Smith said:

> I was asked, not long ago, if I could tell when the Lord would come. I answered, Yes; and I answer, "Yes" now. I know when he will come. He will come *tomorrow*. We have his word for it. Let me read it: ". . . For after today cometh the burning—this is speaking after the manner of the Lord—for verily I say, *tomorrow* all the proud and they that do wickedly shall be as stubble. . . ." [Doctrine and Covenants 64:24; emphasis added]. So the Lord is coming, I say, *tomorrow*. Then let us be prepared. . . . We are living in the "Saturday Evening of Time." [One day for the Lord is equal to a thousand years of our time; see Doctrine and Covenants 77:6-7.] This is the sixth day now drawing to its close. When the Lord says it is today until his coming, that, I think, is what he has in mind, for he shall come in the morning of the Sabbath, or seventh day of the earth's temporal existence, to inaugurate the millennial reign and to take his rightful place as King of kings and Lord of lords, to rule and reign upon the earth, as it is his right.[1]

We Know Exactly When the Second Coming Will Be . . . **TOMORROW!**

MONDAY	TUESDAY	WEDNESDAY	THURSDAY
4000 BC– 3000 BC	**3000 BC– 2000 BC**	**2000 BC– 1000 BC**	**1000 BC– AD 0**

FRIDAY	SATURDAY	SUNDAY
AD 0– AD 1000	AD 1000– AD 2???	Second Coming and Millennium

If the Lord is coming tomorrow, we definitely need to prepare today.

But what if Jesus really *did* come tomorrow? What would you do? Elder Dallin H. Oaks said: "What if the day of His coming were tomorrow? If we knew that we would meet the Lord tomorrow—through our premature death or through His unexpected coming—what would we do today? What confessions would we make? What practices would we discontinue? What accounts would we settle? What forgivenesses would we extend? What testimonies would we bear? If we would do those things then, why not now?"[2]

What Can I Do to Prepare for the Second Coming?

Let's look at three keys to preparing for the Second Coming:

1. **Take the Holy Spirit as our guide.**
2. **Stand in holy places.**
3. **Look to the modern prophets to discern the signs and times of the Second Coming.**

Take the Holy Spirit as Our Guide

Perhaps the best thing we can do to prepare for the Second Coming is to live so that we have the Holy Ghost with us in our daily life. We read in *True to the Faith,* "Do not concern yourself with the exact timing of the Savior's Second Coming. Instead, live so that you will be prepared whenever He comes."[3] We can know we are prepared for the Second Coming if we have the Spirit of the Lord with us. The Lord gave us this key when He said of His Second Coming: "For they that are wise and have received the truth, and *have taken the Holy Spirit for their guide,* and have not been deceived—verily I say unto you, they shall not be hewn down and cast into the fire, but shall abide the day" (Doctrine and Covenants 45:57; emphasis added). As we live worthy of the Spirit, we will be guided, strengthened, and protected in the days leading up to the Second Coming.

MORE PROTECTIVE THAN A SPACESUIT

Spacesuits are designed to prepare and protect astronauts for and from all kinds of dangers—including temperatures as low as -150 degrees Celsius (-238 degrees Fahrenheit) and a complete lack of oxygen. But when it comes to the Second Coming, the best protection and preparation comes from being led by and filled with the Holy Ghost.

Stand in Holy Places

Doctrine and Covenants 45 gives us another key to prepare for the Second Coming. The Lord said, "My disciples shall stand in holy places, and shall not be moved" (Doctrine and Covenants 45:32). Elder Dallin H. Oaks explained: "What are those 'holy places'? Surely they include the temple and its covenants faithfully kept. Surely they include a home where children are treasured and parents are respected. Surely the holy places include our posts of duty assigned by priesthood authority, including missions and callings faithfully fulfilled in branches, wards, and stakes."[4] Clearly, standing in holy places includes *not* standing in *unholy* places. By avoiding the evil that is all around us, we will have the Spirit in greater abundance. As we stand in holy places, our lives, homes, wards, and stakes will "be for a defense, and for a refuge from the storm" (Doctrine and Covenants 115:6). Stay active in the Church and in the gospel, and you will be actively ready for the Second Coming.

Holy Places

Think about the places where you have "stood" (literally—or perhaps figuratively through the Internet or other media) in the past week. Were they holy places? Were there any holy places that you should have stood in but didn't? Based on your analysis, make a plan to stand only in holy places this next week.

Invitation to Act

Look to the Modern Prophets to Discern the Signs and Times of the Second Coming

The scriptures tell us that "the Lord will come as a thief in the night" (2 Peter 3:10). Many people will be caught totally by surprise and unprepared when Jesus comes again. Anyone who tells you that they can calculate or know the hour or day of the Second Coming is leading you astray. Joseph Smith taught, "Jesus Christ never did reveal to any man the precise time that He would come. Go and read the Scriptures, and you cannot find anything that specifies the exact hour He would come; and all that say so are false teachers."[5]

However, the scriptures also tell us that although "the hour and the day no man knoweth" (Doctrine and Covenants 49:7), the faithful will not be caught totally off guard. Listen to what the Lord said to the Saints: "The coming of the Lord draweth nigh, and it overtaketh the world as a thief in the night—therefore, gird up your loins, that you may be the children of light, and that day shall not overtake you as a thief " (Doctrine and Covenants 106:4–5).

Just as a woman may not know exactly when her baby will come, because she knows the signs, she usually knows when the time is getting close.

The Apostle Paul gave an analogy of the Second Coming, likening it to a woman who is expecting to have a baby. She may not know the exact day she will deliver the child—and the day she goes into labor may be unexpected—but as she pays attention to the time and also the signs of her body, she can know for certain when the time is close (see 1 Thessalonians 5:3). Paul said, "But ye, brethren, are not in darkness, that that day [of the Second Coming] should overtake you as a thief. Ye are all the children of light, and the children of the day: we are not of the night, nor of darkness" (1 Thessalonians 5:4–5). As we become "children of light" by studying the scriptures and following the modern prophets, the Second Coming will not be a surprise to us.

We testify that the Lord will come again, and that it will be a glorious time for the faithful. Let us continue to prepare ourselves, and continue to "prepare the world for the Second Coming of the Savior."[6]

TELL ME ONE MORE TiME!

What Happens at the Second Coming?

Jesus will return to this earth to rule and reign as its King and set it right. This is called the Second Coming.

There are many "signs," or events, that the scriptures teach us must happen before the Second Coming. These signs prepare us.

The Second Coming will be tomorrow! (figuratively)

To prepare for the Second Coming as if it will be tomorrow we must (1) take the Holy Spirit as our guide; (2) stand in holy places; and (3) look to modern prophets.

Cont.

What if the Second Coming happens before I can have a family?

Some teenagers worry that they will never have the opportunity to have a family because the Second Coming will bring about the end of the world. President Boyd K. Packer said to the youth, "Sometimes you might be tempted to think as I did from time to time in my youth: 'The way things are going, the world's going to be over with. The end of the world is going to come before I get to where I should be.' Not so! You can look forward to doing it right—getting married, having a family, seeing your children and grandchildren, maybe even great-grandchildren."[7]

You in 50 years!

How does paying my tithing relate to the Second Coming?

While we might not think of tithing as being connected to the Second Coming, it is. In the Doctrine and Covenants we read, "Behold, now it is called today until the coming of the Son of Man, and verily it is a day of sacrifice, and a day for the tithing of my people; *for he that is tithed shall not be burned at his coming*" (Doctrine and Covenants 64:23; emphasis added). The Lord has promised that if we are faithful tithe payers and have the spirit of sacrifice and obedience, we will not be burned at the Second Coming.

NOTES

EPIGRAPH

Dieter F. Uchtdorf, "President Dieter F. Uchtdorf: The Reflection in the Water," *LDS Church News,* 1 November 2009; ldschurchnewsarchive.com.

CHAPTER 1: HOW CAN I INCREASE MY FAITH IN JESUS CHRIST?

1. Thomas S. Monson, "The Call to Serve," *Ensign,* November 2000, 49.
2. *True to the Faith: A Gospel Reference* (Salt Lake City: The Church of Jesus Christ of Latter-day Saints, 2004), 54.
3. Henry B. Eyring, "Spiritual Preparedness: Start Early and Be Steady," *Ensign,* November 2005, 39.
4. *Lectures on Faith* (Salt Lake City: Deseret Book, 1985), 1.
5. David A. Bednar, "Seek Learning by Faith," Address to CES Religious Educators, 3 February 2006, 2.
6. Neil L. Andersen, "Faith Is Not by Chance, but by Choice," *Ensign,* November 2015, 67.
7. James E. Talmage, *Articles of Faith* (Salt Lake City: Deseret Book, 1981), 87; emphasis added.
8. See Wayne Rice, *Hot Illustrations for Youth Talks* (Grand Rapids, Mich.: Zondervan Publishing House, 1993), 206–7.
9. See *Lectures on Faith,* 38.
10. Joseph Smith, quoted in Milton V. Backman, Jr., *Joseph Smith's First Vision: Confirming Evidences and Contemporary Accounts,* 2d ed. rev. (Salt Lake City: Bookcraft, 1980), 157.
11. Richard G. Scott, "The Sustaining Power of Faith in Times of Uncertainty and Testing," *Ensign,* May 2003, 76.
12. Bednar, "Seek Learning by Faith," 2.

CHAPTER 2: WHY SHOULD I KEEP THE COMMANDMENTS?

1. Shankar Vedantam, "Science Confirms: You Really Can't Buy Happiness," *Washington Post,* 3 July 2006, A2.
2. Dale G. Renlund, "Constructing Spiritual Stability," Brigham Young University devotional, 16 September 2014; speeches.byu.edu.
3. Bruce C. Hafen, "The Waning of Belonging," *Ensign,* October 1989, 69.
4. See E. Ann Carson, "Prisoners in 2013," available at http://www.bjs.gov/content/pub/pdf/p13.pdf.
5. Medicinenet.com; see http://www.medterms.com/script/main/art.asp?articlekey=8575.
6. Ezra Taft Benson, quoted in Donald L. Staheli, "Obedience—Life's Great Challenge," *Ensign,* May 1998, 82; emphasis added.
7. *For the Strength of Youth* (Salt Lake City: The Church of Jesus Christ of Latter-day Saints, 2001), 42.

CHAPTER 3: WHY SHOULD I LISTEN TO AND FOLLOW THE PROPHET?

1. *History of the Church of Jesus Christ of Latter-day Saints,* edited by B. H. Roberts, 2d ed., 7 vols. (Salt Lake City: The Church of Jesus Christ of Latter-day Saints, 1932–51), 5:85.
2. Joseph Smith, quoted by Wilford Woodruff, in Conference Report, April 1898, 57.
3. "The Family: A Proclamation to the World," *Ensign,* November 2010, 129.
4. "Same-Sex Marriage"; en.wikipedia.org/wiki/Same-sex_marriage.
5. "The Family: A Proclamation to the World," 102.
6. Bruce R. McConkie, "Stand Independent above All Other Creatures," *Ensign,* May 1979, 93.
7. Ibid.
8. See Jon Krakauer, *Into Thin Air: A Personal Account of the Mt. Everest Disaster* (New York: Villard, 1997).
9. Smith, quoted by William G. Nelson, in "Joseph Smith, the Prophet," *Young Woman's Journal,* December 1906, 543.
10. Wilford Woodruff, *Discourses of Wilford Woodruff,* edited by G. Homer Durham (Salt Lake City: Bookcraft, 1946), 212–13.
11. Harold B. Lee, "Closing Remarks," *Ensign,* January 1974, 128.

CHAPTER 4: HOW CAN I KNOW WHEN THE HOLY GHOST IS SPEAKING TO ME?

1. David A. Bednar, "That We May Always Have His Spirit to Be with Us," *Ensign,* May 2006, 30.

2. Spencer W. Kimball, "Revelation: The Word of the Lord to His Prophets," *Ensign,* May 1977, 78.

3. Richard G. Scott, "Using the Supernal Gift of Prayer," *Ensign,* May 2007, 9.

4. Scott, "To Acquire Spiritual Guidance," *Ensign,* November 2009, 9.

5. See http://www.thefreedictionary.com/enlighten.

6. Bednar, "That We May Always Have His Spirit to Be with Us," 30.

7. Dallin H. Oaks, "Teaching and Learning by the Spirit," *Ensign,* March 1997, 13; emphasis added.

8. Kimball, *The Teachings of Spencer W. Kimball,* ed. Edward L. Kimball (Salt Lake City: Bookcraft, 1982), 454–55.

9. Howard W. Hunter, *The Teachings of Howard W. Hunter,* ed. Clyde J. Williams (Salt Lake City: Bookcraft, 1997), 184.

10. Franklin D. Richards, "The Importance of Prayer," *Ensign,* July 1972, 66.

11. Boyd K. Packer, "Personal Revelation: The Gift, the Test, and the Promise," *Ensign,* November 1994, 61.

12. Scott, "To Acquire Spiritual Guidance," 8.

CHAPTER 5: HOW CAN I STRENGTHEN MY TESTIMONY?

1. Thomas S. Monson, "Be of Good Cheer," *Ensign,* May 2009, 92.

2. Gordon B. Hinckley, "Testimony," *Ensign,* May 1998, 69–70.

3. Robert D. Hales, "Seeking to Know God, Our Heavenly Father, and His Son, Jesus Christ," *Ensign,* November 2009, 32.

4. Ezra Taft Benson, *A Witness and a Warning* (Salt Lake City: Deseret Book, 1988), 18.

5. Benson, "I Testify," *Ensign,* November 1988, 86; emphasis added.

6. Hinckley, "The Power of the Book of Mormon," *Ensign,* June 1988, 6.

7. List adapted from Kay W. Briggs, *Brother Joseph* (Salt Lake City: Bookcraft, 1994), 13–15.

8. George Cannon, in Jeffrey R. Holland, "Safety for the Soul," *Ensign,* November 2009, 89.

9. Benson, "The Book of Mormon Is the Word of God," *Ensign,* May 1975, 64.

10. Howard W. Hunter, in Conference Report, April 1967, 115–16; emphasis added.

11. Brigham Young, in Junius F. Wells, "Historic Sketch of the Y. M. M. I. A.," *Improvement Era,* June 1925, 715.

12. Richard G. Scott, "The Power of a Strong Testimony," *Ensign,* November 2001, 87.

CHAPTER 6: WHAT IS AGENCY AND WHAT DOES IT MEAN TO ME?

1. David O. McKay, *Teachings of Presidents of the Church: David O. McKay* (Salt Lake City: The Church of Jesus Christ of Latter-day Saints, 2003), 208.

2. Guide to the Scriptures, "Agency"; scriptures.lds.org.

3. *Gospel Principles* (Salt Lake City: The Church of Jesus Christ of Latter-day Saints, 2009), 20.

4. The material in this section is drawn in part from the seminary movie *Act for Themselves* and its accompanying curriculum (available at http://www.lds.org/media-library/video/2012-08-1260-act-for-themselves).

5. Robert D. Hales, "To Act for Ourselves: The Gift and Blessings of Agency," *Ensign,* May 2006, 6.

6. *For the Strength of Youth* (Salt Lake City: The Church of Jesus Christ of Latter-day Saints, 2011), 2.

7. Ibid.

8. Paul V. Johnson, "Understanding and Living Gospel Doctrines," CES Satellite Training Broadcast, August 2003; http://si.lds.org/library/talks/training-broadcast/understanding-and-living-gospel-doctrines.

9. Harold B. Lee, "A Sure Trumpet Sound: Quotations from President Lee," *Ensign,* February 1974, 78.

10. Thomas S. Monson, "School Thy Feelings, O My Brother," *Ensign,* November 2009, 68.

11. David A. Bednar, "And Nothing Shall Offend Them," *Ensign,* November 2006, 90.

12. Lynn G. Robbins, "Finding Your Sweetheart," BYU–Idaho devotional, February 12, 2002; http://www2.byui.edu/Presentations/Transcripts/Devotionals/2002_02_12_Robbins.htm.

13. Viktor Frankl, *Man's Search for Meaning* (Boston: Beacon Press, 2006), 75.

14. *For the Strength of Youth,* 2.

15. Richard G. Scott, "He Lives," *Ensign,* November 1999, 87.

CHAPTER 7: HOW CAN I SET STANDARDS THAT WILL KEEP ME SPIRITUALLY SAFE?

1. Thomas S. Monson, "Decisions Determine Destiny," CES Fireside for Young Adults, 6 November 2005; http://www.lds.org/library/display/0,4945,538-1-3310-1,00.html.

2. Richard G. Scott, "Do What Is Right," BYU fireside, 3 March 1996; speeches.byu.edu.

3. Spencer W. Kimball, *Teachings of Spencer W. Kimball,* ed. Edward L. Kimball (Salt Lake City: Bookcraft, 1982), 164.

4. Henry B. Eyring, "Teach with Spirit to get gospel into hearts of youth," *Church News,* 15 February 2003, 5; emphasis added.

5. Scott, "To Acquire Spiritual Guidance," *Ensign,* November 2009, 8; emphasis added.

6. Scott, "Do What Is Right," *Liahona,* March 2001, 16.

7. See http://en.wikipedia.org/wiki/Lindsey_Jacobellis.

8. *For the Strength of Youth* (Salt Lake City: The Church of Jesus Christ of Latter-day Saints, 2011), 36.

9. Eyring, "Do Not Delay," *Ensign,* November 1999, 34.

CHAPTER 8: HOW CAN I BREAK BAD HABITS?

1. Richard G. Scott, "Finding the Way Back," *Ensign,* 75.

2. Thomas S. Monson, "School Thy Feelings, O My Brother," *Ensign,* November 2009, 68.

3. Scott, "Finding the Way Back," 75.

4. See "Ivan Pavlov," en.wikipedia.org.

5. Scott, "Finding the Way Back," 75.

6. See Brian Wansink, *Mindless Eating* (New York: Bantam Books, 2006), 85.

7. Scott, "Finding the Way Back," 75.

8. See Tara Parker-Pope, "What Are Friends For? A Longer Life," *New York Times,* 20 April 2009; nytimes.com.

9. David A. Bednar, "In the Strength of the Lord," *Ensign,* November 2004, 77.

10. Dallin H. Oaks, cited in "Same-Gender Attraction," newsroom.lds.org.

11. Boyd K. Packer, *That All Might Be Edified* (Salt Lake City: Deseret Book, 1982), 196.

12. L. Tom Perry, "'Thy Speech Reveals Thee,'" *New Era,* August 1986, 7.

13. Ibid.

CHAPTER 9: HOW CAN I KNOW WHEN I'VE BEEN FORGIVEN?

1. F. Burton Howard, "Repentance," *Ensign,* May 1983, 59; emphasis added.

2. *For the Strength of Youth* (Salt Lake City: The Church of Jesus Christ of Latter-day Saints, 2011), 29.

3. Jeffrey R. Holland, "'Remember Lot's Wife,'" *Brigham Young University Speeches 2008–2009,* 13 January 2009, 5; see speeches.byu.edu.

4. Dalai Lama; see http://www.achieving-life-abundance.com/inner-peace-quotes.html.

5. Henry B. Eyring, *To Draw Closer to God* (Salt Lake City: Deseret Book, 1997), 49–50.

6. See Gordon B. Hinckley, "Forgiveness," *Ensign,* November 2005, 83–84.

7. *For the Strength of Youth*, 29.

8. Richard G. Scott, "Peace of Conscience and Peace of Mind," *Ensign,* November 2004, 18.

9. Eyring, "Come unto Christ," in *Brigham Young University 1989–90 Devotional and Fireside Speeches* (Provo, Utah: University Publications, 1990), 45.

CHAPTER 10: HOW CAN I HAVE MORE MEANINGFUL PRAYERS?

1. Henry B. Eyring, "The Lord Will Multiply the Harvest," in *Teaching Seminary: Preservice Readings* (Salt Lake City: The Church of Jesus Christ of Latter-day Saints, 2004), 95.

2. David A. Bednar, "'Quick to Observe,'" BYU Devotional, 10 May 2005; speeches.byu.edu.

3. Richard G. Scott, "Learning to Recognize Answers to Prayer," *Ensign,* November 1989, 31; emphasis added.

4. Ibid., 30–31.

5. Dallin H. Oaks, "The Language of Prayer," *Ensign,* May 1993, 15.

6. F. Michael Watson, "His Servants, the Prophets," *Ensign,* May 2009, 108.

7. See Bednar, "Pray Always," *Ensign,* November 2008, 42.

8. Ibid., 42–43.

9. *The Tonight Show with Jay Leno,* 13 May 2005; http://www.flixxy.com/sms-text-messaging-vs-morse-code.htm.

10. Gordon B. Hinckley, *Teachings of Gordon B. Hinckley* (Salt Lake City: Deseret Book, 1997), 469.

11. M. Russell Ballard, *When Thou Art Converted* (Salt Lake City: Deseret Book, 2001), 67.

12. Matthew Eyring, in Gerald N. Lund, "Elder Henry B. Eyring: Molded by 'Defining Influences,'" *Ensign,* September 1995, 15.

13. Bruce R. McConkie, *Mormon Doctrine* (Salt Lake City: Bookcraft, 1966), 586.

14. J. Reuben Clark, Jr., in Conference Report, October 1944, 160; emphasis added.

15. Boyd K. Packer, "Prayer and Promptings," *Ensign,* November 2009, 46.

16. H. Burke Peterson, "Adversity and Prayer," *Ensign,* January 1974, 19.

17. Henry B. Eyring, *To Draw Closer to God* (Salt Lake City: Deseret Book, 1997), 70; emphasis added.

CHAPTER 11: WHY SHOULD I FAST?

1. Plato, *Laws,* Book I, section 626E.

2. *For the Strength of Youth* (Salt Lake City: The Church of Jesus Christ of Latter-day Saints, 2011), 39.

3. *Gospel Principles* (Salt Lake City: The Church of Jesus Christ of Latter-day Saints, 1997), 165.

4. See Richard G. Scott, "We Love You—Please Come Back," *Ensign,* May 1986, 10–12.

5. David O. McKay, *Pathways to Happiness: Inspirational Discourses of David O. McKay* (Salt Lake City: Bookcraft, 1957), 120.

6. Joseph B. Wirthlin, "The Law of the Fast," *Ensign,* May 2001, 73.

7. See Spencer J. Condie, "Becoming a Great Benefit to Our Fellow Beings," *Ensign,* May 2002, 44–46.

8. See World Resource Institute, wri.org.

9. "Frequently Asked Questions," http://www.freerice.com/faq.html.

10. Wirthlin, "The Law of the Fast," 74.

11. See *For the Strength of Youth,* 35.

12. *History of the Church of Jesus Christ of Latter-day Saints,* edited by B. H. Roberts, 2d ed., 7 vols. (Salt Lake City: The Church of Jesus Christ of Latter-day Saints, 1932–51), 7:413; spelling standardized.

13. Gordon B. Hinckley, "The State of the Church," *Ensign,* May 1991, 52–53.

14. See http://www.squidoo.com/world-hunger.

15. *For the Strength of Youth,* 39.

CHAPTER 12: WHY SHOULD I HONOR MY PARENTS?

1. *Expenditures on Children by Families, 2007,* United States Department of Agriculture, March 2008, 20.

2. Russell M. Nelson, "Listen to Learn," *Ensign,* May 1991, 22–23.

3. Gordon B. Hinckley, "Some Lessons I Learned as a Boy," *Ensign,* May 1993, 59.

4. Thomas S. Monson, "Be Thou an Example," *Ensign,* May 2005, 112.

5. M. Russell Ballard, *When Thou Art Converted* (Salt Lake City: Deseret Book, 2001), 203.

6. Ezra Taft Benson, "To the Young Women of the Church," *Ensign,* November 1986, 81.

7. Benson, "To the Elderly in the Church," *Ensign,* November 1989, 6.

CHAPTER 13: WHY SHOULD I BE GRATEFUL?

1. Joseph Smith, quoted in Ezra Taft Benson, *God, Family, Country* (Salt Lake City: Deseret Book, 1974), 199.

2. See Chad M. Burton and Laura A. King, "The health benefits of writing about intensely positive experiences," *Journal of Research in Personality* 38, no. 2 (2004): 150–63.

3. Joseph B. Wirthlin, *Press On* (Salt Lake City: Deseret Book, 2007), 218.

4. *For the Strength of Youth* (Salt Lake City: The Church of Jesus Christ of Latter-day Saints, 2011), 18.

5. Wirthlin, *Press On*, 218.

6. Marvin J. Ashton, "And in Everything Give Thanks," 1 September 1991; speeches.byu.edu.

7. Henry B. Eyring, "Remembrance and Gratitude," *Ensign,* November 1989, 12.

8. Wirthlin, *Press On,* 224.

9. Ibid.

10. International Literacy Day, 7 September 2001, "Facts about Illiteracy," http://www.sil.org/literacy/LitFacts.htm.

11. Wirthlin, *Press On*, 218.

12. Ashton, "And in Everything Give Thanks," 5.

13. Gordon B. Hinckley, in Conference Report, October 1964, 117.

14. Hinckley, "A Prophet's Counsel and Prayer for Youth," *Ensign,* January 2001, 4.

15. Ibid.

CHAPTER 14: HOW CAN I GET MORE FROM MY SCRIPTURE STUDY?

1. Howard W. Hunter, "Reading the Scriptures," *Ensign,* November 1979, 64.

2. *Preach My Gospel* (Salt Lake City: The Church of Jesus Christ of Latter-day Saints, 2004), 17.

3. Bruce R. McConkie, *A New Witness for the Articles of Faith* (Salt Lake City: Deseret Book, 1985), 399; emphasis added.

4. M. Russell Ballard, "'Be Strong in the Lord and in the Power of His Might,'" BYU fireside, 3 March 2002; speeches.byu.edu.

5. Hunter, "Reading the Scriptures," 64.

6. Anthony Sweat, "Reading Motivation: Factors Influencing Daily Scripture Study," unpublished paper for Utah State University, Logan, Utah, 2004, 12.

7. Ballard, *When Thou Art Converted* (Salt Lake City: Deseret Book, 2001), 68.

8. First Presidency Letter, "Strengthening Families," 11 February 1999; http://www.lds.org/pa/display/0,17884,5154-1,00.html.

9. Henry B. Eyring, *To Draw Closer to God* (Salt Lake City: Deseret Book, 1997), 151.

10. See Ann M. Dibb, "Hold On," *Ensign,* November 2009, 79.

11. David A. Bednar, "Understanding the Importance of Scripture Study," Ricks College devotional, 6 January 1998; http://www.byui.edu/Presentations/Transcripts/Devotionals/1998_01_06_Bednar.htm.

12. Jeffrey R. Holland, *Summer 1992 CES Satellite Broadcast* (Salt Lake City: The Church of Jesus Christ of Latter-day Saints, 1992), 4.

13. D. Todd Christofferson, "When Thou Art Converted," *Ensign,* May 2004, 11.

14. *Preach My Gospel,* 22.

CHAPTER 15: HOW CAN I KEEP THE SABBATH DAY HOLY?

1. See John Wells, in Conference Report, October 1927, 135.

2. *For the Strength of Youth* (Salt Lake City: The Church of Jesus Christ of Latter-day Saints, 2011), 8.

3. David A. Bednar, "'Heartfelt and Willing Obedience,'" BYU–Idaho Campus Education Week devotional, 27 June 2002; http://www.byui.edu/Presentations/transcripts/educationweek/2002_06_27_bednar.htm.

4. *For the Strength of Youth,* 8.

5. Dallin H. Oaks, *Life's Lessons Learned* (Salt Lake City: Deseret Book, 2011), 24.

6. Henry B. Eyring, "Education for Real Life," CES Fireside for Young Adults, 6 May 2001; http://www.lds.org.

7. Ibid.

8. Joseph Fielding Smith, in Conference Report, October 1927, 143.

9. *For the Strength of Youth,* 33.

10. Ibid., 32–33.

11. Ibid., 32.

12. Ibid., 31.

13. Russell M. Nelson, "The Sabbath Is a Delight," *Ensign,* May 2015, 130.

CHAPTER 16: WHY SHOULD I KEEP THE WORD OF WISDOM?

1. Larissa Hirsch, "Smoking," August 2007, http://www.kidshealth.org/teen/drug_alcohol/tobacco/smoking.html; photos courtesy of American Lung Association.

2. See "Alcohol Facts and Statistics" at http://www.niaaa.nih.gov/alcohol-health/overview-alcohol-consumption/alcohol-facts-and-statistics.

3. See "Smoking," http://en.wikipedia.org/wiki/Image:Cancer_smoking_lung_cancer_correlation_from_NIH.svg.

4. James E. Enstrom, "Health practices and cancer mortality among active California Mormons," *J. Natl. Cancer Inst.* 81, no. 23 (6 December 1989): 1807–14.

5. Heber J. Grant, in *Teachings of the Presidents of the Church: Heber J. Grant* (Salt Lake City: The Church of Jesus Christ of Latter-day Saints, 2002), 192.

6. Brigham Young, in *Teachings of the Presidents of the Church: Brigham Young* (Salt Lake City: The Church of Jesus Christ of Latter-day Saints, 1997), 212.

7. See http://www.drawyourline.com/harms/effects-on-the-brain; photos of brain scans by Dr. Daniel Amen, http://www.amenclinic.com.

8. See "Consequences of Underage Alcohol Use," http://ncadi.samhsa.gov/govpubs/rpo992.

9. The NHSDA Report, "Academic Performance and Youth Substance Use," 6 September 2002; http://www.oas.samhsa.gov/2k2/academics/academics.htm.

10. Anonymous, "Addiction Is," 16 September 2001; addictionis.org.

11. Boyd K. Packer, "The Word of Wisdom: The Principle and the Promises," *Ensign,* May 1996, 19.

12. George Albert Smith, *The Teachings of George Albert Smith,* ed. Robert K. McIntosh (Salt Lake City: Deseret Book, 1996), 103.

13. Grant, in *Teachings of Presidents of the Church: Heber J. Grant*, 192–93.

14. Joseph F. Smith, in *Teachings of Presidents of the Church: Joseph F. Smith* (Salt Lake City: The Church of Jesus Christ of Latter-day Saints, 1998), 324.

15. For an expanded discussion on this question and a great story about alcohol and eating manure, see "Questions and Answers," *New Era,* June 2008, 16–17.

16. Quoted in "Policies and Procedures," *New Era,* May 1972, 50.

17. See Thomas J. Boud, "The Energy Drink Epidemic," *Ensign,* December 2008, 49–52; see also Russell Wilcox, "Energy Drinks: The Lift That Lets You Down," *New Era,* December 2008, 30–33.

18. See James O'Keefe and Joan O'Keefe, *The Forever Young Diet and Lifestyle* (New York: Andrews McMeel, 2006), 233.

19. Thomas S. Monson, "True to the Faith," *Ensign,* May 2006, 19.

20. See http://www.statista.com/statistics/275525/us-dollar-sales-of-energy-drink-beverages-and-shots.

21. See http://www.caffeineinformer.com/is-energy-drink-overdose-in-teens-really-a-problem.

CHAPTER 17: WHY SHOULD I DRESS MODESTLY?

1. Thomas S. Monson, "Peace, Be Still," *Ensign,* November 2002, 53.

2. See http://www.yourdictionary.com/modesty.

3. Robert D. Hales, "Modesty: Reverence for the Lord," *Ensign,* August 2008, 35.

4. *For the Strength of Youth* (Salt Lake City: The Church of Jesus Christ of Latter-day Saints, 2011), 7.

5. Dallin H. Oaks, "The Aaronic Priesthood and the Sacrament," *Ensign,* November 1998, 39.

6. Jeffrey R. Holland, "'This Do in Remembrance of Me,'" *Ensign,* November 1995, 68.

7. Oaks, "Pornography," *Ensign,* May 2005, 90; emphasis added.

8. Jill C. Manning, *What's the Big Deal about Pornography?* (Salt Lake City: Shadow Mountain, 2008), 82.

9. Holland, "To Young Women," *Ensign,* November 2005, 29–30; emphasis added.

10. *For the Strength of Youth,* 6.

11. Ibid., 6–7.

CHAPTER 18: WHY SHOULDN'T I DATE UNTIL I'M 16?

1. International Communications Research National Omnibus Survey, "Parents of Teens and Teens Discuss Sex, Love, and Relationships: Polling Data," April 1998; http://www.icrsurvey.com/Study.aspx?f=Teenpreg.html.

2. *For the Strength of Youth* (Salt Lake City: The Church of Jesus Christ of Latter-day Saints, 2011), 4.

3. Carrie P. Jenkins, "Making Moral Choices," *BYU Today,* April 1985, 39.

4. Bruce Monson, "Speaking of Kissing," *New Era,* June 2001, 36.

5. Spencer W. Kimball, *The Miracle of Forgiveness* (Salt Lake City: Bookcraft, 1969), 223.

6. See Kate Fogarty, "Teens and Dating: Tips for Parents and Professionals," University of Florida IAF Extension; http://edis.ifas.ufl.edu/fy851.

7. See Claudia Wallis and Kristina Dell, "What Makes Teens Tick," *Time Magazine,* 10 May 2004; time.com.

8. *For the Strength of Youth*, ii.

9. See Deborah A. Cohen et al., "When and Where Do Youths Have Sex?" *Pediatrics* 110, no. 6 (December 2002): 2.

10. See Monson, "Speaking of Kissing," 36.

11. See Cohen, "When and Where Do Youths Have Sex?" 2.

CHAPTER 19: WHY SHOULDN'T I STEADY DATE IN HIGH SCHOOL?

1. Larry R. Lawrence, "Courageous Parenting," *Ensign,* November 2010, 99.

2. Bruce Monson, "Speaking of Kissing," *New Era,* June 2001, 36.

3. *For the Strength of Youth* (Salt Lake City: The Church of Jesus Christ of Latter-day Saints, 2011), 36.

4. Gordon B. Hinckley, "A Prophet's Council and Prayer for Youth," *New Era,* January 2001, 13; emphasis added.

5. Spencer W. Kimball, *Teachings of Spencer W. Kimball,* ed. Edward L. Kimball (Salt Lake City: Bookcraft, 1982), 287–88; emphasis added.

6. Larry Elder, "Kids, Guns, and Dr. Phil," *WorldNetDaily,* 28 November 2002; http://www.worldnetdaily.com/news/article.asp?ARTICLE_ID=29811; emphasis added.

7. Kimball, *The Miracle of Forgiveness* (Salt Lake City: Bookcraft, 1969), 66; emphasis added.

8. See *Adolescent Brain Development: Vulnerabilities and Opportunities,* eds. Ronald E. Dahl and Linda Patia Spear (New York: The New York Academy of Sciences, 2004).

9. John Fetto, "First Comes Love," *American Demographics,* 1 June 2003; http://findarticles.com/p/articles/mi_m4021/is_5_25/ai_102102599/pg_1.

10. Kate Fogarty, "Teens and Dating: Tips for Parents and Professionals," University of Florida IAF Extension; http://edis.ifas.ufl.edu/fy851.

11. Ibid.

12. "Inside the Teenage Brain: Interview: Deborah Yurgelun-Todd"; pbs.org; photo courtesy of Dr. Deborah Yurgelun-Todd.

13. Ibid.

14. *For the Strength of Youth*, 4.

15. Boyd K. Packer, "You're in the Driver's Seat," *New Era,* June 2004, 8.

16. Hinckley, "A Prophet's Council and Prayer for Youth," 13.

17. Ezra Taft Benson, "To the Young Women of the Church," *Ensign,* November 1986, 82–83; emphasis added.

18. Anonymous, http://dearelder.com/index/inc_name/dear_john_display; read more "Dear John" letters at the same site.

19. "Dating FAQs," *New Era,* April 2004, 24.

CHAPTER 20: WHY SHOULD I BE SEXUALLY PURE?

1. *For the Strength of Youth* (Salt Lake City: The Church of Jesus Christ of Latter-day Saints, 2011), 4.

2. Ibid., 4.

3. Ibid.

4. Ezra Taft Benson, "The Law of Chastity," *New Era*, January 1988, 4–5.

5. *For the Strength of Youth*, 35.

6. Ibid.

7. See ibid., 36.

8. Ibid., 4.

9. Gordon B. Hinckley, "Some Thoughts on Temples, Retention of Converts, and Missionary Service," *Ensign,* November 1997, 51.

10. Benson, "The Law of Chastity," 5.

11. *For the Strength of Youth*, 11–12.

12. Jeffrey R. Holland, "Personal Purity," *Ensign,* November 1998, 76.

13. Richard G. Scott, "Making the Right Choices," 13 January 2002; speeches.byu.edu.

14. Holland, "Personal Purity," 76.

15. *For the Strength of Youth,* 6–7.

16. Holland, "Personal Purity," 76.

17. Hinckley, "To the Women of the Church," *Ensign,* November 2003, 115.

18. *For the Strength of Youth*, 25.

19. Ibid., 26.

20. Hinckley, address to CES religious educators, February 2003, 3; see also D&C 10:5.

21. See Lawrence K. Altman, "Sex Infections Found in Quarter of Teenage Girls," *New York Times,* 12 March 2008; nytimes.com.

22. See "Fragile Families Research Brief," *Parents' Relationship Status Five Years after a Non-Marital Birth,* no. 39 (June 2007): 1–4; http://www.fragilefamilies.princeton.edu/briefs/ResearchBrief39.pdf.

23. "Out of Wedlock Pregnancy Fact Sheet," http://firstthings.org/page/research/out-of-wedlock-pregnancy-fact-sheet.

24. "The Family: A Proclamation to the World," *Ensign,* November 2010, 129.

25. David A. Bednar, "We Believe in Being Chaste," *Ensign,* May 2013, 44.

26. *For the Strength of Youth*, 36.

27. Ibid.

28. Ibid., 35.

29. "The Family: A Proclamation to the World," 129.

30. See Holland, "Personal Purity," 75–78.

CHAPTER 21: WHY IS SAME-SEX MARRIAGE CONTRARY TO GOD'S ETERNAL PLAN?

1. "The Divine Institution of Marriage," http://newsroom.lds.org/article/the-divine-institution-of-marriage.

2. See Aaron Falk and Scott Taylor, "Mormon church supports Salt Lake City's protections for gay rights," *Deseret News,* 11 November 2009; deseretnews.com.

3. Russell M. Nelson, "Let Your Faith Show," *Ensign,* May 2014, 31; emphasis added.

4. "The Family: A Proclamation to the World," *Ensign,* November 2010, 129.

5. Robert D. Hales, "General Conference: Strengthening Faith and Testimony," *Ensign,* November 2013, 7.

6. David A. Bednar, "Marriage Is Essential to His Eternal Plan," *Ensign,* June 2006, 82–83.

7. *Handbook 2: Administering the Church* (Salt Lake City: The Church of Jesus Christ of Latter-day Saints, 2010), 3.

8. "The Family: A Proclamation to the World," 129.

9. "The Divine Institution of Marriage."

10. *History of The Church of Jesus Christ of Latter-day Saints,* 7 vols., edited by B. H. Roberts (Salt Lake City: The Church of Jesus Christ of Latter-day Saints, 1932–51), 5:391.

11. *God Loveth His Children* [manual] (Salt Lake City: The Church of Jesus Christ of Latter-day Saints, 2007); https://www.lds.org/manual/god-loveth-his-children/god-loveth-his-children.

12. "First Presidency Statement on Same-Gender Marriage," 20 October 2004; mormonnewsroom.org.

13. "The Family: A Proclamation to the World," 129.

14. Ibid.; emphasis added.

15. "Interview with Elder Dallin H. Oaks and Elder Lance B. Wickman: 'Same-Gender Attraction'"; mormonnewsroom.org.

16. See http://www.ldsliving.com/Elder-Holland-Talks-Candidly-About-Same-Sex-Attraction-Marriage-Pornography-More/s/81526.

17. Dallin H. Oaks, "Truth and Tolerance," CES Devotional for Young Adults, 11 September 2011; http://www.lds.org/broadcasts/article/ces-devotionals/2011/01/truth-and-tolerance.

18. The language in this paragraph has been adapted from the article, "'But If Not'—A Lesson on Faith from Shadrach, Meshach, and Abednego"; https://www.mormon.org/blog/but-if-not-a-lesson-on-faith.

19. The LDS handbook of instructions for leaders of local congregations says that those "whose circumstances do not allow them to receive the blessings of eternal marriage and parenthood in this life will receive all promised blessings in the eternities, provided they keep the covenants they have made with God" (*Handbook 2: Administering the Church* [Salt Lake City: The Church of Jesus Christ of Latter-day Saints, 2010], 4).

20. "Interview with Elder Dallin H. Oaks and Elder Lance B. Wickman: 'Same-Gender Attraction.'"

21. See mormonsandgays.org.

22. Jeffrey R. Holland, "Helping Those Who Struggle with Same-Gender Attraction," *Ensign,* October 2007, 42; emphasis added.

23. See the home page at mormonsandgays.org.

24. See Sarah McBride, "Mozilla CEO resigns, opposition to gay marriage drew fire," Reuters News Agency, 3 April 2014; reuters.com.

25. "The Divine Institution of Marriage."

26. "Interview with Elder Dallin H. Oaks and Elder Lance B. Wickman: 'Same-Gender Attraction.'"

27. See http://www.mormonnewsroom.org/article/the-divine-institution-of-marriage.

28. "The Family: A Proclamation to the World," 129.

29. Ibid.

30. See http://www.mormonnewsroom.org/article/church-mormon-responds-to-human-rights-campaign-petition-same-sex-attraction.

31. Quentin L. Cook, cited in "Love One Another: A Discussion on Same-Sex Attraction," mormonsandgays.org.

32. Holland, "The Cost—and Blessings—of Discipleship," *Ensign,* May 2014, 6.

33. Neil L. Andersen, "Spiritual Whirlwinds," *Ensign,* May 2014, 19.

34. Holland, "The Cost—and Blessings—of Discipleship," 9.

CHAPTER 22: WHY CAN'T I WATCH WHATEVER I WANT?

1. Henry B. Eyring, "We Must Raise Our Sights," CES Symposium, Brigham Young University, 14 August 2001, 1; emphasis added.

2. See "NOAA Scientists Able to Measure Tsunami Height from Space," 10 January 2005, noaanews.noaa.gov; photos courtesy of DigitalGlobe Inc.

3. See http://www.pewinternet.org/2015/04/09/teens-social-media-technology-2015.

4. *For the Strength of Youth* (Salt Lake City: The Church of Jesus Christ of Latter-day Saints, 2011), 11.

5. Parents Television Council, "Facts and TV Statistics," parentstv.org.

6. See Randal Wright, 25 *Mistakes LDS Parents Make and How to Avoid Them* (Salt Lake City: Deseret Book Distributors, 2007), 95.

7. See Malcolm Gladwell, *Blink: The Power of Thinking without Thinking* (New York: Little Brown & Company, 2005), 53–55.

8. See Committee on Communications, "Media Violence," *Pediatrics* 95, no. 6 (June 1995).

9. See "Addictive Behaviors," commonsensemedia.org.

10. Russell M. Nelson, "Addiction or Freedom," *Ensign,* November 1988, 8; emphasis added.

11. Dallin H. Oaks, "Pornography," *Ensign,* May 2005, 88.

12. *For the Strength of Youth*, 11.

13. Ibid.

CHAPTER 23: HOW CAN I RESIST AND OVERCOME PORNOGRAPHY?

1. Richard G. Scott, "The Sanctity of Womanhood," *Ensign,* May 2000, 37.

2. H. David Burton, "Honoring the Priesthood," *Ensign,* May 2000, 39.

3. Julie B. Beck, "Teaching the Doctrine of the Family," Seminaries and Institutes of Religion Satellite Training Broadcast, 4 August 2009; http://www.lds.org/pa/rs/pdf/CES_2009_Beck_eng.pdf.

4. See http://www.haverford.edu/biology/edwards/disease/viral_essays/redicanvirus.htm.

5. Name withheld, "Addicted to Romance Novels?" *Ensign,* July 2003, 59.

6. Joseph Smith, *Teachings of the Prophet Joseph Smith,* sel. Joseph Fielding Smith (Salt Lake City: Deseret Book, 1976), 181.

7. *For the Strength of Youth* (Salt Lake City: The Church of Jesus Christ of Latter-day Saints, 2011), 12.

8. Jeffrey R. Holland, "Personal Purity," *Ensign,* November 1998, 76.

9. LDS Bible Dictionary, 613, 614.

10. *For the Strength of Youth,* 12.

11. Gordon B. Hinckley, "Some Thoughts on Temple, Retention of Converts, and Missionary Service," *Ensign,* November 1997, 51.

12. List adapted from Dallin H. Oaks, "Pornography," *Ensign,* May 2005, 87; Gordon B. Hinckley "A Tragic Evil among Us," *Ensign,* November 2004, 59–62; Scott, "The Sanctity of Womanhood," 36–38; and *For the Strength of Youth,* 17–19.

13. See "Pornography Addiction May Cause Brain Damage in Kids," *Jakarta Globe,* November 2009, 15–21; addictions awareness.com.

14. Thomas S. Monson, "Pornography, the Deadly Carrier," *Ensign,* July 2001, 2.

15. Scott, "How Can I Find Happiness?" radio.lds.org.

16. Hinckley, "Closing Remarks," *Ensign,* May 2005, 102.

17. M. Russell Ballard, "Be Strong in the Lord, and in the Power of His Might," 3 March 2002; speeches.byu.edu.

18. *Let Virtue Garnish Thy Thoughts* (Salt Lake City: The Church of Jesus Christ of Latter-day Saints, 2006), 4.

19. Oaks, "Pornography," 90.

20. Joseph B. Wirthlin, "Press On," *Ensign,* November 2004, 102.

21. Hinckley, "A Tragic Evil among Us," *Ensign,* November 2004, 59.

CHAPTER 24: WHY SHOULD I USE CLEAN LANGUAGE?

1. Gordon B. Hinckley, "'I Am Clean,'" *Ensign,* May 2007, 62.

2. Leland Gregory, *Idiots at Work* (New York: Andrews McMeel, 2004), 120, 193, 195.

3. See Lenore Sandel, *The Relationship between Language and Intelligence,* Review of Historical Research: Summary #5, April 1998.

4. *For the Strength of Youth* (Salt Lake City: The Church of Jesus Christ of Latter-day Saints, 2011), 20.

5. Henry B. Eyring, "God Helps the Faithful Priesthood Holder," *Ensign,* November 2007, 58.

6. See David Whitmer, in B. H. Roberts, *A Comprehensive History of The Church of Jesus Christ of Latter-day Saints,* 6 vols. (Salt Lake City: The Church of Jesus Christ of Latter-day Saints, 1930), 1:131.

7. *For the Strength of Youth,* 20–21.

8. Spencer W. Kimball, "President Kimball Speaks Out on Profanity," *New Era,* January 1981, 4.

9. *For the Strength of Youth,* 22.

10. Bruce C. Hafen, *A Disciple's Life* (Salt Lake City: Deseret Book, 2002), 148.

11. Neal A. Maxwell, "The Pathway of Discipleship," *Ensign,* September 1998, 10.

12. Author unknown, quoted in Vaughn J. Featherstone, "The Last Drop in the Chalice," 24 September 1985; speeches.byu.edu.

13. *For the Strength of Youth,* 20.

CHAPTER 25: WHY DOES THE MUSIC I LISTEN TO MATTER?

1. Britney Spears, quoted in Michelle Tauber, "Britney's Big Break," *People Magazine,* 21 August 2002, 3.

2. See Kristopher Kaliebe and Adrian Sondheimer, "The Media: Relationships to Psychiatry and Children," *Academic Psychiatry* 26, no. 3 (September 2002): 210.

3. *For the Strength of Youth* (Salt Lake City: The Church of Jesus Christ of Latter-day Saints, 2011), 22.

4. Ibid.; emphasis added.

5. Boyd K. Packer, "The Instrument of Your Mind and the Foundation of Your Character," 2 February 2003; speeches.byu.edu.

6. Snoop Dogg, thinkexist.com.

7. Marilyn Manson and Neil Strauss, *The Long Hard Road Out of Hell* (New York: HarperCollins, 1998), 265.

8. "First Presidency Preface," in *Hymns of The Church of Jesus Christ of Latter-day Saints* (Salt Lake City: The Church of Jesus Christ of Latter-day Saints, 1985), x.

9. Jessica Simpson, brainyquote.com.

10. See Gene R. Cook, "Ways to Avoid Discouragement," BYU–Idaho devotional, 29 November 1988.

11. Tara Parker-Pope, "For Clues on Teenage Sex, Experts Look to Hip-Hop," *New York Times,* 6 November 2007; nytimes.com.

12. Trent Reznor, "Hurt," in *The Downward Spiral,* audio CD (TVT/Interscope Records, 1994).

13. See Randal Wright, *25 Mistakes LDS Parents Make and How to Avoid Them* (Salt Lake City: Deseret Book Distributors, 2007), 80.

14. Madonna, in J. Randy Taraborrelli, *Madonna: An Intimate Biography* (New York: Simon & Schuster, 2001), 8.

15. For one study, see Sophia Turczynewycz, Eric McGary, Ashlae Shepler, Laura Fink, and John Drain, "Rock On! The Cognitive Effects of Music," 19 April 2002; http://jrscience.wcp.muohio.edu/nsfall01/FinalArticles/Draft1.RockOnTheCognitive.html.

16. Gary Toms, "Hip-Hop's Negative Impact on Kids," 1 August 2006; associatedcontent.com.

17. 50 Cent, thinkexist.com.

18. See Frances Rauscher and Gordon Shaw, *Neurological Research* 19, no. 1 (February 1997).

19. *For the Strength of Youth,* 20.

20. Sharon G. Larsen, "Your Celestial Guide," *Ensign,* May 2001, 87.

CHAPTER 26: HOW CAN I SMARTLY USE MY DIGITAL DEVICE?

1. Kelly Wallace, "Teens spend a 'mind-boggling' 9 hours a day using media, report says," *CNN.com,* 3 November 2015; cnn.com.

2. "Average person now spends more time on their phone and laptop than SLEEPING, study claims"; dailymail.co.uk.

3. Wallace, "Teens spend a 'mind-boggling' 9 hours a day using media, report says."

4. Randall L. Ridd, "The Choice Generation," *Ensign,* May 2014, 58.

5. Robert Hackett, "Here's how teens really use their phones," *Fortune,* 27 May 2015; fortune.com.

6. "Cognitive control in media multitaskers," *Journalist's Resource,* 1 August 2011; journalistsresource.org.

7. "Go Forward with Faith," in *For the Strength of Youth* (Salt Lake City: The Church of Jesus Christ of Latter-day Saints, 2011), 43.

8. M. Russell Ballard, "Be Still and Know That I Am God," CES Devotional for Young Adults, 4 May 2014; https://www.lds.org /broadcasts/article/ces-devotionals/2014/01/be-still-and-know-that-i-am-god.

9. Ibid.

10. José A. Teixeira, "Seeking the Lord," *Ensign,* May 2015, 98.

11. "The Family: A Proclamation to the World," *Ensign,* November 2010, 129.

12. David A. Bednar, "To Sweep the Earth as with a Flood," Brigham Young University Campus Education Week address, 19 August 2014; https://www.lds.org/prophets-and-apostles/unto-all-the-world/to-sweep-the-earth-as-with-a-flood.

13. David O. McKay, in Conference Report, October 1966, 4.

14. Dr. Sylvia Hart Frejd, "Nomophobia: The Fear of Being Without Your Smart Phone," American Association of Christian Counselors; aacc.net.

15. Ibid.

16. See Dr. James Roberts' book *Too Much of a Good Thing* (Austin, TX: Sentia Publishing, 2015).

17. Herb Scribner, "Your teen's new favorite drug—their smartphone," *Deseret News National Edition,* 19 September 2015; national.deseretnews.com.

18. Wallace, "How to cut your kids' cell phone addiction."

19. See Charlotte Hilton Andersen, "Cell Phone Addiction Is So Real People Are Going to Rehab for It," *Shape,* 11 May 2015.

20. See Erin Cotter, "Teens and tech: what happens when students give up smartphones?" *The Guardian,* 23 April 2015; theguardian.com; and Chris Berdik, "A class of teenagers gave up smartphones for a week, and lived," *The Hechinger Report,* 10 June 2015; hechingerreport.org.

21. See "Language," in *For the Strength of Youth,* 21.

22. See "Entertainment and Media," in *For the Strength of Youth,* 13.

23. See http://www.latterdaysaintwoman.com/would_your_pinterest_page_pass_the_bonnie_oscarson_test/#more-28.

24. Bednar, "To Sweep the Earth as with a Flood."

25. See Jenny Awford, "The shocking 'text neck' X-rays that show how children as young as SEVEN are becoming hunch-backs because of their addiction to smart phones," *Daily Mail,* 15 October 2015; dailymail.co.uk.

26. See Lindsey Bever, "'Text neck' is becoming an 'epidemic' and could wreck your spine," *Washington Post,* 20 November 2014; washingtonpost.com.

CHAPTER 27: WHY DOES IT MATTER WHO MY FRIENDS ARE?

1. *For the Strength of Youth* (Salt Lake City: The Church of Jesus Christ of Latter-day Saints, 2011), 16.

2. See Philippe G. Schyns and Aude Oliva, "Dr. Angry and Mr. Smile," *Cognition* 69 (1999): 243–65; photo courtesy of Philippe Schyns.

3. Quoted in Brent L. Top and Bruce A. Chadwick, *10 Secrets Wise Parents Know* (Salt Lake City: Deseret Book, 2004), 83.

4. See Top and Chadwick, "Helping Teens Stay Strong," *Ensign,* March 1999, 27–34.

5. Thomas S. Monson, "Pioneers All," *Ensign,* May 1997, 94–95.

6. Monson, "Keep the Commandments," *Ensign,* November 2015, 84.

7. *For the Strength of Youth*, 16.

8. Ibid., 17.

9. Ibid.

10. Henry B. Eyring, "Hearts Bound Together," *Ensign,* May 2005, 77.

11. *For the Strength of Youth*, 16.

CHAPTER 28: HOW CAN I HELP FRIENDS AND FAMILY WHO ARE STRUGGLING WITH SERIOUS PROBLEMS?

1. Harold B. Lee, "Stand Ye in Holy Places," *Ensign,* July 1973, 123.

2. *For the Strength of Youth* (Salt Lake City: The Church of Jesus Christ of Latter-day Saints, 2011), 16.

3. Richard G. Scott, "Healing Your Damaged Life," *Ensign,* November 1992, 62.

4. Neal A. Maxwell, *All These Things Shall Give Thee Experience* (Salt Lake City: Deseret Book, 2007), 72, 81.

5. Robert L. Simpson, "'Strengthen Thy Brethren,'" *Ensign,* December 1971, 103.

6. See Scott, "Now Is the Time to Serve a Mission!" *Ensign*, May 2006, 89.

7. See Spencer J. Condie, *Russell M. Nelson: Father, Surgeon, Apostle* (Salt Lake City: Deseret Book, 203), 26.

8. See Henry B. Eyring, "Elder David A. Bednar: Going Forward in the Strength of the Lord," *Ensign,* March 2005, 17.

9. Scott, "To Help a Loved One in Need," *Ensign,* May 1988, 61.

CHAPTER 29: HOW CAN I STAY FAITHFUL WHEN LIFE IS HARD?

1. Nick Vujicic, "Life without Limbs," lifewithoutlimbs.org.

2. Spencer W. Kimball, *The Teachings of Spencer W. Kimball,* ed. Edward L. Kimball (Salt Lake City: Bookcraft, 1982), 38–39.

3. Boyd K. Packer, "The Choice," *Ensign,* November 1980, 21; emphasis added.

4. Richard G. Scott, "Trust in the Lord," *Ensign,* November 1995, 17.

5. Ibid.

6. Orson F. Whitney, quoted in Spencer W. Kimball, *Faith Precedes the Miracle* (Salt Lake City: Deseret Book, 1978), 98.

7. Scott, "Trust in the Lord," 16.

8. Joseph B. Wirthlin, "The Unspeakable Gift," *Ensign,* May 2003, 26.

9. Wirthlin, "'Choose the Right,'" BYU fireside, 4 September 1994; speeches.byu.edu.

10. See http://www.heartlandlibraries.org/news&clues/archive/S2002/columns.html.

11. "Seeing Burgon: Blind, deaf teen lives her life to the fullest," *Deseret News,* 20 September 2009; deseretnews.com.

12. See Rich Bayer, "Gratitude and Mental Wellness," http://www.upperbay.org/articles/gratitude%20and%20mental%20wellness.pdf, 16.

13. See Catherine Price, "Stumbling Toward Gratitude," The Greater Good Science Center, Summer 2007, peacecenter.berkeley.edu.

14. Jeffrey R. Holland, "The Tongue of Angels," *Ensign,* May 2007, 18.

15. Henry B. Eyring, "Mountains to Climb," *Ensign,* May 2012, 26.

CHAPTER 30: HOW CAN I SET MEANINGFUL PERSONAL GOALS?

1. Howard W. Hunter, *The Teachings of Howard W. Hunter* (Salt Lake City: Bookcraft, 1997), 259.

2. See thinkexist.com/quotation/i_find_the_great_thing_in_this_world_is_not_so/174881.html.

3. Ezra Taft Benson, "Do Not Despair," *Ensign,* October 1986, 5.

4. Richard G. Scott, "Learning to Succeed in Life," BYU devotional, 15 September 1998; speeches.byu.edu.

5. Jeffrey R. Holland, "'Cast Not Away Therefore Your Confidence,'" BYU devotional, 2 March 1999; speeches.byu.edu.

6. M. Russell Ballard, "Keeping Life's Demands in Balance," *Ensign,* May 1987, 14.

7. Ballard, "Go for It!" *New Era,* March 2004, 7.

8. Jonah Lehrer, "Don't—The Secret of Self-Control," *The New Yorker,* 18 May 2009; newyorker.com.

9. See George T. Doran, "There's a S.M.A.R.T. way to write management's goals and objectives," and Arthur F. Miller and James A. Cunningham, "How to avoid costly job mismatches," *Management Review,* Vol. 70, No. 11 (Nov. 1981).

10. Thomas S. Monson, *Favorite Quotations from the Collection of Thomas S. Monson* (Salt Lake City: Deseret Book, 1985), 61.

11. Ballard, "Keeping Life's Demands in Balance," 14.

12. Dallin H. Oaks, "Timing," BYU devotional, 29 January 2002; speeches.byu.edu.

13. See Gordon B. Hinckley, "A Testimony Vibrant and True," *Ensign,* August 2005, 2–6.

14. Holland, "The Best Is Yet to Be," *Ensign,* January 2010, 23.

15. Monson, *Favorite Quotations from the Collection of Thomas S. Monson,* 61; emphasis added.

16. Bruce C. and Marie K. Hafen, "'Bridle All Your Passions,'" *Ensign,* February 1994, 16.

17. Ballard, "Go for It!" 4.

18. Ballard, "Be Strong in the Lord, and in the Power of His Might," BYU fireside, 3 March 2002; speeches.byu.edu.

19. Henry Wadsworth Longfellow, quotationsbook.com.

20. Monson, "Choose You This Day," *Ensign,* November 2004, 68.

CHAPTER 31: HOW CAN I MAKE THE TEMPLE A MORE IMPORTANT PART OF MY LIFE?

1. Anne C. Pingree, "Seeing the Promises Afar Off," *Ensign,* November 2003, 13.

2. Howard W. Hunter, as quoted in Jay M. Todd, "President Howard W. Hunter," *Ensign,* July 1994, 5.

3. *Gospel Principles* (Salt Lake City: The Church of Jesus Christ of Latter-day Saints, 2009), 222–23.

4. Dieter F. Uchtdorf, "See the End from the Beginning," *Ensign,* May 2006, 44.

5. Hunter, "Exceeding Great and Precious Promises," *Ensign,* November 1994, 8.

6. David B. Haight, "Temples and Work Therein," *Ensign,* November 1990, 61.

7. Ezra Taft Benson, *The Teachings of Ezra Taft Benson* (Salt Lake City: Bookcraft, 1988), 256.

8. Haight, "Come to the House of the Lord," *Ensign,* May 1992, 15.

9. Glenn L. Pace, "Spiritual Revival," *Ensign,* November 1992, 12.

10. Joseph Fielding Smith, *Doctrines of Salvation,* comp. Bruce R. McConkie, 3 vols. (Salt Lake City: Bookcraft, 1955), 2:242.

11. Joseph Smith, *Teachings of the Prophet Joseph Smith* (Salt Lake City: Deseret Book, 1976), 367; emphasis added; see also Fielding Smith, *Doctrines of Salvation,* 2:158, 230.

12. Theodore M. Burton, "Salvation for the Dead—A Missionary Activity," *Ensign,* May 1975, 71.

13. Haight, "Come to the House of the Lord," 16.

14. Hunter, *The Teachings of Howard W. Hunter,* ed. Clyde J. Williams (Salt Lake City: Bookcraft, 1997), 236.

15. "From the First Presidency," *Church News,* 22 March 2003; see also http://www.ldschurchnews.com/articles/43389/From-the-First-Presidency.html.

16. Hunter, *Teachings of Howard W. Hunter,* 230–31; emphasis added.

17. David A. Bednar, "The Hearts of the Children Shall Turn," *Ensign,* November 2011, 26–27.

18. Hunter, "Follow the Son of God," *Ensign,* November 1994, 88.

19. Boyd K. Packer, *Preparing to Enter the Holy Temple* (Salt Lake City: The Church of Jesus Christ of Latter-day Saints, 2002); see also Russell M. Nelson, "Prepare for Blessings of the Temple," *Ensign,* March 2002, 17.

20. Thomas S. Monson, "Blessings of the Temple," *Ensign,* May 2015, 93.

21. Richard G. Scott, "Temple Worship: The Source of Strength and Power in Times of Need," *Ensign,* May 2009, 43–44.

22. Ibid., 44.

23. W. Grant Bangerter, "What Temples Are For," *Ensign,* May 1982, 72.

24. Jeffrey R. Holland, "'Abide in Me,'" *Ensign,* May 2004, 31.

25. Hunter, "Follow the Son of God," 88.

CHAPTER 32: WHY SHOULD I SERVE A MISSION?

1. Spencer W. Kimball, "Circles of Exaltation," Address to Religious Educators, 28 June 1968, 2.

2. See http://deseretnews.com/article/865606271/LDS-missionary-numbers-to-peak-at-88000-more-to-use-and-pay-for -digital-devices.html.

3. Thomas S. Monson, "Welcome to Conference," *Ensign,* November 2012, 5.

4. Gordon B. Hinckley, "To the Bishops of the Church," *Worldwide Leadership Training Meeting,* 19 June 2004, 27.

5. See http://mormonnewsroom.org/facts-and-statistics.

6. Hinckley, "Of Missions, Temples, and Stewardship," *Ensign,* November 1995, 52; emphasis added.

7. Hinckley, "News of the Church," *Ensign,* May 1985, 97.

8. Richard G. Scott, "Now Is the Time to Serve a Mission!" *Ensign,* May 2006, 89–90.

9. David A. Bednar, "Becoming a Missionary," *Ensign,* November 2005, 47.

10. Ibid.

11. Ibid.; emphasis added.

12. Kimball, "'It Becometh Every Man,'" *Ensign,* October 1977, 3.

13. Scott, "Now Is the Time to Serve a Mission!" 90.

14. Paraphrased from Hinckley, *Teachings of Gordon B. Hinckley* (Salt Lake City: Deseret Book, 1997), 360–61.

15. Hinckley, "Of Missions, Temples, and Stewardship," 51–52.

16. Brigham Young, in *Journal of Discourses,* 26 vols. (Liverpool: Latter-day Saints' Book Depot, 1854–86), 8:53.

17. Orson F. Whitney, in Conference Report, April 1918, 73.

18. Ezra Taft Benson, *The Teachings of Ezra Taft Benson* (Salt Lake City: Bookcraft, 1988), 213.

19. Heber C. Kimball, quoted in Hinckley, "An Ensign to the Nations," *Ensign,* November 1989, 53; emphasis added.

20. Hinckley, "Some Thoughts on Temples, Retention of Converts, and Missionary Service," *Ensign,* November 1997, 52.

CHAPTER 33: WHAT HAPPENS AT THE SECOND COMING?

1. Joseph Fielding Smith, in Conference Report, April 1935, 97.

2. Dallin H. Oaks, "Preparation for the Second Coming," *Ensign,* May 2004, 9.

3. *True to the Faith* (Salt Lake City: The Church of Jesus Christ of Latter-day Saints, 2004), 161.

4. Oaks, "Preparation for the Second Coming," 10.

5. *Teachings of the Presidents of the Church: Joseph Smith* (Salt Lake City: The Church of Jesus Christ of Latter-day Saints, 2007), 253.

6. *For the Strength of Youth* (Salt Lake City: The Church of Jesus Christ of Latter-day Saints, 2011), iii.

7. Boyd K. Packer, "Counsel to Youth," *Ensign,* November 2011, 19.

PHOTO AND IMAGE CREDITS

Authors' photographs: 12, 29, 34, 36, 61, 69, 97, 98, 121, 157, 162, 173, 181, 183, 184, 187, 192, 193, 220, 227.

Illustrations by Brian Clark:1, 4, 7, 19, 70, 73, 84, 85, 96, 110, 127, 133, 167, 173, 194, 207, 209, 226.

Illustrations by Bryan Beach: 5, 36, 53, 54, 72, 75, 80, 99, 128, 153, 165, 175.

iStock: 2, 7, 8, 10, 11, 13, 17, 18, 20, 22, 28, 33, 35, 42, 46, 52, 53, 55, 57, 61, 63, 64, 68, 73, 76, 81, 82, 90, 95, 100, 101, 103, 109, 112, 114, 115, 121, 130, 150, 151, 161, 171, 176, 189, 199, 200, 201, 203, 212, 214, 217, 218, 221, 225, 228, 232, 240.

Thinkstock: 2, 6, 8, 17, 25, 28, 30, 36, 47, 48, 49, 52, 56, 57, 58, 60, 68, 93, 95, 100, 103, 161, 164, 189, 196, 197, 198, 200, 202, 204, 205, 209, 210, 212, 213, 215, 221, 240.

Jupiter Unlimited: 13, 14, 19, 21, 22, 23, 24, 75, 76, 77, 78, 79, 83, 86, 87, 88, 89, 91, 119, 120, 122, 123, 125, 126, 127, 129, 132, 151, 153, 166, 168, 191, 194.

Shutterstock: 1, 5, 9, 14, 15, 19, 23, 26, 38, 39, 40, 41, 43, 45, 46, 49, 59, 62, 67, 68, 70, 71, 72, 75, 77, 78, 81, 83, 84, 85, 87, 92, 102, 104, 106, 107, 108, 111, 112, 113, 114, 116, 118, 121, 124, 126, 127, 130, 131, 133, 134, 135, 137, 138, 140, 141, 143, 152, 153, 155, 156, 158, 159, 160, 163, 167, 168, 169, 172, 177, 178, 179, 180, 181, 182, 183, 184, 187, 188, 203, 206, 209, 211, 215, 219, 220, 222, 223, 224, 229, 230, 234, 235, 239, 240, 241, 242.

Getty Images: 142, 149, 189, 217, 218, 223, 238.

Page 4, © 2013 Brian Call. Used by permission.
Page 11, 10 Years of Meth Use, provided by the Drug Enforcement Administration.
Page 126, photograph of face, courtesy of Dr. Deborah Yurgelun-Todd.
Page 139, © 1995, Edward H. Adelson, http://web.mit.edu/persci/people/adelson/checkershadow_illusion.html.
Page 140, © 1995, Edward H. Adelson, http://web.mit.edu/persci/people/adelson/checkershadow_illusion.html.
Page 142, © 2011 Brian Call. Used by permission.
Page 149, Tsunami photographs © NOAA; courtesy DigitalGlobe Inc.
Page 158, liar/face based on illustration by Paul Agule.
Page 161, painting of Salt Lake Temple by Anthony Sweat.
Page 169, painting of Christ, Gustave Doré.
Page 192, angry faces photograph, courtesy of Philippe Schyns.
Page 207, photograph of Burgon Jensen, © Tom Smart, Deseret News. Used by permission.
Page 222, painting of Logan Utah Temple by Anthony Sweat.
Page 231, used by permission, Utah State Historical Society.
Page 233, © Brian Call. Used by permission.

About the Authors

John Hilton III is an assistant professor in Religious Education at Brigham Young University. He has degrees in Education from BYU and Harvard and frequently teaches at Especially for Youth and BYU Education Week. John and his wife, Lani, have six children and reside in Utah.

Anthony Sweat is an assistant professor in Religious Education at Brigham Young University. He received a BFA in painting and drawing from the University of Utah and MEd and PhD degrees in education from Utah State University. He is a regular speaker at Especially for Youth and Education Week conferences. He and his wife, Cindy, are the parents of seven children and reside in Utah.

Other Books by John Hilton III and Anthony Sweat

Suit Up

Armor Up

The Big Picture

HOW?

WHY?

By John Hilton III

The Little Book of Book of Mormon Evidences

I Lost My Phone Number, Can I Have Yours?

Please Pass the Scriptures

By Anthony Sweat

Christ in Every Hour

Mormons: An Open Book

I'm Not Perfect. Can I Still Go to Heaven?